PSYCHOANALYZING PSYCHOANALYSIS

Dionysiac Maenads, Vatican Museum

PSYCHOANALYZING PSYCHOANALYSIS

Freud and the Hidden Fault of the Father

MARIE BALMARY

Translated, with an Introduction,
by Ned Lukacher

THE JOHNS HOPKINS UNIVERSITY PRESS
Baltimore and London

Originally published in 1979 by Bernard Grasset, Paris,
as *L'Homme aux statues: Freud et la faute caché du père*
Copyright © 1979 by Editions Grasset & Fasquelle

English translation and translator's introduction copyright © 1982
by The Johns Hopkins University Press
All rights reserved
Printed in the United States of America

The Johns Hopkins University Press, Baltimore, Maryland 21218
The Johns Hopkins Press Ltd., London

Library of Congress Cataloging in Publication Data

Balmary, Marie.
Psychoanalyzing psychoanalysis.

Translation of: L'homme aux statues.
1. Psychoanalysis. 2. Oedipus complex.
3. Freud, Sigmund, 1856-1939—Family. 4. Fathers
and sons. I. Title [DNLM: 1. Psychoanalysis—
Biography. WM 460 B194h (P)]
BF175.B2313   150.19′52   81-18568
Includes bibliographical references.
ISBN 0-8018-2349-8   AACR2

CONTENTS

ACKNOWLEDGMENTS

I had two fortunate opportunities during the course of years of research for this volume. First of all, those who held knowledge within their grasp did not help me. Thus I could work without taking into consideration fads or cliques. Next, seeing me alone on such a long road, friends, neighbors—geographical and professional—came along with me for part of the way, encouraging me and helping me in various ways. I wish particularly to mention, in their respective field of interest or work: Jean-Claude Lalanne in psychoanalysis, François and Marie-Michèle Grolleron in ancient languages, Catherine Verner in German, Joseph Thomas for understanding the Bible, Maurice Clavel for the question he unearthed concerning the link between illness, cure, and conversion.

Deolanda Domenech, Elisabeth Guyonnet, Anne and Benoît Balmary have, amicably, daily, aided and supported me with their interest and questions. Maud Espérou opened new fields of reading to me. Brigitte Dardaud participated in this work at all levels in the documentation, discussion, and preparation of the manuscript, which Jean-Baptiste Grasset helped me to make into a book.

I thank them all profoundly. They also brought me an inestimable aid, of which they are not themselves aware: proceeding with them, I recognized that I wanted this book to be comprehensible to them, in particular to those who have no psychoanalytic training. The "we" who speaks in this book is not a purely formal plural of the university type; it is that of an effective solidarity. Far from hindering me, the simple language in which I endeavor to write led me to ever more elementary questions and made me discover, little by little, a more fundamental level of research.

TRANSLATOR'S INTRODUCTION: FREUD'S PHANTOM

Though a scar on my chin might have reminded me ...

Freud

Marie Balmary describes her *Psychoanalyzing Psychoanalysis: Freud and the Hidden Fault of the Father* as an "interrogation of psychoanalytic theory by psychoanalytic method." Her primary objective is to recover those remains of Freud's analytic method which were not assimilated into his theory and which for precisely that reason still possess the potential to revolutionize clinical practice. Her "interrogation" relies upon two fundamental procedures that characterized Freud's clinical practice throughout his career: (1) to regard an omission in the course of a narrative or an analysis as an effort at concealment; (2) when confronted with a symptom incommensurate with its ostensible cause, to deduce a first scene prior to the second, insufficient, scene. Balmary produces many original insights by using these two very basic elements of Freudian technique to analyze Freud himself and the origins of psychoanalysis. With this understanding of psychoanalytic method, Balmary is able to demonstrate how Freud used psychoanalytic theory to repress his clinical method and the insights it produced. What Balmary calls "Freud's method" signifies those elements in his works to which he was blind when his writing was directed toward the articulation of a theory of the mind. His method is composed of those elements in his writing which he found unreadable and which were left behind precisely because his theory could not be written unless they were put aside, forgotten, or neglected. What Balmary calls "the hidden fault of the father" serves both as a description of Freud's unconscious relation to his father and as a general heading for the inconsistencies, contradictions, and oversights of Freud's writing.

Balmary proposes the provocative hypothesis that the incommensurability between Freud's method and his theory—Freud's inability to read and write his method into his theory—was attributable to his unconscious relation to his father. As in the French *péché* 'sin', 'transgression', guilt is also semantically present in the word *faute* 'fault', 'misdeed'. Freud's theory became a ritual atonement for the unconscious guilt that ensued from his acceptance of responsibility for his dead father's fault.

In the two years following his father's death in 1896 Freud "discovered" Oedipus and lay the foundation for his neologism, psychoanalysis. Balmary's primary interest is in this early period during the formation of Freud's theory. She argues that Freud's theory went wrong because it was the work of mourning. In *Anti-Oedipus* Gilles Deleuze and Felix Guattari write: "Psychoanalysis is like the Russian Revolution; we don't know when it started going bad. We have to keep going back further. . . . To Freud himself, from the moment of the 'discovery' of Oedipus? Oedipus is the idealist turning point."[1] Through a detailed return to "Freud himself" during the 1890s, Balmary reveals both when and why psychoanalysis went bad. Unlike Deleuze and Guattari, however, Balmary does not reject the Oedipal model of desire simply because Freud used it for his own idiosyncratic purposes. Behind Freud's "idealist" appropriation of the myth she discovers another, more rigorously Sophoclean, mode of Oedipal interpretation. She reveals that Freud's emphasis upon Oedipus's incestuous desire is a repressive interpretation, a manifest content meant to conceal the latent and fundamentally Oedipal content of the myth: the transmission of the faults of the father (Laius) to the son (Oedipus). Oedipus is indeed the keystone of psychoanalysis but for reasons that remained inaccessible to Freud himself. *Psychoanalyzing Psychoanalysis* is thus anti-Oedipal in an original way. Rather than dispersing psychoanalysis into the "desiring-energies" on the margins of its discourse, Balmary would restructure psychoanalytic theory by recuperating insights long buried in its foundations.

Freud's first written reference to Oedipus appears in a discussion of Sophocles' *Oedipus the King* in a letter to Wilhelm Fliess on October 15, 1897. The term *psychoanalysis* first appears in Freud's writings in an essay entitled *Sexuality in the Aetiology of the Neuroses,* which he finished on February 9, 1898. Freud's father, Jakob, died on October 23, 1896. In September 1897 Freud made what Balmary regards as the pivotal decision in his career: the decision to abandon the mass of clinical evidence that he had collected since his first year of practice in 1886 and that overwhelmingly indicated that the patient's hysteria was the result of seduction or sexual overtures by the father. Freud announced to Fliess in a letter of September 21 that "I no longer believe in my *neurotica*."[2] Freud's rejection of his first theory, his "theory of seduction" [*Verführungstheorie*], marked the beginning of "the idealist turning point"; for from this moment, on the eve of the first anniversary of his father's death, Freud began to turn away from an *inter*psychic to an *intra*psychic theory of mental disorder. Balmary's thesis is that Freud's first theory was the real discovery and that the subsequent "discovery" of psychoanalysis was a repressive ruse, an idealist artifice that was the unconscious work of Freud's mourning and of the "self-analysis" that began in 1897 soon after Jakob's death. Ernest Jones called Freud's repudiation of the theory of seduction "one of the great dividing lines in the story" of psychoanalysis.[3] Freud's rejection of a notion of intersubjective psychical reality, which was based upon his belief in the discourse of his patients, was the direct result of his own self-analysis. He no longer believed his patients' accounts of seduction by the father because he had "discovered," as he wrote to Fliess on October 3, that "in my case my father played no active role."[4] He found the results of his self-analysis so convincing that, for their sake, he would dispense with the work of a decade. The configuration of his own psychical reality became the basis for the structural model of the mind which he would claim possesses universal significance and thus renders any discourse by patients to the contrary invalid. The idealist model (i.e., superego, ego, id, Oedipus complex, etc.) was the projection of his own psychical reality in the form of what Balmary calls "a phantasmatic 'scientific' theory."

As Freud crossed this crucial dividing line between two theories of the constitution of psychical reality, an apparently insignificant Jewish anecdote came to his mind. From the slender thread of that anecdote Balmary weaves an intricate pattern, gathering together the interpsychic connections between father and son that Freud had so forcefully repressed. In chapters 5 and 6 Balmary demonstrates how repeatedly and, indeed, reluctantly Freud, in *Studies in Hysteria* (co-authored with Josef Breuer and published in 1895) and in other essays during the nineties, confronted the irrefutable evidence that pointed to the father as the cause of hysterical symptoms in the child. Freud's theory of seduction was very coldly received by the Viennese medical community; fewer than seven hundred copies of *Studies on Hysteria* were sold in the decade after its publication; and Breuer had broken completely with Freud. Clearly, a theory based on the misdeeds of fathers was a source of discomfort for Freud. As his professional crisis became increasingly acute, his father died and he plunged into a melancholic period of mourning and self-analysis from whence emerged all the epochal changes in his career. In the letter to Fliess of September 21, 1897, he mentioned a "feeling of triumph" amidst "the general collapse," and then made what Balmary regards as the revealing comparison between his renunciation of seduction theory and an ancient Jewish story:

> One of the stories from my collection occurs to me: "Rebecca, you
> can take off your wedding-gown, you're not a bride any longer."
> [*Rebekka, zieh das Kleid aus, Du bist keine Kalle mehr*].[5]

Why this particular story at this especially critical juncture in Freud's
career? Why did he choose Rebecca from his "collection of little stories"
[*meiner Sammlung die kleine Geschichte*]? Balmary's answer will seem to
some an impertinent attempt to psychoanalyze the master, who has until
now been held in reverence by his disciples; to others her answer is a
provocative hypothesis challenging the apodictic spell that has for too
long preserved Freud as the bedrock upon which other disciplines and
other discourses could rely to support their own endeavors. Balmary's
work explodes the myth that psychoanalysis is a ground or a touchstone
with which to verify research into the mind, history, culture, and textuality. Balmary dispels "the cure of the ground," "the ground of Being,"
which many have sought in psychoanalysis.

Balmary's speculation on this solitary appearance of the name
Rebecca in a letter never intended for publication[6] would not have been
possible before 1968. At that time Josef Sajner and Renée Gicklhorn
examined the State Archives of Freud's birthplace, Freiberg (now in
Czechoslovakia), and discovered that Freud's father, Jakob, was not
married twice as everyone—including Sigmund—had believed, but three
times.[7] They found that the woman assumed to be his second wife
—Freud's mother, Amalie Nathanson—was actually his third. The name
of Jakob's second wife was *Rebecca.* Some will say it is an irrelevant
coincidence, but Balmary combines this recent discovery with numerous
other inconsistencies in the Freud family legend to lead the reader on a
fascinating search for clues.

Balmary describes *Psychoanalyzing Psychoanalysis* as "something of a
detective story"; and indeed, like Dupin in Poe's "The Purloined Letter,"
who recovers the Queen's letter from the Minister D——, Balmary recovers a secret, a well-hidden family secret, which had been purloined
from Sigmund Freud. Balmary retrieves the purloined mystery of
Rebecca; she retrieves the secret message, whose course had been pro-
longed by the detours, deferrals, and repression that constitute the history of psychoanalysis. Alongside the official history of the Freud family,
alongside the official history of psychoanalysis, there is another story
involving both the biblical Rebecca, who was the wife of Isaac and the
mother of Jacob, and the missing Rebecca, who was the wife of Jakob
Freud.

Because the Jewish legend of Rebecca plays an important role in
Psychoanalyzing Psychoanalysis some contextual background may be help-
ful. Max Schur, Freud's friend and doctor during his final years, poses

some of the relevant questions in his *Freud: Living and Dying*, the first study of Freud to take Sajner's findings into account:

> The meaning of this Jewish joke is obvious: "You were once a proud bride, but you got into trouble, the wedding is off—take off your bridal gown."
> Why just this joke at this time? Why a joke in which Freud identifies himself with a disgraced women? And a joke, the punchline of which contains the name of this mysterious second wife of his father?[8]

Throughout the French edition of her book Balmary translates Freud's German *Du bist keine Kalle mehr* into the French *tu n'es plus mariée* 'you're no longer married.' As Schur's comments correctly indicate, Freud's anecdote refers to Rebecca's fate *immediately before* her marriage; she is a bride who is repudiated just before she is to be married. The note to the German edition, which Balmary cites late in her book, clearly states that *Kalle* is a Jewish expression for a bride (*Braut*), not a wife. The passage should read as it does in Eric Mosbacher's translation: "you're not a bride any longer." This detail is important, for it supports Balmary's thesis more than she suspects. As Gicklhorn has noted, even though an Orthodox Jew could divorce on the basis of sterility, the law would have required that the separation be registered; but since there was no account given when Jakob married Amalie in 1855, the possibility that Rebecca suffered any of a number of unpleasant fates, including repudiation, between 1852 (when she appeared on the Freiberg registers as Jakob's wife) and 1855 cannot be ruled out. Balmary has translated the anecdote to read "'you're no longer married'" in order to emphasize the resemblance to Rebecca Freud, whose mysterious fate transpired after she was married.

In Genesis, chapter 24, Rebecca is chosen to be Isaac's wife by a servant sent by Abraham to find a suitable bride for his son. The story of Rebecca and Isaac has been the object of considerable anecdotal embroidery in Jewish lore. According to the account by Robert Graves and Raphael Patai, when the Canaanite servant returned with the bride Abraham told his son to examine her maidenhead in order to be sure that she was still a virgin.[9] Since Canaanite custom allowed the father to sleep with his daughter before her marriage and since Canaanite women were notoriously promiscuous, Canaanite Rebecca's virginity was a source of some doubt for the Jews. The line that Freud cites to Fliess is probably uttered by Isaac after he has examined her maidenhead but before her virginity has been proved. There is, however, no certainty whether Freud is identifying himself with Rebecca, as Schur suggests, or with Isaac. They are, of course, figures of Freud's own internal debate. Is Rebecca a figure for the seduction theory that Freud, like Isaac, now rejects? Or is

Freud, like Rebecca, himself rejected by an undefined Other? In any case, seduction and the faults of fathers are already inscribed within the Jewish tradition of this anecdote. Isaac suspects that Rebecca has been seduced and calls the marriage off: "Rebecca, you can take off your wedding gown, you're not a bride any longer."

In this letter of September 21, 1897, to Fliess in which Freud claimed he no longer believed his first theory he also listed the reasons for his change of mind. Balmary regards these reasons as pretexts and analyzes them closely. I want to look briefly at two of them: (1) "it was hardly credible that perverted acts against children were so general" (literally: "that such dissemination [*Verbreitung*] of perversion against children is scarcely probable"); (2) "it is impossible to distinguish between the truth and emotionally-charged fiction" in the discourse of patients. Because his patients' discourse had not agreed with the results of his self-analysis, he rejected it as being outside the realm of psychical reality. A few sentences later, however, he turned to a fiction about the suspicion and consternation that arise when one considers seduction and the unnatural acts of fathers. Freud's emerging structural theory of psychical reality, which no longer depended upon the intersubjective context to determine anew for each occasion how "to distinguish between truth and emotionally-charged fiction," was itself an "emotionally-charged fiction" (literally: "affect-filled fiction" [*mit Affekt besetzte Fiktion*].[10] Freud's reluctance to confront the always shifting borderline between truth and fiction forced him to posit an a priori structural model that formally and finally excluded fiction. Freud's theory-building succeeded less in excluding affect-filled fictions than in elevating them to a dominant position in the conceptual hierarchy of his psychical reality. Freud's sudden complete inability to believe his patients' discourse may be the fact behind the figure of Isaac's disbelief before Rebecca's account of her broken hymen. While Rebecca can overcome Isaac's doubt by appealing to the traces of her virginal blood, Freud completely rejected his Rebecca-like *Verführungstheorie* and the clinical evidence on which it was based. But if Freud knew the anecdote he must have also known its denouement. This question brings us to the problem of Freud's "choice" of this particular story. Was it the return of a repressed or forgotten secret, emerging under the combined pressure of an intellectual crisis regarding fathers' faults and a personal crisis regarding his mourning for a father who had also committed and concealed certain faults with a woman named Rebecca? By disregarding the denouement of the Rebecca-Isaac story was Freud not tacitly acknowledging that his patients, like Rebecca, spoke the truth? By repressing the act of seduction and Rebecca's appeal to the bloody stump, was Freud not also repressing, once again, his memory of his father's fault with a woman named Rebecca? The name *Rebecca* marked both the return of the repressed and the return of repression.

It is interesting to note that the use of marriage and the repudiation of a mate as figures for the acceptance and rejection of a theory also appeared, seventeen years later, in Freud's *On the History of the Psychoanalytic Movement* (1914). When he described the difference between the role of sexuality in the aetiology of the neuroses according to his mentors, Breuer, Charcot, and Chrobak, and its role in his own thinking, Freud wrote:

> I am well aware that it is one thing to give utterance to an idea once or twice in the form of a passing *aperçu,* and quite another to mean it seriously—to take it literally and pursue it in the face of every contradictory detail, and to win it a place among accepted truths. It is the difference between a casual flirtation and a legal marriage with all its duties and difficulties. "*Epouser les idées de . . .*" is no uncommon figure of speech, at any rate in French.[11]

If the mystery surrounding Jakob's marriage to Rebecca is a decisive factor in determining which ideas Freud will or will not "espouse," then his allusion to "a legal marriage with all its duties and difficulties" is a particularly apt metaphor for this thinker's relationship to his theory. What Balmary calls the father's hidden fault signifies the interminable conflation of literal and figurative readings of every Freudian figure of speech.

When thirty-six-year-old Jakob and thirty-two-year-old Rebecca first appeared on the Freiberg registers in 1852 they were accompanied by Jakob's sons by his first marriage: twenty-year-old Emanuel and sixteen-year-old Philipp. Freud's stepbrothers certainly knew about Rebecca, but even though they lived in the same building during Freud's youth, they apparently kept silent about it. So did Emanuel's wife and Freud's mother, Amalie, who was also a Freiberg resident when it was a small Catholic village of five thousand inhabitants, whose small Jewish minority was under surveillance by officials of the Austrian Empire in the troubled years following the disturbances of 1848. The chances that Amalie knew nothing of Jakob and Rebecca are extremely remote. In his recent biography of Freud, Ronald Clark discusses in broad outlines the problem that Balmary has pursued so thoroughly.

> The . . . alternative is that the young Freud acquired some knowledge of his father's affairs [with Rebecca] but repressed it, for the whole of his life, respecting the family taboo out of filial loyalty and keeping its knowledge secret even from his wife Martha, who always spoke of Jakob Freud as having been married twice, not thrice. This . . . possibility, if correct, would, according to Freud's own beliefs, have significantly affected the development of his own mental life, and it would be ingenuous to believe that it would not have affected the course of psychoanalysis.[12]

Like Sajner and Gicklhorn when they decided to examine the Freiberg registers, Balmary considers most closely all those textual and personal details that, precisely because they have long been open to public scrutiny, have been ignored or simply considered insignificant. Balmary's strategy is to "hypothesize an 'unconscious' Freud in search of a truth which has been denied him." Balmary's "'unconscious' Freud" in search of the phantom Rebecca is a hypothetical deduction, a speculative effort to explain how Freud's texts, as well as his personal manias and phobias, manage at once to proclaim and to conceal the father's fault throughout the son's lifetime.

What remains unreadable, unanalyzable to Freud, constitutes the principle of Freudian textuality which Balmary calls the father's hidden fault and which is transmitted through the agency of the unconscious Freud. In this sense, the fault traverses Freud's discursive and nondiscursive practices. Although he has no conscious memory of his father's fault, Freud's writing, manias, and phobias nonetheless retain its traces. The conscious Freud disavows the reality of the fault while that other Freud repeatedly decries it. What those traces mutely proclaim is the instability of writing itself. The fault is really the fault line, concealed with varying degrees of care within every inscription and awaiting imaginative readers to dismantle the representations of psychical realities which rise boldly from an uncertain foundation. Freud's analysis of Sophocles' *Oedipus the King* is thus dismantled by Balmary as she delineates how carefully inattentive Freud was to the traces of the fault in this textual keystone in the history of psychoanalysis. Freud's emphasis on Oedipus's incestuous desires and his claim that "there must be something which makes a voice within us ready to recognize the compelling force of destiny in the *Oedipus*"[13] appear, after Balmary's reading of the play, astonishingly wide of the mark. What Freud was unable to read in the play is precisely what is everywhere proclaimed: that at every crucial moment Oedipus unknowingly pays for his father's numerous crimes. Balmary's reading focuses on Sophocles' play upon the Greek word for articulation, *arthron,* which links the pierced joints (*arthra*) of Oedipus's feet to the orbits (*arthra*) of Oedipus's blinded eyes. That *arthron* also signifies the male organ leads us to interpret Oedipus's self-blinding as not only symbolic castration but also a link that makes his martyrdom an expiation for his father's sexual misconduct, which includes Laius's violation of the boy Chrysippus and his prohibited procreation of Oedipus. Numerous details, among them the Sphinx's riddle and Oedipus's name, indicate that the figure of the articulation of bodily joints constitutes the mute textual articulation that alone iterates the juncture through which the faults of the deceiving Laius are transmitted to his unperceiving son. Freud's recourse to "a voice within us" saying that each of us was once a "budding Oedipus"[14] is an affect-filled fiction which tries to conceal the fault line of unreadability running through this Sophoclean keystone of psychoanalysis.

Psychoanalyzing Psychoanalysis is an answer to the implied question in Freud's idea that "there must be something which makes a voice within." Since Freud, *oedipal* desire has meant primarily incestuous desire. Balmary would like to reverse that current and to clarify oedipal incest as a repressive concept, which has occluded what is really oedipal: the fault and its transmission. For Balmary, Freud failed to read in Sophocles what he failed to remember in his own family: the father's fault. In the Old Testament she discovers a possible explanation for Freud's insistence on incest, for his inability to read Sophocles' point: that incest was the effect of the father's fault rather than the cause of the tragedy. Freud's emphasis on the incest theme appears as the fortuitous result of the fact that in Genesis the names *Rebecca* and *Jacob* are linked as mother and son. Superimposing the biblical pairing of the two names upon an unconscious memory of a connection between these names and a fault, Freud may have received a certain impetus for his belief that the fault was everywhere and its name was incest. Rebecca and Isaac were Jacob's parents; so once again Freud's interest in biblical legend became crucial to the history of psychoanalysis.

Freud's fascination with the Moses of Michelangelo and Mozart's *Don Giovanni,* his mania for mushroom hunts and collecting statues, his phobia regarding railways and umbrellas, his peculiar table manners, his children's names, his cohabitation with *two* women (his wife Martha and her sister, Minna Bernays), and several other curiosities appear, through the new optic of Balmary's thesis, as a mute language of symptoms that, despite their apparent disparity, are all manifestations of the son's unconscious complicity in his father's hidden misdeed.[15] Like certain aspects of Oedipus's relation to Laius, these symptoms remained strictly unanalyzable to Freud, even those regarding the Moses of Michelangelo to which he devoted an essay. Mushrooms and statues held an unparalleled attraction for Freud. Balmary explains that this is a result of Freud's unconscious identification during the year of mourning of his father with Don Juan. The figure of the stone guest, who visits an awful vengeance upon the licentious Don, became an obsession of Freud's at this time because he feared precisely such a fate might have awaited his Don Juan father. Balmary's analysis of the cluster of symptoms that resulted from this identification make her chapter, "The Freudian Mosaic," a dazzling exercise in the psychoanalytic method. Freud's famous simile in *The Interpretation of Dreams,* "out of one of the denser places of this meshwork, the dream-wish rises like the mushroom [*der Pilz*] out of its mycelium,"[16] appears at once less unmotivated and even more densely provocative after Balmary's reconstruction of Freud's mania for mushrooms and statues.

The Freud who emerges from *Psychoanalyzing Psychoanalysis* is at once a being who is compelled by the ethical imperatives and the sacrificial logic of the unconscious and a writer whose sensibility is unmistakably aesthetic. The fault inscribed wordplay and fiction everywhere in Freud's writing. By virtue of its hiddenness, the fault transformed Freud's life as well as his work into art. In this sense, *Psychoanalyzing Psychoanalysis* is an appreciation in the style of H.D.'s *Tribute to Freud* (1956). Balmary sets out to track down an analytical thinker but somehow manages to reveal a surrealist *avant la lettre.* Psychoanalysis went "bad" because from its inception it was a question of style. Sigmund Freud, officially the eldest son of Jakob's second wife, found a parallel with the eldest son of Rachel, who was also the second wife of the biblical Jacob; the name of that son was, of course, Joseph, the interpreter of dreams. If Jakob, whose name means "one who takes by the heel" or "supplants" (Genesis 25:27), played a role in the phantasmatic, idealist turn that his son's work took during that anxious year of mourning, it can also be said that he thereby contributed to making his son's style so unique that it engendered an institution.

> *I prayed the angel to desist, and he has since done that . . . though since then I have been noticeably limping.*
>
> Freud

Freud called the transference "the mainspring [*Triebfeder*] of the joint work of analysis."[17] The word *Triebfeder* derives from *Trieb* 'drive' 'impulse' and *Feder* 'writing pen' 'spring'. What drove Freud's pen, what compelled Freud's writing to take the particular form it did was the unconscious work of the father's fault, the unconscious speculation about the fate of the phantom Rebecca.[18] Freud's ideas about, as well as his practice of, the transference would doubtless also bear traces of the phantom, and Balmary offers some interesting observations on the difficulty with which the analyst must assume the role of the guilty one, the perpetrator of the fault whose consequences have caused the patient's disorder. The model for this crucial aspect of clinical psychoanalysis thus becomes Freud's assumption of responsibility for Jakob's fault during the period of mourning. This transference of psychical roles between an unconscious memory of a dead father and a conscious intellectual crisis defines the psychical reality within which Freud would remain for the rest of his life. This alone enabled him to renounce his longstanding wish "to pin down a father as the originator of neurosis" [*einen Vater als Urheber der Neurose zu ertrappen*][19] and the seduction theory, its immediate result. Balmary describes Freud's transference of the fault onto himself as a victimizing strategy that René Girard calls the mechanism of "the emissary victim."[20] With characteristic thoroughness, Freud himself provided us with his own version of the emissary victim in *Mourning and Melancholia* (1917). From October 1896 to October 1897 Freud was deciding that the faults of fathers were not factors causing mental disorder; at the same time he was discovering traces of incestuous desire in himself and first heard that "voice within." What he wrote years later in *Mourning and Melancholia* reads like an analysis of the unconscious work that performed the transference of the fault: The melancholic's

> self-reproaches are reproaches against a loved object which have been shifted away [*gewaltzt sind*] from it on to the patient's own ego.[21]

What has occurred is a change in the ego's relation to the loved object. The ego is disappointed by the loved object and has withdrawn its libido from it; the ego then treats part of itself as though it were the abandoned object. Of this identification between the two Freud wrote, "The shadow [*der Schatten*] of the object fell upon the ego." The ego's love for the object continues even after the object has been abandoned. This transformation in the ego results in "a cleavage [*Zwiespalt*] between the critical activity of the ego and the ego as altered by identification."[22] This process, which Freud called "incorporation," thus becomes a model of radical instability threatening to undermine every exercise of the transference. By incorporating within itself the faults of the now absent loved object, the ego is able to preserve a spectral remnant of the object only at the price of self-division. Incorporation is the work of the phantom. Freud could neither denounce his dead father's faults nor renounce the love that bound him to the lost object. Freud's abandonment of seduction theory was the effect of his incorporation of his father's fault. His various fictions and his pervasive wordplay served as defensive gestures that protect and encrypt the site of incorporation and thus assure that the rest of the ego will remain in complete ignorance of the transformation. The homophony between *Trauer* 'mourning', *trauen* 'to marry', and *Ubertragung* 'transference', along with their thematic importance in Freud's work, seem at once to proclaim and conceal the fault.

Balmary's work forces us to pose questions that Freud only vaguely anticipated when he referred to the "overlooked solution" [*übersehene Lösung*] to his self-analysis.[23] Her idea of the father's fault provides new dimensions to Jacques Derrida's suggestion that "the unanalyzed content will have been that on and around which the analytic movement will have constructed and mobilized itself; everything will have been constructed and calculated so that the unanalyzed can be passed on, protected, transmitted intact, properly bequeathed, consolidated, encysted, encrypted."[24] Freud conceived of his rejection of seduction theory as the constitutive move away from the uncertainty of descriptive medical practices of the nineteenth century and toward the structural model of the unconscious. Derrida's "unanalyzed" and Balmary's "fault" are strategies with which to question the psychoanalytic logic of the unconscious and to recover the radical otherness buried in the *Zwiespalt* between the analyst's ego and its "objective" theoretical structure. The future of such work will depend on its ability to situate Freud's work not as a break or a new beginning but as a function of discursive and nondiscursive practices already in place.

In concluding this introduction I would like to use Freud's epigraph to *The Interpretation of Dreams* as an example of how the unanalyzed is properly bequeathed. The Virgilian epigraph demonstrates that Sigmund's identification with Jakob was indeed fully incorporated and, furthermore, that such incorporation has political and social dimensions that *Psychoanalyzing Psychoanalysis* does not explicitly address. The epigraph appears on the title page and again near the end of the book: *"Flectere si nequeo superos Acheronta movebo"* [If I cannot bend the High Ones, I shall move the Underworld] (*Aeneid* 7. 312). The line is spoken by Juno, who wishes to stop Aeneas's progress to Rome. Balmary points out that Aeneas, like Jakob Freud, was officially married twice but was in fact married thrice if one counts his secret nuptials with Dido. That marriage led to the death of the clandestine wife, as may have Jakob's with Rebecca. Dido's suicide thus becomes a speculation about Rebecca's fate. Freud had also intended to use the line from Virgil as a motto for a chapter on "Symptom Formation"; and certainly Juno's efforts to stop Aeneas are a suitable figure for the symptom whose formation is intended to prevent the return of the repressed. I suggest that Freud's reading of Virgil has yet another dimension. Immediately following his citation of *Aeneid* 7. 312, late in the second edition (1909) of *The Interpretation of Dreams,* Freud inserted one of the most memorable passages of Virgilian exegesis: *"The interpretation of dreams is the royal road to a knowledge of the unconscious activities of the mind.''*[25] This Virgilian citation is indeed the royal road to Freud's unconscious, if we, unlike him, are only willing to follow it.

We begin with the singular coincidence that Otto von Bismarck was also very fond of Juno's imprecation, and that he repeatedly quoted *Aeneid* 7. 312, during the early 1860s to express his determination to introduce universal suffrage as a means of counteracting the resistance to his policies by the middle class.[26] Bismarck thought that by extending the vote to the workers he would win support for his policies. During the early 1860s the Freud family was in Vienna, following the mysteriously sudden flight from Freiberg in 1859 (about which Balmary has some very interesting ideas). Bismarck first became prime minister in 1862; he must have been a much discussed figure in Jakob's home for reasons Ernest

Jones explains in his discussion of Sigmund's attitude toward Bismarck during the years before the latter's death in 1898.

> There are only three remarks [in Freud's letters] about public personages, all three concerning their death. The first was where he expressed the opinion that Bismarck like a nightmare (*Alp*) weighed heavy on the whole continent: his death would bring universal relief. This may well have been a perfectly objective political judgment, but it is perhaps pertinent to recall that Freud's father's birthday was the same as Bismarck's (1815) and that Freud once asked his friend Fliess whether his numerical computations could predict which of the two men would die first. Indeed, the figure of Bismarck seemed, perhaps for the reason just hinted, to have exercised a peculiar fascination for Freud. When the great man visited Vienna in June 1892, Freud made several attempts to see him in the flesh, but the nearest he got to it was a glimpse of his back after waiting two and a half hours in the street—behavior one would have thought very atypical of Freud. A still more interesting feature in the story is that Freud's father had been such an ardent admirer of Bismarck, on the grounds of German unification, that when he had to translate the date of his birthday from the Jewish calendar into the Christian one he chose that of Bismarck's. So there were many links between Jakob Freud and Bismarck.[27]

That Freud should choose as his motto for the new science of psychoanalysis the same line from Virgil that Bismarck had used as a motto for German unification, and that Jakob had doubtless repeated in Sigmund's presence, is to acknowledge that the solution of the crisis of self-analysis and the revocation of seduction theory were not properly solutions at all but only the intensification of ambivalence toward the father.[28] Freud's politics were consumed by this ambivalence; for while he anticipated Bismarck/Jakob's death, his motto was a sign of his complicity in the conspiracy to move the forces of the Underworld. Freud must, to some extent, have "realized" the irony of the Latin citation when, in 1909, he added his famous remark about the royal road. Bismarck's *royalist* countermove to resistance by the middle-class intelligentsia against the power of the Prussian crown was his policy of "moving the Underworld" by extending the vote to the workers. As it so happened, Bismarck's policy failed because he mistakenly assumed that the royalist sympathies of laborers on his estates would also exist among industrial workers. Although his policy of moving the Underworld was abandoned, he nonetheless succeeded in his efforts toward unification and Prussian supremacy through his victory in the war against Austria in 1866. The conspiratorial motivation of Bismarck's policy of universal suffrage was no secret to Karl Marx, who, when approached by Bismarck, "refused any co-operation."[29] The royal road is indeed an ironic commentary on the resemblance between the subversive strategy of psychoanalysis and Bismarck's political cunning, and also on Freud's unconscious pursuit of Jakob's secret conspiracy.

Freud's analyses of his own dreams in chapter 6 of *The Interpretation of Dreams* are throughout marked by traces of this unconscious political coalition. To Balmary's innovative readings of Freud's so-called absurd dreams one should also add the dream where Jakob appears sullied on his deathbed by the homonymic play on the word *Stuhl* (which contains the same pun as the English *stool*).

> (I lost my father in 1896). *After his death my father played a political part among the Magyars and brought them together politically.* Here I saw a small and indistinct picture: *a crowd of men as though they were in the Reichstag; someone standing on one or two chairs [Stühlen], with other people round him. I remembered how like Garibaldi he had looked on his death-bed, and felt glad that that promise had come true.*[30]

The allusions to Garibaldi and the Reichstag are unmistakably feeble attempts to conceal the more profound resemblance between Jakob and Bismarck. Freud must have thought of Bismarck as Jakob's reincarnation in the two years between Jakob's death and the chancellor's. In his analysis Freud suggested that his dream condensed a picture of Maria Theresa in the Reichstag and an account he had heard of a daughter's distressing discovery that at "the moment of death, or *post mortem,* [her father] had passed a stool [*Stuhl*]." In his "Underworld" conspiracy with Jakob, Sigmund chose to read the deathbed dream as the expression of a wish "to stand before one's own children's eyes, after one's death, great and unsullied." Concealed/revealed by the post-mortem *Stuhl* is, of course, the fault. The irony is particularly rich here as Freud decried how accustomed we are "to overlook the absurdity" [*wir gewöhnt sind, über die Absurdität hinwegzusehen*] of dreams and of the "figures of speech" [*Redensart*] that generate them. Freud's dream denounced the father, while his dream-analysis encrypted the fault and once again erased the possibility of its revelation. In the same dream-analysis Freud cited two lines from Goethe's epilogue to Schiller's "Lied von der Glocke," naming Freud's secret conspiracy with his father's phantom in words upon which it would be difficult to improve.

> *Und hinter ihm in wesenlosem Scheine*
> *Lag, was uns alle bändigt, das Gemeine.*
> [Behind him, in shadowy illusion, lay what holds us
> all in bondage—the things that are in common.]

The fault ("das Gemeine") rings the death knell of psychoanalysis as a science even as it *bändigt* ("restrains," but also "bands," "binds," "constricts") Freud's work to a primordial structure of repetition which precedes both the unconscious and consciousness, a structure in which they are themselves inscribed. Psychoanalysis is thus preserved on an entirely other scene by becoming the death knell itself, rather than the one for whom the bell tolls. The fault rings the toll for the passing of an autobiographical speculation that would pose as an institutional power even as the fault preserves that speculation as an interminable passage into the abyss of repetition: for that specula-tion was always a specular, autobiographical projection, an apotropaic gesture, a rite of mourning, an effort to ward off the threat of immanent death or madness. That the reinscription in Freud's work of the fault and the phantom that transmits it is as much Bismarck's legacy as it is the father's requires a rethinking of history according to a new logic, according to a structure of repetition that is at once primordial and radically innovative. Following the logic charted by Balmary's rejection, not of intrapsychic Oedipal sexuality as such but of Oedipal sexuality as *the* determinant in the aetiology of the neuroses, we might consider psychoanalysis, not simply as the repetition of Bismarckian imperialism but as the expression of the bondage of structural thought to its own inherent imperialism.

Man speaks, then, but it is because the symbol has made him man.

Lacan, *Ecrits: A Selection*

Symbols in fact envelop the life of man in a network so total that they join together, before he comes into the world, those who are going to engender him "by flesh and blood"; so total that they bring to his birth, along with the gifts of the stars, if not with the gifts of the fairies, the shape of his destiny; so total that they give the words that will make him faithful or renegade, the law of the acts that will follow him right to the very place where he is not yet and even beyond his death; and so total that through them his end finds meaning in the last judgment, where the Word absolves his being or condemns it. . . .

Lacan, *Ecrits: A Selection*

Our wish to think well of man has played many tricks on scientific accuracy, and this study was not begun in defense of man's dignity. But in my work with children I have learned that while little good results from an unjustly high opinion of persons and motives, much and serious damage may result from an unwarrantedly low opinion.

Bettelheim, *Symbolic Wounds*

INTRODUCTION

"Where does it hurt?"

No response.

"Does your head hurt, or your back, or your shoulders?"

After a moment of silence, "Ah! No, Madame, it does not hurt there."

"Then what is it that makes you ill?"

"It is my father who makes me ill."[1]

The response of this child takes us at once to the heart of the archaeological expedition that this book recounts. This is a very special archaeology, since it explores the foundations of an edifice constructed less than a century ago by a man of genius who was himself an archaeologist of the mind, who made the cumbersome and unacknowledged past rise again in our memories. His name was Sigmund Freud.

The doctor asks, Where does it hurt? The psychoanalyst begins by silently questioning, What happened to you that your only memory of it is in your symptoms and your dreams? What were your desires? Then, as a result of Lacan's decisive innovation that one's desire is always the desire of the Other, the next question, always asked in silence and without preempting the preceding questions, becomes, Who made you ill? From one's own body to one's personal history, to one's family history, to one's relation to the Other: a great evolution that leaves no theory of mental life unchanged, regardless how encompassing it may be. Psychoanalysis, which has enabled us to pass in this way from the body to a relational system, now finds itself in a new situation. Wherever psychoanalysis has evolved and extended its influence, be it in classical analysis, child psychoanalysis, psychosomatic medicine, or among researchers in psychosis, the tide is turning; psychoanalytic theory, which was once questioned only by those who opposed it, is now interrogated by those to whom it at first provided answers.

On another front—but is it in fact another front?—biographical studies on Freud have accumulated since his death in 1939; at first eulogistical or critical, they now bring new elements and new questions, particularly concerning the authenticity of the official version of the life of Sigmund's father, Jakob Freud. These investigative psychoanalysts expose us to some troubling facts; their work is especially daring since they can still only formulate questions on the extent of their discoveries.

Thus on two fronts—the research in clinical practice, where mysterious links appear between the indefensible acts of one generation and the suffering of the next, and the research on its founder—psychoanalysis is interrogated by those who *make use* of it, while it is still not interrogated by those who *serve* it, to whom the present work, moreover, can be of no use.

In addition to these two inquiries, coming from within psychoanalysis itself, there is a third form of questioning, which comes from outside and which has been close at the heels of psychoanalysis since its foundation. It is the question philosophers pass to one another by relay: What about consciousness? In the words of Henri Ey,

> Psychoanalytical doctrine could give birth and consistency to the unconscious only on the express condition that its birth and its life depend on the constitution of a conscious being. Psychoanalysis should be reminded of what, in the rapture of its discoveries, it has forgotten of its first founding intuitions: no unconscious without the structure of consciousness.[2]

What can we say in response? No more than Freud do we know what consciousness is, nor even why consciousness is. And yet, is it not our objective to elicit from the patient a "coming to consciousness" [*prise de conscience*]?[3] The efficacy of our treatment leaves us finally astonished—what is it that enables one "to cure" in psychoanalysis? This simple, fundamental question brings us, as Lacan says, to "some mysterious resistance which conceals the question in relative darkness." Some kind of repulsion prevents its conceptualization. "There, perhaps more than elsewhere, it is possible that the completion of the theory and even its progress are perceived as a danger."[4] Is not the philosopher's question regarding consciousness tied to our astonishment as clinicians regarding the coming to consciousness? Why and how does one cure in psychoanalysis? Is the transmission of disorders from one generation to another connected to these questions? These surely are the questions we must ask when presented with new biographical information on Freud: How did he bear the secrets veiling his father's life? Will we discover that Freud's avoidance of the question of consciousness was synonymous with his avoidance of these secrets?

The confluence does not stop at the knot of clinical, biographical, and philosophical questions. Another current of research, by Hellenists and specialists on the ancient world, joined it many years ago. A youthful psychoanalysis has for long made too much noise to pay much attention to the reservations that these discrete people expressed when they refused to follow Freud in his use of *Oedipus the King* as an explication that was immediately clear and could be transposed directly from Greece in the fifth century B.C. to the nineteenth- and twentieth- century West.[5]

In addition to all this we must still consider the sociological evolution of the clients of psychoanalysis. The first were of the Viennese bourgeoisie of the late nineteenth century, in a period when the weight of morals and religion made itself felt very differently and with a force other than that of our epoch. That clientele submitted to physical and mental exigencies that are well enough represented by the fashion of that age; in all seasons the body was covered and restrained by corsets. As a child, Freud's son Martin did not know that under their skirts women had legs.[6] These first patients found in psychoanalysis liberation from their shackles. They found in psychoanalysis the possibility to understand what they had really felt in their own lives and bodies; the opportunity to understand those things that did not correspond to what was officially prescribed; those things that had been ruthlessly repressed or forgotten, by themselves and by others, as if they had never been experienced.[7] Through psychoanalysis they could recognize all those things that, if not shared verbally with another, return, like unsepulchered souls, to haunt human lives—the image is Freud's.

Times have changed; religion, morals, manners, what an overthrow in less than a century! Psychoanalysis has contributed much in the direction and speed of this change. We have applauded the new beginning of educational methods, the diminution of "sexual taboos," the disappearance of a certain hypocrisy, the rediscovery of the body, the recognition of desire from childhood on, the end of the yoke of religion and of the terrorism of virtue.

Of course, all this does not take place on a unified front. Analysts still see patients who are stifled and corseted. But now they also see the children of an education which, either directly inspired by analysis or having indirectly profited from its influence, has produced beings very different from the Viennese of 1900. Have we passed from the excess of the corset to an absence of the backbone? One sometimes wonders. These are the children of the "everything-is-permitted" generation; but if everything is permitted, why do they sometimes ask, Is anything possible? Joyous innocence of a generation "without complexes"; but then why do patients who are no longer even ill but completely worn out and lost come to analysts?

Briefly put, Freud described the neurotic as one who is unable to work or to enjoy; inhibited and afflicted by a culpability linked to unconscious desires, he suffers under psychic impotence. Are there still such people today? The answer is evidently yes. Now, however, their problem lasts longer—they are culpable to the second power; they feel guilty about feeling guilty. Guilt is not diminished. It is often tragically displaced; no longer guilty of doing, or desiring, one is now guilty of being. Is there a cure? What can analysis say to those whom drugs accompany in the terrifying feeling that is the total indignity of a so-called innocent?

Analysts have often energetically protested that excessive liberalism in education is a misinterpretation, rather than the fruit, of Freud's theories; and we agree.

Among those for whom psychoanalysis is applied with the utmost rigor and in all its purity, that is, among analysts themselves in the course of their formation, things become so difficult, even tragic, that we are not about to have the last word.[8] We are thinking of that "infinite analysis," that interminable dependence of the apprentice upon his master, who goes so far as to devour, little by little, the life of his student. Has psychoanalysis, founded by a new Oedipus who solved a famous riddle, become itself the sphinx, the "devourer of men?"[9]

Must we think that, paradoxically, the most intensive, the purest, analysis runs the greatest risks? If that is the case, then analytic theory and method could not be blameless. Happily, we know of many people whom analysis has awakened to themselves, to others, and to the world. The success of the analytic process, however, does not seem to be in relation either to its purity or its length. Freud already regretted this; for, with the exception of his earliest cases where he had considerable trouble persuading his patients to continue for at least a few months, he had afterward rapidly to recognize that the great difficulty was to convince them to terminate the analysis.

We are therefore vigorously advised on all sides to explain ourselves and to move on—or, if we are prevented from doing so, to find again the point where we went astray. When an admirably constructed house becomes cracked on every floor, one has the right to inquire into its foundations. At the beginning, the first-floor tenant sees the fissure; he recalls that one day he made an unlucky stroke of the hammer while installing the laundry rack, and feeling vaguely responsible, patches it up and says nothing. The second-floor tenant also sees the crack; he finds another explanation, acts just like his neighbor, and so on. Next, on the ground floor the cupboard suddenly comes loose, causing a service of Limoges china to fall. Then all the tenants can state their common misfortunes and ask for the architect.

Psychoanalysis is an edifice in which questions are posed at every floor. But the architect is dead. We have no alternative but to examine the foundations and to try to understand. These foundations are the life and work of Freud, and the relation between them. Fortunately for us, there is probably no mortal about whom so much information is available; he published a very important body of work, recounted to us his dreams, his parapraxes, his omissions, and his lapses of memory, and his disciples have collected everything up to the slightest trace of his name on a register. He taught us himself to decipher and interpret; we have therefore both the method and the material. And yet how can we find anything new in these places where so many have visited so often? Our project is to descend into the foundations of psychoanalysis—but by which route? Which among Ariadne's threads will guide us?

Perhaps we should look elsewhere to discover how other edifices are built, and then apply to psychoanalysis what we have learned about other narrow passageways scarcely noticed until now: to return to the Freudian edifice only after we have learned to read very small signs long covered by dust. In short, we must change radically our research habits, since we are looking not toward the heights but toward the depths, and not at what psychoanalysis wishes to show but at what it has perhaps covered up.

It is not a question of explicating Freud, that is, of linking elements of his life to another symbolic system that would be exterior to him as others have done—not without rousing our interest: for example, David Bakan's study of Freud and the Jewish mystical tradition.[10] One can, through that method, prepare a new idea, but nothing is established.

We attempt here an interpretation and not an explication. According to us, the two things are to be distinguished. Explication is a simple equivalence. Two terms are in play. To explicate is to say $T=I$ or $D=O$. In interpretation there are no longer two but three terms: the conjunction of two elements constitutes a third. To interpret is to say $T+I=TI$ or $D+O=DO$. A new meaning then appears (in this case musical) whose elements were already present but that only their conjunction reveals. The third term, the result, is in no way exterior to the first two. One can thus distinguish between an *inter*-pretation and an *ex*-plication.

To explore foundations. We feel that in order to reread Freud in a new way, we need a new insight and a new investigative tool. Without it, we will proceed as did Charcot, who, on repeated visits to the hospital wards, saw only what he had been taught to see. How can we understand what Freud really said and not simply what the psychoanalytic tradition and first of all, Freud, have taught us to understand? Where, for a while, can we unlearn analysis? Where can we go to cleanse our too habituated eyes? To which epoch? To which country?

Because it was from Sophocles' tragedy *Oedipus Rex* that Freud named the famous complex, we can justifiably regard the play as the keystone of psychoanalysis. The play's language, ancient Greek, a dead language, would suit our estrangement.

Since our method is to concentrate our attention upon what until now has been ignored, we can begin with this tragic story, on the condition that we put it on its reverse side: here also, we must look to its foundations. What happened before the birth of Oedipus?

In 1953 a psychoanalyst began his article by observing, "It is striking to remark that psychoanalytic theory pays extremely little attention to certain complexes which, in the strictest meaning, complete the Oedipus complex."[11] He wished to discuss the sadistic and homosexual components that appeared in Oedipus's parents. A quarter century later, other writers observed that Freud seemed to have ignored that Oedipus had invented neither the murder of a parent nor the union with a forbidden person; that the first murder was committed not by the son but by the father; and that the first sexual crime is not attributable to Oedipus.[12]

In conjuction with the recent revelations concerning Sigmund's father, Jakob Freud, his son's inattention to the foundations of the Oedipean myth immediately suggests a hypothesis: Would he have failed to recognize in the myth what he must have failed to recognize in his own family? If that were the case, however, what function would the discovery of the unconscious and the elaboration of analytical theory have had in his life? And reciprocally—the question then is of the greatest interest to us—what role would Freud's life have played in the discovery and construction of psychoanalysis if, unknown to him, it had comprised such a fundamental misapprehension [*méconnaissance*]? Was it due to his father that Oedipus became ill? Is it because Freud suffered from the same disorder that he was unable to recognize it in Oedipus?

Our journey to Greece is not therefore a simple change of countries. If we find there something other regarding Oedipus than what Freud said about him, we should then have reversed the habitual movement: to Sophocles, this time, to pose some questions.

a diabolic, divisive act that separates him from what is his own, there is only a symptom where there should be a symbol. Such is the result of the father's willful disavowal of his fault and of his effort to protect himself from its consequences. *The symptom originates from the fault that ruptures the symbol from what it entails.*

Is there a Greek word that would be to *symptom* what *diabolic* is to *symbolic*? The Greek word *diaptoma*, which combines the verb *piptō* and the prefix *dia*, means "fall," "mistake," or figuratively, "fault."

diabolē (false testimony)	*sumbolē* (symbol)
diaptoma (fault)	*sumptoma* (symptom)

Freud and Lacan have already stated that the symptom appears in the absence of the symbol. To this we add that the symbol is missing because a dia-bolic separation has intervened in its place. The dia-bolic is itself a consequence of the fault (*diaptoma*).

Laius $\xrightarrow{\text{diabolē}}$ sumptoma
diaptoma   ~~sumbole~~   Oedipus

The symptom, an effort to overcome the dia-bolic word, would appear as the trace of a broken, disrupted symbol. Swollen feet are all that remain of Oedipus's filiation. It was Laius, not Oedipus, who was under an interdiction. Oedipus was only bound and cast out. For him there was no *interdiction* against incest, only an *obstacle*.

To compare briefly the Greek myth to the biblical myth in Genesis, we see that there were no obstacles to the fault in the Garden of Eden: Adam and Eve were free and unbounded in their movements. God withdrew himself from the site of the ordeal; he neither controlled nor intervened in their actions. In Genesis there is an interdiction without obstacles.

Nothing is said directly to Oedipus. It is the father who hears the oracle before Oedipus is even conceived. (According to Sophocles, Laius hears it a little later, after the child's conception.) The oracle makes no demands of Oedipus. The utterance is neither addressed to, nor does it reach, Oedipus. Oedipus is sentenced to death by Laius, but not to death by human hands. It is not to a speaking subject but to chance, to the wild, that Oedipus is to be delivered to die. But the servant charged with this task hands the child over to some passing shepherds. They bring him to

---

CHAPTER 1

OEDIPUS HAS STILL MORE TO TEACH US

Lao-Tzu asks: "To what would you first give your attention if the Prince of Wei awaited your ruling on public matters?"
"To give each thing its true name," answers the Master.

Confucius

We all share this wish of Confucius. But how would we go about fulfilling it? We can try to discover the true name of each thing by seeking, not its figurative, but its literal meaning, by seeking a concrete sense that refers to material things. This line of inquiry leads us to etymologies rather than definitions. Our most abstract words are built on distant, but visible, tangible realities. In order to make our way into the myth, we will use a simple tool: a verb and two prefixes.

Pivotal to our research and to psychoanalysis is the word *symbol* and its derivatives (*symbolic, to symbolize*). According to the old Bailly dictionary, the ancient Greek *sumbolon* signifies first a "sign of recognition" and originally meant "an object cut into two, of which two friends each keep half, which they pass on to their children; these two halves identify the bearers when they meet one another and attest to the hospitable relations contracted earlier."[1] This drawing together is synonymous with the meaning of the verb *sun-ballō* (composed of *sun* 'together' and *ballō* 'to throw'), whose meaning, "to throw together," "to end at the same point," is already inscribed in the *sumbolon*. In its origins, the symbol is a sign whose double meaning, when reunited, serves to facilitate the recognition not so much of a person as of a relation that unites one person to another. Is that not in fact precisely the nature of every sign of recognition? The word *sumbolē* signifies bringing together two things that belong together, that are fitted to each other, like lips or eyelids.

The often ignored antonym of *symbolic,* in Greek, is *diabolic.*[2] It is formed from the verb *ballō* and from the preposition *dia,* which means the opposite of *sun.* While *sun* is the preposition of unity, *dia* is the preposition of separation. In the etymology of the words *diabolic, diable* (French for "devil"), etc., we find the idea of throwing or flinging, but in the sense of separating, of rendering asunder. *Diabolos* literally means "one who disjoins," from which come the meanings of scandal and calumny (*diabolē*).

The Origin of the Curse

Oedipus was a foundling, an adopted child. He was named after what had characterized his condition when he was first discovered: *Oidipous* 'swollen feet'. His ankles were transpierced, and a strap was strung through them, but no sign of recognition, no *symbol* was found with him. The mark on his body, the mark that would later enable him, despite all obstacles, to recognize who he is, constitutes the first sign of *méconnaissance.* His father, Laius, marked him thus so that he might die of exposure. The father rejected his son in order to escape the fulfillment of the oracle's prophecy, which, according to Sophocles, predicted that the son would slay the father. "But according to Aeschylus and Euripides, the oracle would have intervened before the conception of the child in order to prevent Laius from fathering a child, warning him that if he had a son, that son would not only murder him, but would be the cause of a series of frightful calamities."[3]

Instead of following the story of Oedipus downstream, we are going to go backward to what happened before his birth for such a prediction (or according to other versions, interdiction) to have been pronounced. We must therefore investigate the life of Laius. Laius was very young when his father, King Labdacus, died, and he had to flee when the regent was killed. He sought refuge with King Pelops. "There he developed a passion for young Chrysippus, Pelops' son, and thus, by some accounts, he conceived unnatural passions. Laius ran off with the young man and was cursed by Pelops. . . . Chrysippus, from shame, committed suicide."[4] Such is the origin of the curse of the Labdacidae. The whole story now appears under quite a different light. It is neither Oedipus's desire, nor blind destiny, that constitutes the profound motive behind the tragic events that will befall him. At the origin is the fault committed by Laius; the abduction and homosexual violation of the young son of his host and the suicide that follows constitute the mainspring of the Oedipean myth. Even the name of the young man should be noted: it means 'golden horse' *Chrusippos.*[5]

The original fault in this story is therefore committed not by Oedipus, murderer of his father and husband of his mother, but by

Laius. In addition to his first series of faults, Laius commits y[...] fault when he violates the interdiction not to have children, [...] imposed as a result of his first offense against Chrysippus ar[...] Laius's third fault is of a different order: having nevertheless f[...] son, Laius tries to conceal his violation by exposing his son to[...] ments. His intended murder of his son fails, and thus the way is[...] the fulfillment of the oracle. His ankles pierced and tied toge[...] birth, Oedipus is thus exposed to death. Instead of bearing a [...] recognition *on* him, as one might expect of a newborn child, Oed[...] identifying mark is inscribed *in* his body; and, ironically, the lin[...] "joining together" of the symbol, does not attach him to another[...] only binds him to himself. The drawing together of two identical th[...] —the ankles—does not, at least apparently, form a new sign. Only a[...] the drama is complete, when it is too late, will this sign play its role.[...] his effort to evade the consequences of his transgression, Laius breaks th[...] relation which joins him to the son who is the embodiment of his faul[...] He does not name him. Oedipus does not have either a name or an[...] origin; there is no symbol which binds him to anyone. And yet, from the[...] treatment which should have led to his death, there remains a sign: his[...] swollen feet. Not a symbol, but a symptom.

The Symptom and the Fault

The Greek word for symptom, *sumptoma,* means "subsidence" or "coincidence"; in general it signifies a fortuitous event. Formed from *sun* 'together,' and *piptō* 'to fall', it conveys the idea of an involuntary or partially involuntary fall as in French (or English) reflexives that express attitudes governed by a strong emotion or passion: *je me précipite, je me jette* 'I rush, I throw myself'. While the verb *ballō* means to cause something to fall. *piptō* means "to fall," "to take a fall." The subject of *ballō* is active, while the subject of *piptō* is passive. Likewise, *sumbolon* and *sumptoma,* 'symbol' and 'symptom', reach the same end through different means. The symbol actively produces the joining of two halves, which enables meaning to appear. In the symptom that union is produced accidentally. Men are the authors of symbols, but they are the spectators of symptoms. It is as though the symptom were a subsymbol, a chance return of what could not be symbolized. Does Lacan not say that what cannot be symbolized reappears in the realm of the real?

Oedipus, to whom all symbols are refused, is therefore passively marked by a bodily symptom. His name does not come from the treatment he has been subjected to—he is not called "pierced feet"—but from his body's response to this treatment: its swelling. Instead of a symbolic name, Oedipus is given a symptomatic name. For Oedipus, victimized by

their master, the king of Corinth. Just as Laius was sheltered by Pelops, so is Oedipus by Polybus. Why will Oedipus leave him one day? "The most ancient version of the story appears to be the following: Oedipus leaves in order to recover some stolen horses, and it is then that he meets, without knowing it, his real father, Laius."[6] According to another, better known, version, that of the Tragic poets, Oedipus learns from a fellow citizen, full of wine and wrath, that he is not Polybus's son, and goes to consult the oracle to discover who his true parents are.

First Scene of Suffering: The Bodies of Father and Son. Signs of the Father's First Fault

We adopt here the opinion of Claude Lévi-Strauss that "all versions belong to the myth" and should be considered.[7] Does Oedipus leave to seek his father or to recover the stolen horses? What if these two questions are really only one? Did not Laius "steal" Chrysippus, the golden horse, from his host, King Pelops? What follows brings the questions of the father and the horse still closer together. Laius and Oedipus meet at the intersection of three roads. There is little space between the rocks. "And then Polyphontes, Laius' herald, ordered Oedipus to let the king pass and killed one of his horses because he had not obeyed quickly enough; furious, Oedipus slew Polyphontes and Laius."[8] The theme of the narrow passage where father and son struggle has been explicated by psychoanalysis as symbolizing the female sexual organs. If we reject explication for interpretation, however, we might notice the murder of the horse: Chrysippus is also a murdered horse. On his quest for his father, Oedipus first finds a slain horse. Or, seeking the stolen horses, Oedipus meets his father, on whose account a horse is killed. An intersection of three roads forms a *lambda*, the first letter of Laius's name (λ, formed also by Oedipus's legs fastened at the ankles). Oedipus arrives at the crossroads because of his father and the stolen horses; and what first takes place is the murder of a horse. Indeed, Chrysippus had himself been stolen, and had died because of Laius.

In Euripides' play *The Phoenician Women* things are clearer yet. In the following passage, Jocasta describes what happened after her marriage to Laius.

> When he still was childless
> after long marriage with me in the palace,
> he went to Phoebus asking and beseeching
> that we might share male children for the house.
> But he said, "Lord of Thebes and its famed horses,

> sow not that furrow against divine decree.
> For if you have a child, him you beget
> shall kill you, and your house shall wade through blood."[9]

Phoebus's reference to the "famed horses" clearly suggests Laius's fault; what better way to remind him of Pelops's curse and the interdiction against procreation. Jocasta goes on to recount that only after Laius, lustful and drunk, "begot a child on me" did he realize that "his sex was a sin, as the God had said it" (l. 24).

Thus, according to Euripides, Oedipus was conceived by accident. As the word *sumptoma* suggests, his conception took place in a state of unintentional oblivion. Having realized what he had done, he pinned his son's ankles and sent him to be exposed in the wild. But "Polybus' herdsmen-riders took the child/ and brought it home" (l. 29); thus, again the horse motif. The king's horsemen assume responsibility of the child who, due to his father's theft of a "horse," is left in the nonsymbolizable void. They bring the child to Polybus's wife, who, in Jocasta's words, "took my labor's fruit to her own breast/ and told her husband that it was her own" (l. 30-31). Again, it is false testimony that prevents Oedipus from being recognized for what he is: in this case, an abandoned child. Jocasta goes on to describe how Oedipus and Laius leave to search for one another.

> When his red beard was growing, my young son,
> who had guessed or heard the truth, set off to learn
> at Phoebus' house, his parents. So did Laius,
> seeking to learn if the child he had exposed
> were still alive. They met in middle journey
> at the same spot in the split road of Phocis.
> Then Laius' runner ordered him away:
> "Stranger, yield place to princes." But he came on,
> silent, in pride. So with their sharp-edged hooves
> the mares of Laius bloodied up his feet.
> And so—why give the detail of disaster?—
> son slew father, and he took the team
> to give to Polybus, his foster parent. (ll. 32-44)

In bloodying Oedipus's feet, Laius's mares repeat what their master had done to his son. In offering the horses to Polybus, his host, is Oedipus not making a "blind" reparation for the theft of Chrysippus from Pelops?

We have tried to discover whether Freud was familiar with the various versions of the Oedipus tragedy which we possess today. Although he cites Sophocles frequently, he refers to Euripides only once, apparently ignoring *The Phoenician Women*. And to Aeschylus there is no reference. "It might easily be supposed that the material of the [Oedipus] legend had in view an indictment of the gods and of fate; and in the hands of

Euripides, the critic and enemy of the gods, the tragedy of Oedipus would probably have become such an indictment. But with the devout Sophocles there is no question of an application of that kind."[10] Where did Freud get this idea? Besides, in the texts available to us, the oracle that concerns Laius and announces his guilt appears before the two tragedies, Sophocles' *Oedipus the King* and *The Phoenician Women* of Euripides. In the French edition it appears in translation before Euripides' play:

> Labdacide Laius, you want happy children:
> You will engender a son, but your destiny will be
> To lose your life by his hand; Zeus the Cronide
> Ratifies the fatal warnings of Pelops;
> You stole his son: he has cursed you.[11]

We do not know if this oracle appeared before the texts that were accessible in Vienna at the end of the nineteenth century. According to the English and German indexes of Freud's work, however, we can state that the name of Laius does not appear anywhere in his writings (except where it is a question of Oedipus's crime).

Let us return to Oedipus's destiny. Apparently only the product of chance and coincidence, the meeting of Oedipus and Laius is full of signs indicating that it is the result of destiny and fate. Mindful of the father's hidden fault and the words that represent it in the "fortuitous" event, one might say that destiny determines the *sumptoma*, the coincidence. Every detail counts and fits together in a circular way. Everything that was hidden in Oedipus's destiny is revealed through the repetition of numerous motifs. What had been concealed now becomes reality: the horsemen, the stolen horses, the three branches of the crossroads in the form of the letter *lambda* (as in Laius), the slain horse, Oedipus's bloody heels, the team of horses given to Polybus, the return to Polybus of horses in place of Pelops's horse-son, etc. There is even the assonance in Greek between Pelops and Polybus.

Like Laius, as he silently prepared his son's death, Oedipus kills his father without saying a word. Oedipus does to his father what his father wanted to do to him. Without knowing it, Oedipus fulfills a double vengeance: Pelops's and his own. We can now embark in a new direction. A new inquiry into Sophocles' *Oedipus the King,* which has been analyzed so often, is indeed possible because we can now assert that the life of the son cannot be considered apart from the life of his father. For, unrecognized and rejected by his father, Oedipus will find on his search for him all the signs representing the sin that led to his rejection. And he will perform an act that not only renders to the father what he had wanted to give to his son but also revenges the death that Laius was responsible for, once again indirectly: namely, the death of the young Chrysippus.

After Laius's death Oedipus heads toward Thebes and vanquishes the Sphinx by answering her riddle, thus liberating Thebes from that devourer of men. Interestingly, her riddle also has much to do with feet. "There is on earth a being of one voice who first walks on four feet, then on two feet, and finally on three feet; it alone, among all the beings which live on earth, in the air or in the sea, goes through these changes; but this being is weakest when it uses more than two feet to walk." Oedipus's own name can help him to find an answer. Indeed, we just saw that a horse could represent a child. Here the Sphinx presents a unique being—a voice—that can have two, four, or three feet and that we must always identify as the same. Leaving aside this enigma, let us proceed to Thebes. Oedipus has been placed on the throne by the Thebans in gratitude for their liberation and has married Queen Jocasta. All is well. Then comes the plague.

Second Scene of Suffering:
The Social Body.
Signs of the Father's Second Fault.

Athens had suffered a frightful visitation of the plague in 430 B.C. Instead of exploring this element of *Oedipus the King* in terms of Greek history, however, we would rather investigate it from within the text itself. What are the Thebans suffering from? In the opening scene of Sophocles' tragedy, the priest of Zeus describes the symptoms to Oedipus.

> King, you yourself
> have seen our city reeling like a wreck
> already; it can scarcely lift its prow
> out of the depths, out of the bloody surf.
> A blight is on the fruitful plants of the earth,
> a blight is on the cattle in the fields,
> a blight is on our women that no children
> are born to them.[12]

The epidemic subsequently evoked is as vague as the previous sentence was precise. Further on the Chorus continues in its lament.

> There are no children in this famous land;
> there are no women bearing the pangs of childbirth. (l. 171-172)

Here, too, we find a more nebulous description of the countless dead.

> In the unnumbered deaths
> of its people the city dies;
> those children that are born lie dead on the naked earth
> unpitied, spreading contagion of death; and grey haired

mothers and wives
everywhere stand at the altar's edge, suppliant, moaning. (ll. 182-85)

If we read carefully, it seems that only the men of Thebes are struck by
death, whereas all that is feminine or carrying fruit in its womb is struck
with sterility. As the editor of the French translation of the play notes,
this is indeed a curious epidemic. "The 'plague' in *Oedipus the King* is no
ordinary epidemic. It's one of the great mythical 'evils' evoked by the
old ritual imprecations whose essential characteristic is the sterility which
strikes every fertile being. . . . In describing it, Sophocles, perhaps unconsciously, included some details of the plague that ravaged Athens at
the beginning of the Peloponnesian war."[13]

Here once again we find superimposition, as if two curses were
intertwined. These afflictions of Thebes set the whole drama in motion.
The oracle declares that they are linked to some taint. The "plague" is
thus directly linked to the fault; the *sumptoma* here also refers to a
diaptoma. The question is: which fault? We know that it is the murder of
Laius by Oedipus, but as a result of the parallels between the lives of
father and son, we should ask ourselves if there is a link between this
epidemic of feminine sterility and masculine mortality and the life of
Laius.

The plague at Thebes corresponds, point by point, to Pelops's curse
and to the interdiction of the god. Like Laius, Thebes is barred from
procreating. Were Laius to violate this edict, his son would kill him; and
now the citizens of Thebes die. Just as Oedipus's meeting with his father
was a return to Laius's original fault, so too is the plague as much a
return to the father's (voluntary?) transgression as it is to the son's (involuntary?) crime. If Thebes under Oedipus suffers evils that sympto-
matically represent Laius' fault, then perhaps this is related to the missing
symbol between Oedipus and Laius: the abortive symbol that deteriorates
into the symptom. The symptom also joins two half-signs together, but
this transpires without speech in the realm of the real. This process
knows no sovereign; everyone submits to it. It is precisely what escapes
the sovereignty of Oedipus.

The misfortunes of Thebes are inseparable from the life of Oedipus.
Its citizens are his subjects, and from the beginning he claims that these
calamities are more closely connected to himself than to anyone else:

> I know you are all sick,
> yet there is not one of you, sick though you are,
> that is as sick as I myself.
> Your several sorrows each have single scope
> and touch but one of you. My spirit groans
> for city and myself and you at once. (ll. 59-64)

The social body is here identical to the physical body since it bears the symptoms of its ruler's illness. Paraphrasing the child of whom Françoise Dolto spoke, the Thebans could say: "my king makes me ill" or even "my kings make me ill." The figure of Oedipus as head of the body that is Thebes is also present. After his interview with Teiresias, Oedipus, who believes nothing that the blind prophet has told him, bursts out with accusations against his brother-in-law, Creon. Learning of the scene, Creon comes, in Oedipus's absence, to ask the Chorus what condition the king was in when he made these accusations:

> *Creon:* Were his eyes straight in his head? Was his mind right
> when he accused me in this fashion?
> *Chorus:* I do not know; I have no eyes to see what princes do.
> (ll. 528-31)

Just as the body is unable to see its own head, the social body has no eyes, no way to judge what its head is doing. Oedipus is the eyes of Thebes.

Third Scene of Suffering:
The Eyes of Oedipus.
Signs of the Father's Third Fault.

To understand this metaphor we must return, following the play, to a previous moment of suffering, a moment outside the history of Oedipus since it was lived at a time that he does not remember. At the end of his quest to find the murderer of Laius, the taint upon his land, Oedipus succeeds in finding the sole witness to the drama, an old shepherd. The revelation of the truth occurs when a messenger from Corinth arrives to announce the death of Polybus and to proclaim Oedipus king of Corinth. The Corinthian messenger and the Theban shepherd had been involved with the adventures of the infant Oedipus. Oedipus asks many questions of the Corinthian, who believes he is re-assuring Oedipus by telling him that he need not fear committing incest upon his return to Corinth because he is not the son of Polybus and Merope. The messenger tells him that it was he who found him in a valley in Cithaeron and returned him to be adopted by Polybus.

> *Oedipus:* What ailed me when you took me in your arms?
> *Messenger:* In that your ankles should be witnesses. (ll. 1031-32)

In the Greek text, it is written as *podo an arthra* 'the articulations of the feet', i.e., the ankles. In the preceding scene, Jocasta, in order to prove that the oracles were not fulfilled, had described to Oedipus the fate of her first child, Laius's son, who had not had the chance to become his father's murderer because:

before three days were out
after his birth King Laius pierced his ankles
and by the hands of others cast him forth
upon a pathless hillside. (ll. 717-20)

Again, the same expression appears in the Greek text: *arthra podoin* 'the articulations of the two feet'.

What more can we discover about the wound from which Oedipus derives his name? According to Jocasta in *The Phoenician Women*, Laius used "sharp iron" to pin the ankles (l. 27). Elsewhere, we find references to "golden needles."[14] All these versions of the story mention the same part of the body (the ankles), the same action (piercing), a similar instrument (a metal needle, a pointed tool which might well have been a prod or spur that one associates with horses and cattle).

Before Oedipus's investigation is over, Jocasta realizes the truth and hurriedly returns to the palace. Soon afterward, Oedipus realizes that the child exposed by Laius and supposed dead, the child adopted by Polybus and now king of Thebes, and the murderer of Laius are in fact the same person. Here also we find an intersection of three roads; three lives, three identities cross and join one another. The Sphinx had maintained that a being could walk in three different ways and still have but one voice.

Crossroads are decidedly dangerous places; and Oedipus has yet one more to cross alone. He is alone under the eyes of time, or as the Chorus puts it after the scene of discovery: "Time who sees all has found you out against your will" (l. 1213). Then suddenly, as if "some god showed him the way," he flings open the doors, "wrenching the hollow bolts out of their sockets," and finds Jocasta hanging by the neck.

When he saw her, he cried out fearfully
and cut the dangling noose. Then, as she lay,
poor woman, on the ground, what happened after,
was terrible to see. He tore the brooches—
the *gold chased brooches* fastening her robe —
away from her and lifting them up high
and dashed them on his own eyeballs. (ll. 1265-70, emphasis ours)

The significance of the Greek words cannot be realized in translation. First of all, there is only one golden brooch; the Greek is singular. Only the translator can explain why multiplying the brooch should make the text more coherent. For our part, in our way of proceeding, we will consider that there are no errors in the original text which need to be corrected. Everything that appears incoherent is actually meaningful. What, then, is the Greek word for a brooch or clasp? The Greek word is *peronē,* the point that goes through the object and fastens into the clasp or buckle. Whence by analogy, we derive its anatomical meaning present in the French *péroné*, and the English *peroneal*, both of which refer to the fibula, the smallest of the two bones below the knee. Once more we are led to the ankle; for the bottom of the *péroné* forms the external malleolus, or the rounded projection of the bones that we call ankles. Oedipus gouges his eyes out with an instrument that evokes not only the needle Laius used to pierce his ankles, but, still more intimately, the very bone Laius transpierced. Yet another surprise awaits us in the expression Sophocles uses for what the English translator renders as "eyeballs." Sophocles' phrase is *arthra tōn kuklōn*, "articulation of the eyes"; again, the same word, *arthra*, he employed to designate the articulation of the feet that Laius had transpierced. The word *arthron* 'articulation', when used alone, discreetly designates the male sexual organ. Herodotus uses it in this way. In Greek literature *arthron* is usually used in combination with the words feet, mouth, and eyes.

Even though the word is unfamiliar, we can easily understand that *arthra* designates any juncture of two parts, one concave and the other convex, which makes movement possible. Thus the cavities of the mouth and of the eye sockets, as well as the joints of the limbs, permit the free movement of the tongue, the eyes, and the hands and feet. Although we would no longer explain the erection of the male organ as the articulation of a joint (around the testicles?), it is surely not difficult to understand that this was assumed to be the case in 500 B.C.

Laius's initial fault was indeed a sexual fault. Psychoanalytic thought, which sees in Oedipus's mutilation the equivalent of castration, certainly is echoed in the Greek words themselves. The third site of suffering in this tragedy, Oedipus's gouged eyes, recalls the third sin of Laius. The son punctures the articulation of the eyes with a needle (a *peronē*) whereas the father had used a needle—the kind of needle used as a prod for horses—to puncture the articulation of the son's ankles, which is to say the lower part of the fibula (*peronē*).

Transmission

We have seen how the life of Oedipus, at three tragic moments, repeats the three faults of Laius: (1) Laius seduced, abducted, and caused the death of another's son; his own son kills him, seduces his wife, Jocasta, and causes her death (suicide again); (2) Laius violated the divine interdiction against procreation; his son's subjects become sterile or die; and (3) Laius transpierced his son's ankles (*arthra*) with a *peronē*; his son pierces his own eyes (*arthra*) with a *peronē*. Perhaps the Greeks would not have regarded Laius's exposure of the infant Oedipus as a fault, but certainly the manner in which it was done raises questions. There is no risk that the three-day-old Oedipus, who has been abandoned in the forest, would even have a chance to return home by foot, like Tom Thumb. Laius's treatment of his son's ankles links this act to the first fault and the ensuing curse of the Labdacidae. The fault is a "fault of articulation" in the primary meaning of the word *arthron:* male sexual organ. The rape of Chrysippus and the procreation of Oedipus are sexual activities.

Although all the events of the Oedipean story appear to be unconnected, we can see the formation of an extremely tightly knitted network when we consider the words themselves. From behind the apparent coincidences, behind the chance disorder, beyond the apparent innocence of the individual, hidden in the most simple and concrete words, there arises a new network of meaning. Like a new path in the circulation of blood, like the discovery of the confluence of two riverbeds long since dried up, what now appears are subterranean passages from one life to another, from one destiny to another.

Is it really alien to us, this vision of human destiny caught in a system of hidden faults (Laius), expiated sins (Thebes), repeated sins (Oedipus), and reproduced ones (from Oedipus to his sons)? Laius's first fault is avenged by his death in a similarly concealed way. His second fault is expiated by a stricken city, but the citizens are unaware of it. The third fault, the deferred murder of the son, will be unknowingly repeated, when Oedipus pierces himself as his father had done. This will also be reproduced: Oedipus will send his own sons to death; cursing them, he will inflict upon them the destiny of dying at the hands of one another. Transpierced by a father who had "transpierced" another's son, Oedipus will, in his turn, transpierce his own sons. Oedipus's ankles, eyes, and the fruit of his sex (we could substitute the word *arthron* in each case) are all transpierced; his two sons will pierce one another with their weapons and die together.

Much remains to be discovered in this story. What, for example, will we find if we look upstream, as it were, toward Laius's origins? What do we know of his father, Labdacus, whose very name evokes the act of limping? What is the role of the feet in his story? What fault might be concealed there? If we look in the other direction, to Oedipus's sons Polyneices and Eteocles, how is their conflict linked to the preceding faults and to the curse cast upon them by their father, which, according to one version of the legend, he uttered after they had given him the hip to eat rather than the shoulder of the sacrificial animal? Again, we note the articulation of the joint. The texts and the legends are both so rich and so precise, each word is so specific, that we cannot possibly follow all these paths of investigation. We hope that others, with a better knowledge of Greek language and civilization, will have more success than us in finding the meaningful elements that abound.

The child whose response opens this book could be Oedipus himself. It is indeed Oedipus's father who makes him ill. The son bears the burden of the father's evil deeds throughout his life in his flesh and blood. It is not therefore without good reason that the spectacle of Oedipus before the people of Thebes, his eyes gouged out, his face covered with blood, evokes the figure of Jesus of Nazareth when he is presented to the people of Jerusalem after his flagellation. *Ecce homo,* said Pilate, Behold, this is the man. In his book on Sophocles, Karl Reinhardt makes the following comment on this aspect of Oedipus's tragedy: "Within this *ecce* there remains a silent question, that the man of future ages—who begins in Euripidean man—when his universe has become tragic, will no longer be able to avoid: where is the fault?"[15] Inasmuch as he was unable to see that Euripides had begun to ask this question, Freud's inability to ask it is not surprising. He was unable to see that *Oedipus the King* involves many more questions than the one concerning Oedipus's desires. Much more frightening than Oedipus's desires is the recognition of the transmission of the original fault from generation to generation. This is an inexorable machine without forgiveness or redemption; the father's evil will be expiated by the son, who will transmit it to his sons, and so on, until their lineage is extinct. There is no name by which they can be saved, no god to take the fault upon himself. As the Bible says:

> The fathers have eaten sour grapes,
> and the children's teeth are set on edge.[16]

The prophet predicts that when the Messiah comes this will no longer be said; when that time comes each man will pay for his own crime.

Before going on to investigate Freud, with the understanding that he neither studied nor analyzed the very text that was nevertheless one of the bases of his theory, we want to articulate the question that arises from our reading. Could it be that the series of faults and suffering, which extends across generations, is only readable in Greek tragedies of the fifth century B.C., and that Freud was therefore right not to undertake the brief investigation we have just carried out? The pattern we have deciphered, however, corresponds to the great mythical and religious explanations of human existence: an original fault, the punishment of the guilty party and the transmission of this punishment through generations. We cannot put all this aside. Moreover, we will see later that psychoanalysis itself is linked, at its origin, to the idea of the fault.

For the moment, we will see if, outside Freud's work, anyone in our time has gathered clinical data corresponding to what we found in *Oedipus the King.*

LACAN'S MAN WITH THE SEVERED HAND

The strongest echo comes from Lacan's first *Séminaire,* which contains his lectures for the year 1953-54. This is particularly curious because, outside his doctoral thesis, case histories are extremely rare in Lacan's writings. This is perhaps the only place where a clinical example is presented at such length. In the context of our argument, this fact is indeed noteworthy. What follows are the main points of Lacan's account.

> It concerns one of my patients. . . . He had particularly unique symptoms having to do with the use of his hands. . . . An analysis had been conducted along classical lines without success, organizing, at all cost, his symptoms in terms of infantile masturbation, of course, and the prohibitions and repression that it would have brought with it. . . . The patient was . . . of the Islamic religion. But one of the most striking aspects in the history of his subjective development was his estrangement from, his aversion to the law of the Koran. . . . Something struck me in passing, in relation to an idea that I consider quite sane, namely that one can not ignore [*méconnaître*] the symbolic appurtenances of a patient. That led us straight to what was in question here.
>
> In a word, to one found guilty of theft the law of the Koran states: *Your hand will be cut off.* During his childhood, the patient, privately and publicly, had been cast into a whirlwind, which resulted from his having overheard—what was all playacting, for his father was a civil servant who had been dismissed—that his father was a thief and should therefore have his hand cut off.
>
> A long time had indeed passed, and the sentence was still not executed. . . . But it nonetheless remained inscribed in the symbolic order of intersubjective relations which one calls the law.[17]

This takes us to the heart of the same problem we encountered in ancient Greece. The form of the symptom is linked to a divine prescription. Lacan's patient fulfills through his unusable hand what his father should have suffered as punishment for his fault; the son now has the severed hand. The subject's symptom is a representation of the father's punishment—and therefore, to take it one step further, a representation of the fault. The equivalent to this in *Oedipus the King* is the plague in Thebes. According to the classical method of interpretation, here exemplified by Teiresias and the oracle, the plague is caused by the murder Oedipus has committed. In exactly the same way classical analysis interpreted the Moslem patient's problem as the effect of masturbation. In both cases, a first level of interpretation of the problem leads back to a fault committed on the suffering subject himself, suffering through his own body or through the social body of which he is the head. In both cases, the fault, even if it is known, is not recognized. The one who suffers is not supposed to know it. If, however, he does know it — and we could argue that otherwise there would be no symptoms — it is without anyone making an accusation. He overheard by coincidence that the father — or the king? — was at fault.

Lacan's patient was "in a whirlwind" when he accidentally discovered the fault; and Oedipus first heard himself called an adopted child by a drunkard. Word of the scandal, which divides and breaks relations between people, is a "diabolic" discourse without an author. Perhaps in the uncertain, unidentifiable author of the accusation we begin to approach what is most powerful, most unavoidable, and most diabolic in the inexorable machine that transmits the fault.

It is quite in the direction of our hypothesis of a correlation between illness and fault that Lacan concludes his case history: "It is the same for every human being: every personal experience is determined by the individual's relation to the law which binds him." And then, addressing his audience of analysts, Lacan comments: "I hope that this brief observation will have been striking enough to give you the idea of a dimension that analysts rarely pursue in their reflections, but which they should not completely ignore."[18] Lacan returns to this idea a little later, as though he were calmly driving home the point, concerning precisely the famous complex: "The fact that the structure of the Oedipus complex is always essential does not mean that we should not also notice that other structures, which are on the same level in the design of the law, can play just as decisive a role in determining a case." Whether we look upstream to Oedipus' genealogy or downstream to his progeny, we see very clearly that "other structures, which are on the same level in the design of the law," have played a role. And if we consider Greek myth in a broader sense than did Freud, we are able to see Oedipus as a moment, a structure, universal perhaps but not unique, in a much larger process. Thanks to the tools of Freud's analysis, however, we are able to venture on to other ideas. We are led to what Lacan invites analysts to consider: the question of "the whole symbolic system in which the subject is called, in the full meaning of that word, to take his place."[19]

Oedipus, the Child without a Place

The word *place* is perfectly apt, for the story of Oedipus is indeed the story of a child without a place. Rejected by the father, Oedipus also rejects the father in turn and takes his place. Why this absence of place for Oedipus? Is it because his father had not been in the right place in relation to his son? What does it mean to take one's place in relation to the entire symbolic system? Is it to be able clearly to make known the signs that together form the symbol, that is to say, the sign of recognition? Laius cannot declare himself the father of anyone because, by begetting a son, he transgresses the oracle and brings disaster upon himself. As a result, Oedipus cannot clearly be assigned a place in the genealogy; and the words of a drunkard are enough to unleash his doubts about his supposed parents and to send him to Corinth to consult the oracle.

Rethinking the events that brought about the curse of the Labdacidae in terms of "place" could help us to understand the transmission of the curse. In the symbolic system where the subject is to take his place, each place is symbolic: it is defined by the fact that others besides the subject recognize it. And indeed, around Oedipus, no one recognizes his rightful place. His father denies being his father and wants to kill him. Consenting to this crime, his mother fails to assume her true place with respect to her son. By pretending to be his real parents, his foster parents are also displaced from their proper place. Oedipus is finally placed only in relation to the symptom he bears: his swollen feet. Earlier, Laius had not occupied his place as a man, in the normal, virile sense, in his relation to young Chrysippus, unless it was that he denied Chrysippus his place as a boy. In relation to Pelops, Laius should have put himself in the place of an adopted son, since Pelops replaces his dead father. A son and, therefore, a brother for Chrysippus. Instead, Laius, through abduction and rape, takes the place of Chrysippus himself—and the boy dies as a result. Laius's acts put him outside any relational system. The curse that follows does not finally impose his fate; it does nothing more than to announce the continuation of this situation.

The words *replacement* and *displacement* are closely linked to the problem of place. If we see here that the displacement of people—their failure to assume their proper place—constitutes a fault, then we must also state that the fault brings displacement in its wake. Because Laius failed to recognize Chrysippus's place as a boy and as the son of his host, he would also fail to recognize his own son. Because Oedipus has been displaced from his role as son, he would one day fail to recognize his father and would instead take his place. Because Oedipus will have occupied his father's place, the royal, conjugal place, he too will be displaced by his sons from his place as father and as king. They will fail to recognize him. As a result of having displaced their father, the brothers will not recognize one another as brothers and, each wanting to occupy the same place, they will kill each other. Thus the story of the Labdacidae ends as it began; whether by sword or by sex, it is a case of fratricidal murder.

But why did Laius not recognize the place of the other? Was he himself displaced? And if so, in relation to whom? To his father Labdacus, who died when Laius was still a child? To Pelops, himself born of tragedy, who, as a child, was killed by his father, Tantalus, cut into pieces, offered as food for a feast, and finally restored to life by Hermes?

A childish voice says to us: "Where will you end if you continue like this?" And truly we are seized by vertigo when we thus consider the chain of human generations.

CHAPTER 2

THE
FREUDIAN MOSAIC

We have seen that Oedipus had more to contend with than his parricidal and incestuous desires. He was not himself the source of his tragic actions. They were like a foreign language that he spoke without being able to understand. These actions spoke of his father, or rather, Oedipus was himself acted upon by the past actions of his father.

FREUD BLINDED: LAIUS AND JAKOB FREUD

This simple rereading of the Oedipean myth, done without research into recondite sources and without a complex critical apparatus, leads to a vision of the myth which is quite different from what Freud transmitted to us. The simple psychoanalytic method that we have applied works well here. Provided that we take into consideration the entire legend and not only the destiny of the hero of *Oedipus the King*, this method enables us to discover a latent meaning behind the manifest meaning. Freud never carried out this simple task of decipherment; it seems that he never even attempted it. Without any effort at interpretation, Freud accepted the Oedipean myth as a direct revelation. Why? ask the Hellenists. We join them in their astonishment, especially when we recall that Freud knew Greek — infinitely better than we do. Yet Freud's work is not lacking in psychoanalytical interpretations of masterpieces. It is as if *Oedipus the King* were a fundamental postulate, an original explication; it is by means of this work of Sophocles — why this one rather than another? — that all the others (Shakespeare's tragedies, Ibsen's plays) can be explained. This tragedy would speak directly of that which is most hidden in men, while all the others would be only its disguised representation.

How is it possible that in applying Freud's method while forgetting his theory we find that the efficacy of the former leads us to question the validity of the latter? At this point in our itinerary we can formulate our project as an interrogation of psychoanalytic theory by psychoanalytic method, or rather, using Freud to interrogate himself—or yet again, using Sophocles, along with Freud and Lacan, to analyze Freud.

We shall make no effort to disabuse those who will see in the argument that follows an enterprise whose objective is the demolition of psychoanalysis. For them, the edifice built by Freud is still perhaps a sacred temple of which not a stone should be displaced. What follows can be of no interest to those whose understanding of psychoanalysis is on unconditional terms. We can only advise them to read no further. Our position is different, for we believe that by pursuing Freud's work as we are doing, we remain faithful to his creative genius. He is presented to us in his biography as a man who thoroughly fulfilled Goethe's saying: "The first and the last thing one must demand of genius is the love of the truth." For Freud, everything had to be sacrificed in this quest. If the search for the truth now leads to a reinterpretation of psychoanalytic theory, we believe that if Freud were alive today he would be the first to undertake it. By seeking with him the truth about him, we are not going against what Freud valued most of all.

Besides, we can leave the task of presenting our work to Freud himself. What follows are the opening words of his study of Leonardo da Vinci.

> When psychiatric research, normally content to draw on frailer men for its material, approaches one who is among the greatest of the human race, it is not doing so for the reasons so frequently ascribed to it by laymen. "To blacken the radiant and drag the sublime into the dust" (Schiller) is no part of its purpose, and there is no satisfaction for it in narrowing the gulf which separates the perfection of the great from the inadequacy of the objects that are its usual concern. But it cannot help finding worthy of understanding everything that can be recognized in those illustrious models, and it believes there is no one so great as to be disgraced by being subject to the laws which govern both normal and pathological activity with equal cogency.[1]

Let us return for a moment to our archaeology. We have just made a visit to Greece, into the foundations of Sophocles' work, and therefore, in a certain sense (if Oedipus is the keystone of psychoanalysis), into the foundations of psychoanalysis itself. What we discovered there astonished us and altered our understanding: *Oedipus the King* indicates in every possible way (and with what incredible skill) the closest links between the lives of the father and the son. How then can this tragedy serve as the foundation of psychoanalysis through the "Oedipus complex," a theory where the son alone is in question? More precisely, our rereading of the tragedy would lead us to develop *a theory of the father's hidden fault* and of its transmission across generations, through symptoms, violent acts, and unconscious faults of all sorts. Analytic theory, quite to the contrary, is *a theory of the son's hidden desires,* where the son himself is the origin of his own symptoms and his own acts of violence (against himself or against others).

How can we resolve this contradiction? The solution that follows is simple, even if it goes against all our habits and perhaps even against our immediate feelings. What we had presupposed at the beginning now becomes true: this voyage to Greece, into the foundations hidden beneath the foundations of psychoanalysis, reverses the situation. It is no longer Freud who explains everything through Oedipus; it is Oedipus who questions Freud. Why did Freud retain only that part of the legend which makes Oedipus the only guilty one? Why did Freud ignore everything that came before? One cannot reproach him for not having read Lacan or Bateson or Laing. And we, who use his discoveries to call one of his postulates into question, cannot, without deriding ourselves, doubt Freud's good faith any more than one who mounts a staircase could, while making a step ahead, deny the existence of the step from which one rises. Freud sought the truth at all costs. The continuity of his research and the integrity of his life leave us only one hypothesis concerning his misapprehension [*méconnaissance*] of Oedipus: namely, that it was involuntary.

It can only be for "unconscious"—a word we may need to redefine —reasons that Freud accepted the manifest content of the Oedipean tragedy without looking for its latent content, as if it were a noninterpretable, founding myth, as if it were the universal key to the unconscious. Here we are led to ask, What made Freud retain less of Oedipus than Sophocles had? Psychoanalysis itself, having applied this idea many times, permits us to answer: When someone thus omits telling part of a story, it is because the omitted section resembles some repressed elements of his personal life. Freud himself often applied this very simple reasoning to his own failures of memory. Freud has therefore "forgotten" Laius. This is not insignificant, but why? We have spent a long time on this question.

In 1968 Josef Sajner discovered that Freud's father had not been married twice, as everyone including Freud had said, but three times.[2] It was also discovered that the birth register in the town hall at Freiberg, where Freud was born, attributes to him a different birth date than the one that, until then, had been known and widely recognized. These revelations have made their way from one study of Freud to another (e.g., those by Schur, Anzieu, and Granoff).[3] In bringing together all the new elements and in daring to pose the fundamental questions, Granoff, above all, enabled us to take the decisive step in our research. These questions were not meant only for analysts: Why had people lied about the number of Freud's father's wives, and about the son's birth date? Did Freud know about it? What influence did the secrets enveloping the adventurous life of the father have upon the son?

At the appropriate time we will look again in detail at these new findings concerning the Freud family and especially the father. For the moment we only mention them to clarify the basic motif of our research. Our archaeological expedition consists of bringing together these two facts: Freud ignored Laius and what he had done; Freud had also probably ignored what Jakob Freud had done. We could explain here, from the outside, that Freud, who must have repressed whatever he might have been able to guess about his father's faults, failed, because of this, to recognize the origin of the Oedipean myth and of the curse that Laius's faults brought upon him. Having said this, however, what more could we add? What would we establish if we manage to construct a discourse on this subject? Our project is not simply to produce words but to extend Freud's research by returning to the point where his research went wrong.

Only one method presents itself to us, the most difficult one: starting from the interior of Freud's life to try to discover what was no doubt incomprehensible to Freud himself. If Freud failed to see, if he repressed something concerning a blameworthy father, then these repressed elements must have returned in some disguised way in his life, and perhaps even in his work. We should find some trace of them in his biography, not, of course, in those things presented most clearly, not in broad strokes, but in the small details, in the margins or in what was presented to us as marginal. We are going to visit the "Freud household" as might some impolite guest who opens the doors before which the masters of the house pass, rapidly saying: here are the bathrooms, here is the basement . . .

FREUD AND THE ABSURD.
TWO PRANKS: MUSHROOMS AND STATUES

Since we want to begin with unutilized details—those pieces of the Freudian puzzle which have not found a place in the great works dedicated to his memory—we must find in Ernest Jones's monumental biography some trifle that would not have been used to interpret the Viennese genius but that the honest biographer would have noted in his concern to tell everything. A chapter entitled "Mode of Life and Work" collects precisely these details of Freud's daily life. Jones goes on to recount a typical day in the master's life: the friends he visited, the places where he liked to walk, his habits, his tastes.

We learn, as an aside, that Freud never left Vienna during the nine months he spent there each year and that "he had a strong dislike of the famous Wienerwald. . . . His children, who were all fond of it, could never drag him there. Whether this was because it grew no mushrooms, or whether it was too close to his hated Vienna, I cannot say, but he preferred to divide his life sharply between enforced work in the town and a complete change in the holidays to a distant and quite different country scene."[4] Mushrooms must have occupied a very particular place in Freud's life to justify his aversion to a forest just because of their absence. Jones has already reported the very strong taste Freud had for these plants and, to show what an excellent household Sigmund and Martha Freud formed from the beginning, he even notes: "The only sign of 'war' recorded in all the ensuing [fifty-three] years was a temporary difference of opinion over the weighty question whether mushrooms should be cooked with or without their stalks [in French, *pieds* 'feet']."[5] The biographer's humor. Jones, an Englishman, is perhaps less appreciative when the passion for mushrooms—with or without their stalks —is transformed into a hatred of umbrellas. "He had a special aversion to umbrellas. I remember his asking me in a slighly irritated tone, 'Why ever do you carry an umbrella?' When I said I supposed it was a habit from having to wear a silk hat he replied: 'Then try to give up the habit.' He once told my wife that all an umbrella did was to keep its stick dry."[6] Freud's dislike of umbrellas can be considered a small mania, like we all have, but is there not something in common between mushrooms and umbrellas? Are they not both made in the same way, of a stalk, or handle, with a hat on top? On the same page we are brought back to mushrooms and led ahead to statues.

> The most characteristic feature of Freud's holiday pursuits was his passion for mushrooms, especially for finding them. He had an uncanny flair for discovering where they were likely to be, and would even point out such spots when riding alone in a train. On an expedition for the purpose he would often leave the children and they would be sure to hear soon a cry of success from him. He would then creep silently up to it and suddenly pounce to capture the fungus with his hat as if it were a bird or butterfly. So Freud could be boyish enough on occasions. Another example of it was his habit of bringing his latest purchase of an antiquity, usually a small statuette, to the dinner table and placing it in front of him as a companion during the meal. Afterwards it would be returned to his desk and then brought back again for a day or two.[7]

Again, Granoff's book, so rich in new material and in remarks on what are usually classified as "details," confirmed for us the importance of mushrooms. He offers comments made by Martin Freud, the eldest son, concerning this strange chase.

> This activity was carried out in a style Martin describes as quite military. The family patrol was supposed to deploy itself as light infantrymen on a wide front. And, once the mushroom was sighted, usually by the father, the latter pulled a whistle out of his pocket. He threw his hat over the mushroom, small hat imprisoned beneath the larger one, then sounded the whistle, the signal for the infantrymen to immediately converge on the hat and to take away the captive.[8]

Thus, Freud wanted the hat to be over the mushroom and not beneath it like Jones's top hat sheltered by the umbrella.

Our first questions emerge from these details of Freud's life, from his pranks, as Jones calls them. Why does Freud "capture" these mushrooms as if they were animals who might escape? Why did he invite the statues he had bought to dinner? Jones presents these two strange details about Freud in the same paragraph. Although he makes no interpretation, a juxtaposition is possible by superimposing them in our reading (as we did in the Oedipus legend, concerning the search for the father and for the stolen horses).

Mushrooms and statues are both made up of top and bottom parts. Mushrooms have a stalk or foot and a hat or cap; statues have a foot or pedestal and the statue proper. Although a mushroom is secured by its stalk, Freud acts as if he expected to see it run away. He captures it to eat in the course of a meal — with or without its stalk? A statuette, an inanimate thing, is also fixed on a foot or pedestal; Freud invites it to dinner as if it were a human being. Three elements are therefore common to these two objects: their forms, their positions of being fixed on a foot or base, their presence — as part of the meal or as a guest — at Freud's dinner table. Only one thing seems to differentiate the two objects: Freud's attitude toward the mushrooms reveals that he expects them to be mobile, yet he does not "capture" the statuette. If we look more closely, however, his dinner invitation to them reminds us of another famous story of a statue that walks.

A statue that is invited to dinner and arrives on foot — is this not the conclusion of *Don Giovanni*? Is the guest not the statue of the Commander, the murdered father? We remember the story: The Commander is the father of a young girl, Anna, whom Don Juan wanted forcibly to seduce; the father, in protecting himself and his house against the seducer, dies in his fight with Don Juan. Sometime after the death Don Juan and his valet, Leporello, pass at night through the cemetery where the tomb and the statue of the victim is located. While Don Juan is telling the valet the story of his latest villainy, a voice is heard: it is the Commander's voice. Leporello is terrorized; at this point, the statue comes to life and looks at them. Don Juan forces Leporello to read the inscription on the pedestal: "I await vengeance upon the impious one who killed me." Don Juan, refusing to be impressed by the miracle and insensitive to the prediction of his own approaching death, responds with such impertinent mockery that Leporello invites the Commander (the statue) to dinner. In the last scene of the opera, the dinner scene, the statue ominously arrives on foot. Don Juan refuses the invitation that the Commander offers in turn, signifying his refusal to be converted. He dies after the statue takes his hand, offered as a final gesture of defiance. The ground opens and swallows Don Juan, already gripped by the terror and the torments of hell.

It is strange that the founder of psychoanalysis was so passionately taken with this story. Strange also is the little detail about the mushrooms and the statues. If we pursued the hypothesis, mixing together the characteristics of the two objects that Freud treated so bizarrely, would we not be led to equate the dish of mushrooms to be eaten—with or without the stems?—and the statue-guest? The mushroom-statue would be an assassinated father, which one eats, and also an animal that one captures according to a certain ritual, in the course of which a hat is thrown over the prey. Would one not call all this a bad joke? *Totem and Taboo* revisited, with the murder of the father, the return of the repressed memory (the statue), the substitution of the animal for the father, the totem-animal, the mushroom, which is captured and eaten according to ritual. If in fact the body of the father-statue is eaten, obviously one should not eat the stalk-pedestal. Martha Freud, however, cannot understand that. And Sigmund cannot explain it to her—a good reason for the sole conflict of their married life.

This fiction does surprise us a little. It could constitute, despite its fantastic character, an interpretation, if we were provided with other factors that supported it. The German language associates hatstands (*Hutständer*) with mushrooms. The word *Hut* 'hat' employed alone also signifies "mushroom" in botany. *Hut* has another meaning: "the surveillance kept over someone." The word *Ständer*, which is part of the compound word *Hutständer*, means "foot" or "support." Is it surprising that *Standbild* means "statue"? Three objects appear in the repeated, ritual gestures of Freud: mushrooms, hats, and statues. In German, hat constitutes precisely this link between mushrooms and statues. We note these little details completely by chance, in order not to neglect anything on our way which might be significant.

Freud Ill

Let us return to Don Juan, to try to see what role this myth played in Freud's life. Freud, who detested music, was extremely fond of Mozart's opera based on the myth. He said one day that he "was shocked to find that his friend Schönberg did not know that *Don Giovanni* was composed by Mozart, so he insisted on taking him to see it; he referred to the irresistable 'Lucca' who played Zerlina," the young peasant seduced by Don Juan.[9] Freud knew this opera well enough to recognize the brief musical citation of *The Marriage of Figaro* that occurs in *Don Giovanni*. This is surprising for a man so notoriously unmusical, although he did love *The Marriage of Figaro* and *Carmen*. These two operas, along with *Don Giovanni*, actually share three Don Juans, three seducers (Don Juan, Almaviva, Carmen), who, comically or tragically, are prevented from pursuing their evil ways and are punished. What can this theme of Don Juan have to do with Freud? It seems as if nothing can justify any particular link between the scientist and the seducer, except that which unites contraries. All accounts agree, and Freud's own is no less explicit, in establishing a portrait of a chaste young man and a scrupulously faithful husband. A sentence from a letter to his friend Fliess even suggests that Freud's sexual activity did not continue beyond his forties and that after that he became the scholar whose entire libido was sublimated into intellectual research.

Are we going to upset the mass of evidence which seems, in advance, to block all research in this direction, just for a few strangely captured mushrooms and some dinner invitations to statues? No. But something still prevents us from renouncing the attempt to examine this enigmatic detail thoroughly. It is the strange account that Schur, the doctor who cared for Freud until his death, gives us in his book and that, this time, brings Freud's mysterious relation to the statue of the Commander into the realm of symptoms rather than inoffensive whims.

Death Anxiety

In a letter of April 16, 1896, to his friend Fliess, Freud complains of crises of death anxiety. This happens so rarely in Freud's letters that Schur was struck by it. What could be the cause of it? "Tilgner's cardiac death is probably more responsible for that than the time period," writes Freud (referring to numerically determined periods that, according to Fliess's hypotheses, control human destinies).[10]

Schur then gives us an account in a few pages of the article that appeared that same day in a Viennese newspaper Freud read regularly.

It basically contained, together with Schur's commentary, the following: Tilgner, a sculptor, is commissioned to do a statue of Mozart for the city of Vienna. This man resembles Freud in many features of his personal history and tastes: the childhood of a poor emigré in Vienna, creative success, dreams of going to Italy. Tilgner consecrates all his time to the statue of Mozart; it is to be his great masterpiece. Then cardiac symptoms appear. He will not rest, however, until his Mozart is unveiled. "He began to be beset by anxious doubts and premonitions, stating: 'My gratification will be complete only if I can see [the statue] free and fully unveiled.' This was countered with: 'Of course, there isn't the slightest doubt that I shall live to see my Mozart free, in full daylight.' After a moment of silence came the assertion that after the festivities were over, he would go to Italy instead of dying in his studio."[11] Schur relates Tilgner's attitude to Freud's doubts of living long enough to write the books he expected to write, and to see Rome. Would he see the promised land, as he will say a propos of the completion of his book on dreams? Schur continues: "Freud feared that, like Moses, he would die within sight of his goal. This is what actually did happen to Tilgner,"[12] who died six days before the unveiling. After having given his last instructions to have a few measures from *Don Giovanni* engraved on the pedestal of the statue, he spent the rest of the night playing Tarock—Freud's favorite card game—then had repeated attacks of very strong heart pain, accompanied by shortness of breath, and died in the morning.

Schur remarks, "Curiously enough, Freud, who was anything but a music lover, was very fond of Mozart's operas, particularly of *Don Giovanni.*" Then, still according to the Viennese daily newspaper, Schur tells us, "The bars to be engraved on the monument were taken from the final scene of the opera: the scene in which the ghost of the Commander, whom Don Giovanni has murdered after having seduced his daughter, appears before the villain who dies under the impact of the apparition."[13] What Schur calls the "ghost" is obviously the statue of the Commander. Freud explicitly relates the fear of dying he experienced that evening to the death of the sculptor. It occurs the very night of Tilgner's death, after Freud had read the details in the newspapers.

Is it possible that Freud identified with the victim of this astonishing and tragic episode? A sculptor dies, struck down by the statue he has made, or rather by that which is evoked at the foot of the one he has carved. Why does Tilgner take himself for Don Juan, threatened by the vengeance of heaven for having committed too many crimes? Above all, why does Freud put himself in the place of the dying artist, to the point of experiencing a death anxiety (*Todesangst*)?

There is yet another little detail to add concerning Freud's relationship to Don Juan. The year after this dramatic episode, Freud writes to

Fliess: "Dear Wilhelm, I send you herewith *il catalogo delle belle,* etc."[14] This "catalog of wonders" refers to the catalog of his works, his bibliography. Freud is citing a phrase from Leporello, Don Juan's valet, who reads aloud from the notebook in which he has recorded his master's "one thousand and three" feminine conquests—the list therefore of the seducer's misdeeds. In this letter to Fliess, Freud is at the same time Don Juan, the author of his works—and Leporello, who relates them to another. In the libretto by Lorenzo da Ponte to Mozart's *Don Giovanni* the exact line is "Madamina, il catalogo e questo delle belle che amo il padron mio" (Madam, this catalog is of the beauties whom my master has loved). Thus, Freud's works would occupy the place of Don Juan's feminine conquests. Is Freud sending to his friend Fliess, with whom he never really shared his theories, the list of his works as so many infidelities that Freud the writer would have committed toward him?

How can we go forward on this path? We cannot erase our impression that this must have been a very important theme, at least at a certain moment in Freud's life. Yet we cannot illuminate any of these peculiarities or unexplained symptoms by referring only to Freud himself. The Don Juan myth could have explained the prankish eccentricities. We grasped its importance through the anxiety crises. And then, nothing; the trail is lost, we do not see its origin.

We are tempted, therefore, to appeal to what we have discovered in the story of Oedipus: what makes no sense in someone's life may be meaningful when that life is related to those that preceded it. Who could be the secret Don Juan in Freud's life, whose nonsymbolized crimes would reappear in him as symptoms?

It is not even necessary to make a hypothetical leap. The situation during this period when Don Juan assumed such importance for Freud already reveals to us the identity of his Don Juan. The anxiety crisis at Tilgner's death dates from April 1896; the "catalog" letter to Fliess is from May 1897. These two dates frame a third, very important date: the death of Freud's father on October 23, 1896. This period of particular sensitization to Don Juan corresponds in Freud's life with his father's old age and illness, then to his death and the period of mourning which followed. Freud makes no mystery about it: this death is the most striking event in his adult life.

The Secret Don Juan

Authors like Schur, Anzieu, and Granoff who made the facts concerning Sigmund Freud's family known, have done more than simply provide new information. The official version of the life of Jakob Freud suddenly appeared as a pious legend. With the publication of their respective books, these authors questioned, with increasing insistence, the conscious or unconscious impact on Freud of the secret events in his father's life. On the basis of what these men have accomplished, especially Granoff, and by assembling the elements already noted in the mass of Freudian documents, we now feel able to give an answer—just one answer —to their question and to ours.

"What is simple is always wrong. What is not, is unusable." Paul Valéry's humor gives us a good warning just as we embark into simple facts, or supposedly simple ones.

The life of Jakob Freud contains secrets that were apparently hidden from everyone, at least from Sigmund Freud and his first disciples. They appeared only when psychoanalysis and its author became so important that pilgrimages were made everywhere the name of Freud might be inscribed. Then the new evidence, which was not expected, was discovered in civil registers and census records. We want to make it clear at the outset that we are not concerned with judging these new pieces of information, or with deciding whether they are valid or invalid in themselves. The same elements could be judged as either important or unimportant. The only criterion that makes us think this could constitute a fault for those who committed these actions is that it was concealed. Perhaps here we are touching on the fundamental problems of the fault and its consequences. Does the fault's value as a scandal, which is carried into the following generation, not consist in something other than the nonrecognition of this fault by its author? Someone other than the dominated usually learns of the fault of the dominating. If the dominant person recognized his fault, perhaps he would cease being dominant, but then he would not be the "occasion for the fall" of the person dominated, which is the real meaning of scandal. He would recognize himself as fallen. Does the dominated person always fall when the dominant one fails to recognize his fault? We propose the following formulation: The dominated carries out the repressed [*la refoulé*] of the dominant.[15] Perhaps we will rediscover this by another path as we return to Jakob Freud.

Freud's official biographer begins his great work thus: "Sigmund Freud was born at 6:30 p.m. on the sixth of May, 1856." Further on: "[His father] married twice."[16] These are two very simple statements of fact, which do not usually cause problems in a biography. It so happens, however, that these two statements are false. It was discovered in the Freiberg birth register a few years before Freud's death that he was born March 6, 1856. Jones believes the notation was a clerical error. When Freud was asked about it he "was angry that someone wanted to age him by two months. But he added (say the Bernfelds, who questioned him about it) that it was his mother who had told him the date, and if anyone should know it, it would be she."[17] If, as Jones supposes, it was a *lapsus calami*, we are very surprised, along with Granoff, who, "having seen photocopies of these registers, . . . found this *lapsus calami* not just in one place but in everything that concerned the child in question, that is to say concerning not only his birth but also his circumcision."

All this is of no interest unless we observe at the same time that, since the parents were married on July 29, 1855, the discrepancy between the two birth dates leads to questions about the date of the conception of the child: Was it before or after the marriage? Was Jakob Freud re-married, at forty years of age—at least according to what he says—to a twenty-year-old pregnant woman, and was this fact subsequently erased by advancing the child's birthday two months?

What about Jakob himself? If his birthday is exact—the one he himself chose when he had to adapt it from the Jewish to the Christian calendar, and which is the same as Bismarck's, April 1, 1815—then Jakob Freud was married for the first time, to Sally Kanner, at the age of sixteen. His first child was therefore born when he was seventeen. We do not know the precise date. Jakob and Sally had two sons: Emanuel (1832) and Philipp (1836). Jones tells us that the first wife died in 1852, but neither Schur nor Granoff find any trace of this Sally or of her death at Freiberg in the registers at Freiberg where Jakob and his sons settled in 1840.

"On the other hand," Granoff adds, "the register of the Jewish population of Freiberg for the year 1852 gives us the following list: Jakob Freud, thirty-eight years old, his wife *Rebecca*, thirty-two years old" (emphasis mine), his two sons, and the wife of the oldest son. Rebecca cannot be the mother of Emanuel, who was then 21 years old. "In 1854, Rebecca is no longer listed on the register. Either she died, or the marriage has ended in divorce. According to Schur, the former possibility is more plausible. But the second, scandalous possibility explains as well the dis-appearance of the name."[18] Then comes Amalie, the mother of Sigmund— the third, not the second, wife of Jakob Freud.

At least some questions have been posed. Let us resume with Max Schur's formulation of them.

> Discrepancies between a family legend and actuarial history may develop either through distortion or the complete blotting out of certain facts. It would seem, for instance, that the existence of Jakob Freud's second wife was subjected to such a blotting-out mechanism.
> Obvious questions now arise: who *must* have known about the marriage and who *probably* knew about it? In addition to Jakob

Freud, his two sons Philipp and Emanuel as well as Emanuel's wife must have known. It is possible, but not likely, that Freud's mother, Jakob's third wife, was completely unaware of the second marriage.[19]

Each author takes a step forward, just when one was getting used to the preceding revelations. To the question, Did Freud know about it? Schur answers, "Certainly not consciously." Granoff does not so easily grant the "psychic status of the absent representations," all the more so since he found an allusion to a Jewish story in a letter Freud wrote to Fliess: "Rebecca, take off your wedding gown, you are no longer married." Granoff indeed remarks that this Jewish story does not appear for no reason at this point in the Freud-Fliess correspondence. We are going just a bit further when we emphasize that the letter mentioning Rebecca is central for psychoanalysis—and also for our hypothesis: it is precisely in this letter that Freud tells Fliess he is abandoning his first theory, the theory of the father's fault.

It is not yet time, however, for us to return to psychoanalysis. We found the hidden Don Juan in the life of Freud: his father. If it were only a question of a mistake on the registry, one could say that Ernest Jones was right. The half-effaced traces are too numerous, however—the mistakes, the appearances and disappearences of women, the surprising ages. Their varying degrees of authenticity, practically unverifiable, are finally without importance. One indeed feels that something there is not at all right. The figure that begins to take shape is that of a Jakob Freud who is a seducer, a transgressor of the sexual laws of his milieu and of his time—otherwise, why all these mysteries?

Denounce, Renounce

Is Sigmund Freud thus caught in a story of seduced and then disappearing women, just as Oedipus was caught when he had to leave Corinth because of the stolen horse? For Oedipus, the horse is the sign of a hidden fault of the unknown father. Chrysippus, the golden horse, was stolen from his father in spite of the laws of hospitality—a signifier whose signified is hidden from Oedipus and for which he is in quest.

Freud is probably no more aware of the relation between his father and the story of Rebecca than Oedipus was of the relation between his father and the stolen horses. It is only that Freud finds himself at first seeking "to pin it on the father," as he says to Fliess, looking in the past memories of the hysterics who consult him for a father (or a brother) at the origin of their neurosis. In so doing, Freud builds a first theory of the seduction of his patients by their fathers. Then one fine day he renounces it—he "no longer believes it," and it is then that "Rebecca, remove your marriage gown" comes back to his mind. The context of this first theoretical elaboration and Freud's sudden turnabout will thus be extremely important for us, and we will have to examine with the closest attention the period of his life in which this great change takes place—from which psychoanalysis originates.

All psychoanalysts agree, in effect, on the point that Freud's major discovery occurs after the renunciation of the "error," which was the theory of seduction by the father. What Freud took to be reality, the rape of all hysterics by their father, would afterward be revealed as a phantasy. Freud would then realize that it was a question of repressed desires of the patient alone. He would "discover," after having believed the father to be guilty, that, in fact, the repressed desires of the son toward his mother would force him to become the murderous rival of the father. It is not the real fault of the father, but the fantasized one of the child.

The way opened to us by the thorough investigation of the Oedipus legend leads now to a curious reversal: Freud's first theory would be on the right track, and what is usually presented as decisive progress, the renunciation of an error, would on the contrary constitute a repression and a displacement onto himself of the father's fault—and this by a mechanism that Jones describes perfectly but evidently did not apply to Freud:

> When an analyst loses insight he had previously had, the recurring wave of resistance that has caused the loss is apt to display itself in the form of pseudo-scientific explanations of the data before him, and this is then dignified with the name of a 'new theory.' Since the source of this is on an unconscious level it follows that controversy on a purely conscious scientific level is foredoomed to failure.[20]

Freud in the Shadows

We must now take a small step back and bring the pieces of our Freudian mosaic together. The reader, now familiar with our way of working, will be better able to judge the connections of meaning.

Just as Oedipus's life could be explained through the knowledge of the faults of his father, we have picked up some fragments in Freud's life—incomprehensible in themselves, but meaningful thanks to the new facts about the life of his father, Jakob. If Jakob Freud is a Don Juan, the son might well fear for this father as the hour of his death approaches. Consciously, or unconsciously? How can we decide? What is the psychic state of that which is experienced without being clearly recognized? The inner division alone appears certain. The invention of psychoanalysis is agnostic, but it certainly seems that something, someone, in Freud believes in the possibility of divine punishment. Otherwise, how can we explain the crisis of death-anxiety at the moment of Tilgner's death?

Freud's Son Speaks

We can be a little more precise about the relation between the mysterious capture of mushrooms and the death-anxiety. Martin Freud, the eldest son, provides some indications in the troubling book devoted to his father. Jacques Trilling, the author of the preface to the French edition of the book compares it to a garden sprayed with herbicide. In her two-page presentation to the French edition, Marie Bonaparte says, "Martin evokes, in all their freshness, impressions of his childhood lived in the shadow of the great man who was his father; their mountain vacations, perfumed by the odor of wild strawberries and those large mushrooms (*Herrenpilze*) that Freud so loved to discover beneath the large evergreens of the forest he loved so much."[21] We learn that the mushrooms Freud seeks carry the signifier *Herr:* mister, master, lord, and finally, God.

Why still insist on those mushrooms? A small object of interest for such a genius. Martin himself, however, insists on them in a curious way.

> In late summer our subject was the collection of edible fungi; but we never discussed this with local people outside our circle. They would have thought the spending of many hours day after day gathering mushrooms a very dull business, something only poor old women did with big dilapidated baskets which they carried to the local market to earn a few kronen.[22]

The phrase "we never discussed this" surprises us a little, as it does not correspond to the rest of the picture he gives of the Freud family. The Freud children also felt that there was something in the life of their father that he himself could not explain: all the more reason why they could not explain it themselves. Martin continues,

> Our attack on the mushroom was never haphazard. Father would have done some scouting earlier to find a fruitful area; and I think one of the pointers he used was the presence of a gaily coloured toadstool, red with white dots, which always appeared with our favorite, the less easily seen *Steinpilz*, which my dictionary tells me is the yellow edible *boletus*.[23]

Here the words and the things speak for themselves. In German *Stein* means "stone." Therefore it is the "stone mushroom" that Freud seeks. Martin also names the *Herrenpilze* in order to say that they no longer picked these mushrooms when they had become very ripe and were then called *alte Herren* 'old men'. Martin describes the technique of capture, the dispersion of the children "like a well-trained infantry platoon attacking through a forest. We played that we were chasing some flighty and elusive game; and there was always a competition to decide on the best hunter. Father always won." Boyish pranks, as Jones would say; since Freud had gone on ahead in reconnaissance, could it be anything else?

Martin then mentions the hat that his father suddenly threw down when he found a perfect specimen—the scene we already mentioned —with the call of the whistle to reassemble the little group: "Only when the concentration was complete would father remove the hat and allow us to inspect and admire the spoils." Mrs. Freud and her sister, at home, had their own duties: cleaning and peeling the mushrooms "before showing the cook precisely how they were to be cooked"—decidedly a whole ceremonial. Martin ends his description of it with this commentary (that those who know the task of the daily feeding of children will appreciate): "In a good season we had mushrooms nearly every day; but we never tired of them."

Herrpilz, Steinpilz: these are the two names transmitted to us. It can no longer be a matter of chance. Jones, who presented together as two of Freud's pranks the capture of the mushrooms and the invitation of the statues, had thus—no doubt unconsciously—understood very well what Freud displayed there, also unconsciously. As for Martin, after the story of the hunt he suggests the difficulty his mother and his aunt would have had in participating. He had never seen them dressed in anything but long flowing skirts, to the point where he never imagined that his Aunt Minnie "had legs." Were they also statues on pedestals who walked?

The stone guest could indeed have been present through the form, through the movement that Freud fantasized and, above all, through the names of these mushrooms that were so sought after. To pick and eat the *Herrenpilze,* to capture and taste a *Steinpilz*—is not that to eat the words that designate the master of stone, the stone gentleman? How much closer can we get to the statue of the Commander? And as in the French word *seigneur,* or the English *Lord* or *nobleman,* the German *Herr* can lead us all the way to God; "the day of the Lord" is *der Tag des Herren* in German.

To finish with these disparate pieces of the mosaic, we must mention in passing a particularly dear friend of Freud's, Königstein—literally, "King's stone." Must we reverse it? "King of Stone"? We have led our readers through many unusual details in a book that proposes to study a great man seriously, but perhaps they will allow us nonetheless to bring to their notice the following small coincidence. We remember that the sculptor Tilgner spent his last evening playing tarock before dying of a

Herztod (literally, "heart-death"). From 1901 on, almost until his death, Freud went to have dinner and play tarock at his friend Königstein's house every Saturday night. Jones talks about these Saturday evenings as an institution to which Freud was religiously devoted. Perhaps Jones does not know how true that is. One can imagine that Freud himself provoked what he went through with great anxiety in the Tilgner episode in all those situations where the encounter with the Commander is repeated like a game in which he is master. He resembles the child who, hospitalized after an accident in which he was ejected through the door of a green car, asks his mother to bring him a toy—"a green car with doors that open." He needs to master the trauma; to replay it until the subject is no longer passively acted upon by what has happened, by what has terrified him; to repeat it in order finally to master it. Again, it is Freud himself who has described this psychic mechanism in *Beyond the Pleasure Principle.*

QUESTIONS ABOUT THE FREUDIAN MOSAIC

While by day Freud constructs his theory, makes discovery after discovery, writes and publishes, in the shadows he has a rendezvous with death. It is mixed with the shadow life of his father, with the seductions that his lies were not entirely able to hide. He is confronted with the hour of punishment that awaits Jakob, the hour of the Last Judgement. At the moment of Jakob's death, Freud has nevertheless discovered facts of which he is certain (*quod erat demonstrandum* 'that which must be demonstrated', he writes at the bottom of a letter to Fliess,[24] as if he were concluding a mathematical proof). Everything fits. For the moment he sees only the sexual fault of the father, committed directly with the hysterical daughter. Later on, he would perhaps come to understand that it might concern a fault of which the child has been the witness, and not simply the object, in the case of what we call obsessional neurosis. But Jakob dies, and in one year Freud's whole initial discovery is repressed. Could he reveal the fault of the father at the moment when his father was appearing before his judge?

Freud does not say, of course, what we are saying here; nor do the psychoanalysts of our time. We do not think, however, that by so saying we are being innovative. From Freud to Lacan, from Jones to Granoff, we find here and there all the constitutive elements of our hypothesis, and even all the models for the meaningful conjunction of these elements. Many authors, beginning with the pious biographer and the eldest son, have left indications in their works, small, astonishing notations left out of the indexes, from which they apparently draw no conclusions. But these notations are like bottles in the sea that a boat off course would leave in its wake. Our work is singularly aided by them.

We have arrived at a point in our path where we must make a decision, since, in effect, several ways are open to us. We can consider what we simply find interesting, even ingenious, but we can also feel that this displeases us, and claim to be shocked that such a requestioning of Freud could be based at first on an anxiety crisis, on two family secrets and three whims—and stop there. It is an attitude we understand well enough since it was our attitude at first.

A second position is possible: to accept as certain what we have already been able to establish, and to draw negative conclusions from it right away as to the value of Freud's work—and stop there. This is the attitude of the traditional enemies of Freud. They were horrified at psychoanalysis, and that was certainly their privilege. But they did not find anything better; horror is not enough to prevent the development of a theory.

A third possibility remains: to become interested—from now on, or gradually—in this reversal of roles between Freud and Oedipus, between the error and the discovery, between the desire of the son and the fault of the father; to try, in an attitude of conditional acceptance, to go yet further. If our hypothesis is correct, other faults should await us in Freud's private life, and, in his works, other words, which will again evoke the repressed truth, will speak to us of his father.

This time, Sophocles will be our guide. A father fails to acknowledge his son: this is Laius. A father recognizes his son but hides from him an important fact about his (i.e., the father's) own life; he also conceals the circumstances in which his son was conceived and the date of his birth: this is Jakob. Oedipus's question is, Who are my parents? He sets out to ask the oracle, the divine voice. At this moment he encounters his father and, at the same time, the signs of the fault which made him conceal himself as father. Freud's question concerns his father's second wife: Who is she? What happened to her? And what is his place in this secret story? Why was he lied to about his date of birth?

There is apparently no sign that Freud knew anything about this. But he himself always insisted that human beings can hide nothing. He who silences his lips speaks with his fingers. No analyst, familiar with the anomalies of Freud's biography can imagine that these secrets had no influence on Freud. We can therefore hypothesize an "unconscious" Freud, in search of a truth that has been denied him. Let us return to the model provided by Sophocles: What does a son do when he learns that the truth has been hidden from him? He goes off to question the divine voice. Oedipus leaves Corinth to consult the Delphic Oracle. The father and his fault obstruct the way.

The Metamorphoses of the Sphinx (from the Commander to Moses).

In the same way, after the death of his father, Freud tries for five years to go to Rome. As we shall see, the obstacle is an inner one. He is obsessed with the trip to Rome. Who is he going to consult? Who will speak to him, like an oracle, in allegorical fashion, of his father's second wife and of his own place in the family—unless it is the Sphinx who awaits him there—the Sphinx that one encounters after the death of one's father, the Sphinx that one must conquer in order to succeed? We can verify our itinerary by making the point in another way, without going through Sophocles, simply by following a word from Freud's pranks: the word *statue*. Occupying himself with statues was his principle pastime, together with picking mushrooms and wild flowers. Throughout his life, Freud bought antique statues, especially Egyptian ones, statues that he invited to dinner.

The Don Juan theme seems to leave Freud's life the year after his father's death. Nevertheless, the strong emotional charge of this theme could not purely and simply disappear, because it was in part unconscious. Freud has taught us that the unconscious is atemporal and that there is no forgetting or usury associated with what arises from it. One might suppose that the terrifying statue of the Commander must have been replaced in Freud's mind by another, equivalent object. During this period Freud dreams of going to Rome, but cannot do it; he writes *The Interpretations of Dreams* and finally, in 1901, is able to go to the eternal city. Who will he visit most often? A statue of Moses.

We enter here into the realm of Freudian contradictions. After many visits to Rome, Freud publishes an article in 1914 on the Moses of Michelangelo, in which he presents himself as a simple amateur in art who is informed about psychoanalysis. He does not sign the article. His disciples, Jones among them, make spirited protestations, to which Freud responds, "Why disgrace Moses by putting my name to it?"[25]

The strange answer becomes still more enigmatic for us when we consider that between 1887 and 1895 Freud had six children: Mathilde, Martin, Oliver, Ernst, Sophie, and Anna (or Hanna, to write this Jewish first name, given after some of Freud's Jewish friends, in the Jewish manner). Is it by chance that one can write the name *Moshe*, that is, Moses, with their initials?

Let us reflect again upon the mysterious meaning of the statues in Freud's life; aided by David Bakan's *Freud and the Jewish Mystical Tradition*, we will interrogate the contradiction that a statue of Moses presents for a Jew. Let us keep in mind that the divine law transmitted by Moses himself to the Jewish people—the Decalogue—begins thus:

> You shall have no other god to set against me.
> You shall not make a carved image for yourself nor the likeness of anything in the heavens above, or on the earth below, or in the waters under the earth.
> You shall not bow down to worship them.[26]

Doubtless, Freud does not "worship" the idols that he collects. But can a collection of statues be considered by a Jew as a simple and innocent pastime?[27]

What a surprise it is for us to read, immediately following in the Biblical text, these words:

> For I, the Lord your God, am a jealous god. I punish the children for the sins of the fathers. To the third and fourth generations of those who hate me. But I keep faith with thousands, with those who love me and keep my commandments.

Although we wanted to interpret and not to explicate, we cannot help posing the question, Is it to annul the conclusion of the Second Commandment—the punishment across generations—that Freud transgresses the beginning of the commandment in such a provocative way?

All these coincidences invite us to give the greatest attention to Freud when he leaves Vienna for Rome. They induce us to follow him right up to the statue, to listen to what he has to say of this tête-à-tête, without losing sight of our question: Where has the Don Juan myth gone? Could the statue of Moses also be a representation of the Commander (unless it might just as well be the reverse)? If Jakob Freud is Don Juan, and since the latter has no children, what will Freud's place and identity be before Moses? Why has he lost his name before him? Will we find in Freud's work on Moses noticeable traces of Jakob's fault and of Freud's assimilation of Moses and the Commander?

Our interrogation will not be too lengthy. What awaits us in Rome, in the church of St. Peter in Chains, surprised us to the extent that it was no surprise at all.

CHAPTER 3

THE
POPE'S TOMB

We are better equipped for this trip, on which we shall follow
Freud to Rome, than when we were in Greece and followed Oedipus
leaving Corinth. This time we have a competent guide, Sophocles himself,
who knows what it means for a son to bear the iniquities of his father. The
question of hidden faults was formulated for Freud, at first, through
another myth, that of Don Juan. We have to go to the end of the metamorphoses of this myth in the life of Freud, remembering that Don Juan
has no son but a valet, Leporello—and that it was with him that Freud
identified when he sent the list of his works to his friend.

Freud before Rome

In Freud's life there is a "before" and an "after" Rome. Jones speaks
of this in the following terms:

> In the late summer of 1901 there took place an event which had the
> highest emotional significance for Freud, one which he called "the
> high-point of my life." It was the visit to Rome, so long yearned for.
> It was something vastly important to him and consideration of it
> must therefore yield some secret of his inner life.[1]

It took Freud years to reach Rome. Before going there he published *The
Interpretation of Dreams* and edited the first version of *The Psychopathology
of Everyday Life*, works in which Freud revealed himself. He would afterward do it no longer—at least not in the mode of public self-analysis.
Also after visiting Rome his long relationship, his long dependence on
his friend Fliess, would end. Again, after Rome—and he himself wrote
this to Fliess—his "zest for martyrdom" would disappear and he would
finally dare to do what was necessary to triumph over an obstacle:
challenge the antisemitism that barred his nomination to a professorship.

Jones himself says that we "must" discover some intimate secret of Freud's in Rome. This suspicion, however, has not been entirely confirmed until now. One hundred elements of proof do not constitute proof. Jones collected all the hypotheses that had been advanced to explain Freud's inhibition about going to Rome: unconscious emotional relationship to the Sacred Cross, to the Pope, to the Trinity; nostalgia displaced from Jerusalem to Rome; a desire to convert to Catholicism. All these explanations, however, seemed most unlikely to Jones. He believed that Freud found himself caught in an internal conflict nourished by two contradictory feelings: his love for ancient Rome and his hatred for, and fear of, Christian Rome.

What prevented Freud from going to Rome? In Jones's words,

> There is plenty of evidence that the fulfillment of this great wish was opposed by some mysterious taboo which made him doubt if the wish could be realized. . . . At times he tried to rationalize his inhibition by saying that the climate in Rome in the summer made it impossible, but all the time he knew there was something deeper holding him back. So his years of extensive travels in northern and central Italy brought him little nearer to Rome than Trasimeno (in 1897). Thus far and no farther said the inner voice, just as it had spoken to Hannibal at that spot two thousand years ago.[2]

What did Freud himself say, how did he feel during the period preliminary to "the high point" of his life?

Let us follow this question in the letters he wrote to Fliess during the year preceding his trip to Rome. (The letters from earlier years contain still more allusions to Rome, but we cannot reconsider all of them here.)

> *Letter 133* (April 16, 1900): Otherwise Vienna is Vienna, that is to say extremely revolting. If I closed with "Next Easter in Rome," I should feel like a pious Jew.
> *Letter 134* (May 7, 1900): No critic . . . can see more clearly than I the disproportion there is between the problems and my answers to them, and it will be fitting punishment for me that none of the unexplored regions of the mind in which I have been the first mortal to set foot will ever bear my name or submit to my laws. When breath threatened to fail me in the struggle I prayed the angel to desist, and that is what he has done since then. But I did not turn out to be the stronger, though since then I have been noticeably limping. Well, I really am forty-four now, a rather shabby old Jew.[3]

This allusion to the fight with the angel is worth noting. Sigmund Freud is in fact the son of a Jakob, and in the Bible, the patriarch Jacob struggles with the angel without relenting; for this reason, he receives the name of *Israel* 'strong against God'.

Letter 136 (May 20, 1900): I do not stick even to my hobbies, but alternate between chess, art history and prehistory, but keep at none of them for long. I should like to disappear for a few weeks to somewhere where science does not exist—apart, of course, from the congress with you. If only I had money or a travelling companion for Italy!

Letter 138 (July 10, 1900): I am completely exhausted with work and with everything connected with it that is germinating, tempting and threatening. . . . The big problems are still unsettled. It is an intellectual hell, layer upon layer of it, with everything fitfully gleaming and pulsating; and the outline of Lucifer-Amor coming into sight at the darkest centre.

Letter 139 (October 14, 1900): For the psychology of everyday life I should like to borrow from you the superb quotation: *Nun is die Welt von diesem Spuk so voll* [the world is now so full of this phantom]. . . . Otherwise I am reading Greek archaeology and revelling in journeys which I shall never make and treasures which I shall never possess.

Letter 141 (January 30, 1901): In the midst of this mental and material depression I am haunted by the thought of spending Easter week in Rome this year. Not that there is any justification for it—I have achieved nothing yet, and in any case external circumstances will probably make it impossible.[4]

Letter 142 (February 2, 1901): I shall no more get to Rome this Easter than you will. . . . I have become entirely estranged from what you are doing.

Letter 143 (May 3, 1901): I am correcting the first pages of The Everyday Life, which has turned out to be about sixty pages long. I have taken a tremendous dislike to it, and I hope others will take an even bigger dislike to it. It is entirely formless and contains all sorts of forbidden things.

We have now reached the summer vacation of 1901. The last letter before the journey to Rome—at least among those published—begins thus:

Letter 145 (August 7, 1901): The weather is horrible today for the first time in three weeks, and makes it impossible to do anything else; tomorrow we are going to Salzburg for a performance of *Don Giovanni*. . . . That is how I come to be answering you at once, or at any rate beginning an answer. . . . There is no concealing the fact that we have drawn somewhat apart from each other. . . . In this you came to the limit of your penetration, you take sides against me and tell me that "the thought-reader merely reads his own thoughts into other people," which deprives my work of all its value.

If I am such a one, throw my Everyday Life unread into the wastepaper basket. It is full of references to you: obvious ones, where you supplied the material, and concealed ones, where the motivation derives from you.[5]

Our supposition that *Don Giovanni* and Rome cannot be separated in Freud's life already finds an echo in this trip to Salzburg, a month before the great Roman meeting.

Freud finally leaves for Rome. He sees many things, but above all, "He caught his first glimpse (first of how many later!) of Michelangelo's statue of Moses. After staring at it for a while he suddenly had a flash of intuition, at reflecting on Michelangelo's personality, that gave him an understanding of it."[6]

What had he understood? It is only in 1913, after having returned to Rome several times, that he writes the article about Michelangelo's statue, signing it with three asterisks; we will come to it later. What we already see is that something decisive happened to Freud in Rome. In March 1902, Freud writes:

> I am glad to be able to tell you that at last the long-withheld and recently really desirable professorship has been conferred on me.[7]

Fliess congratulates him. Freud then answers—and it is the last (published) letter to this friend.

> It was my own doing, my zest for life and work had somewhat grown and my zest for martyrdom had somewhat diminished. I found that my practice had melted away and I withdrew my last work from publication because in you I had recently lost my only remaining audience. I reflected that waiting for recognition might take up a good portion of the remainder of my life, and that in the meantime none of my fellow-men were likely to trouble about me. And I wanted to see Rome again and look after my patients and keep my children happy. So I made up my mind to break with my strict scruples and take appropriate steps, as others [in German, *andere Menschen Kinder* 'other children of men'] do after all. One must look somewhere for one's salvation, and the salvation I chose was the title of professor. For four years I had not put in a word about it. . . .
> I have obviously become reputable again. . . .
> If I had taken those few steps three years ago I should have been appointed three years earlier, and should have spared myself much. Others are just as clever, without having to go to Rome first.[8]

The first trip to Rome took place in 1901. The last would take place in 1923, and the circumstances in which Freud decided to go deserve to be noted: following the first operation—the first of what again is a long series—which revealed the cancer that overtook Freud and from which he would die in September 1939. Marked by death, Freud had one thought the day following the operation: Rome.

Freud in Rome

Freud arrives in the city on September 2, 1901. Jones recounts that he visits Saint Peter's in the Vatican the next day. "He soon tossed a coin into the fountain of Trevi, vowing that he would soon return to Rome, which indeed he did the very next year. He also thrust his hand into Bocca della Verita in S. Maria in Cosmedin, a superfluous gesture for a man of such integrity."[9] Freud had written the above anecdote to Fliess, from which letter Jones probably took it. But Jones has normalized the texts somewhat on one small detail. What Freud asks at the Bocca della Verita is to be told if he is lying when he swears to return. We ask ourselves, Has the wish that one usually makes at the fountain become, for Freud, a question for the stone's mouth which, it is said, devours the hands of liars? In swearing to return—without saying precisely where—is Freud asking the stone Pythia if he will return *to* Rome or *from* Rome? Let us listen to him giving his impressions of Rome to a friend upon his return.

> It was an overwhelming experience for me, and, as you know, the fulfillment of a long-cherished wish. It was slightly disappointing, as all such fulfillments are when one has waited for them too long, but it was a high-spot in my life all the same. But, while I contemplated ancient Rome undisturbed (I could have worshipped the humble and mutilated remnant of the Temple of Minerva near the forum of Nerva), I found I could not freely enjoy the second Rome [i.e., medieval and Renaissance Rome, Christian Rome as distinct from ancient Rome]; I was disturbed by its meaning, and, being incapable of putting out of my mind my own misery and all the other misery which I know to exist, I found almost intolerable the lie of the salvation of mankind which rears its head so proudly to heaven.
>
> I found the third, Italian, Rome hopeful and likeable.[10]

Let us stop at this passage for a moment. Freud has three Romes before him. The first, with its ruins of temples dedicated to ancient divinities, provokes in him a sense of adoration; for him, ruins, beautiful and miserable things, are compatible with humanity. The third Rome, the contemporary city of 1901, inspires sympathy in him and agreeable expectations. But he is troubled by the second—Christian—Rome, which, from the time of triumphant Christianity, had proudly reared its head. Freud, however, does not speak accusingly here—which we would understand, for many reasons; this Rome does not anger him but troubles him—he cannot stand it. What exactly bothers him? He explains the meaning of this Rome as the falsehood of the redemption of man. In his opinion, the second Rome bears a lie about the redemption of a fault, a lie because it does not correspond to what he knows about misery, in himself and in others. It is a lie; the fault has not been redeemed. Misery remains.

Let us muse a little; we pass from the second Rome to the second wife—Rebecca Freud, the father's second wife; there too we find a lie. Is Freud also troubled by a fault that has not been redeemed?

We now know the climate in which Freud awaited this journey, his state of mind after his return, and his general impressions while there. We are ready to join him at the church of Saint Peter in Chains, where we find the tomb of Pope Julius II and the famous statue of Moses. The tomb and the statue certainly belong to this second Rome, which Freud cannot stand.

He goes to the church on the third day of his stay in Rome, after a storm "of the kind that Michelangelo might have made."[11] The only way for us to see Freud standing in front of Moses is to go back to the text he devoted to him, where, behind the amateur that he pretends to be, we can detect, here and there, Freud the man, hidden.

The Pope's Tomb

The author of *The Moses of Michelangelo* presents himself as a simple amateur of art, who is informed about psychoanalysis and is trying to understand the strong impression that works of art, particularly plastic or literary ones, make on him. If he cannot understand why he is moved or what grips him, as in music, for example, he cannot enjoy it. The greatest works, such as the statue of Moses, remain the most enigmatic. That which grips us so could only be the intention of the artist. Perhaps this response is not possible without the application of psychoanalysis.

Having left his city five years after the death of his father, Freud encounters an enigma in Rome, of which he can only speak by becoming enigmatic himself—by losing his name. Is this not close to the situation of Oedipus leaving Corinth, who finds himself before the Sphinx, poser of enigmas, after the death of his father—and he too without a name?

Freud continues thus: "As we know, it is only a fragment of the gigantic tomb which the artist was to have erected for the powerful Pope Julius II."[12] In German the word *Pope* is intensified *"den gewaltigen Papst-herrn Julius II."* The word *Herr*, which is added here, is already familiar to us as part of the name of the mushrooms so sought after by Freud. Sir Pope, the Lord Pope, who is buried under Moses, is, in addition, named Julius, which presents a coincidence. The brother who immediately followed Sigmund was named Julius. He died the year after his birth. Thus, beneath Moses a pope is buried, a *Herr* who carries the name of the dead brother Julius, and in the same numerical order: the second pope, the second son.

We want to know everything we can about this tomb because it seems possible that not only the statue is enigmatic for Freud. Would he give us still other details? A few pages later:

> The figure of Moses was to have decorated the bases of the tomb together with five other statues (or according to a later sketch, with three). Its immediate counterpart was to have been a figure of Paul. One other pair, representing the *vita activa* and the *vita contemplativa* in the shape of Leah and Rachel—standing, it is true—has been executed on the tomb as exists in its sadly aborted form.[13]

Finally, the monument presents itself thus: on the tomb of Julius II are Moses, seated, and, on each side, two standing statues, Leah and Rachel.

Leah	MOSES	Rachel

Pope Julius II

Leah and Rachel

A moment ago there were three Romes, one of which troubled Freud. Here, there are only two women, sisters. Having no direct historical link to Moses, they nonetheless are also biblical characters, who belong to an earlier epoch. The two sisters married successively the same man following a trick of their father who, on the wedding night, substituted the oldest, the unattractive Leah, for Rachel, the youngest, who had been asked in marriage. After waiting for seven years, the oldest, who was less loved, conceived numerous children, while the second remained sterile for a long time. Thus Leah represents the active life and Rachel the contemplative one. We find this allegory repeated in Christian iconography with the two wives of the New Testament, Martha and Mary. Freud, so well informed about Rome, must have known all this.

A bridge suddenly emerges between Rome and Vienna, between the pope's tomb and the Freud family. The husband of Leah and Rachel is none other than the famous patriarch Jacob (Genesis, chapter 29). The tomb of Julius II already comprises, in Freud's eyes, many comparisons with the story of his family.

Jacob

The man buried in the tomb is called pope (*il papa*), the father (*Herr*): *Papstherr*, which could evidently suggest a dead father. Freud's father's name was Herr Jakob Freud. The first name of this pope is Julius, the same name as the only dead child in the Freud family, and the number two represents the second Freud son. On the tomb is the statue of Moses, legislator of the Jewish people and before whom whoever has acted badly can feel himself gripped, seized, apprehended as an evildoer, as Freud anonymously claims to be seized (the same word in German)[14] by this enigmatic masterpiece. At the sides of Moses stand the two wives of Jacob. Sigmund Freud's father, Jakob, also officially had two wives.

(Does it not seem that this quest unfolds itself like a child's song, where at each new couplet one repeats what has already been learned, until the story has developed its entire meaning?)

The tomb of Julius II presents Freud in 1901 with a representation of the official version of his family history. In reality, Jakob, the father, is dead. So is this father's second son, Julius, and in the work of art, a pope (father) named Julius is buried. In the pretended reality the father Jakob had two wives; in the work of art are Leah and Rachel, the two wives of Jacob.

All this is perhaps only a coincidence. But if so, then how could it disturb Freud so much, and how could the presence of Moses, in the middle, fascinate him so? An answer presents itself, as much by following our hypothesis as by applying what Freud himself has taught us: If Freud is so disturbed and fascinated, it is because this monument introduces, in doubtless a disguised and coded way, the presence of what must not be named, of what was hidden. The monument that Freud sees must show him something that he knows without knowing that he knows it, something that he must have repressed.

The presence of Moses fascinates him so much that, in the course of the article, he inquires not so much into the intentions of Michelangelo as into those of the statue itself. Said even more directly, this statue must contain something that contradicts the lies of the Freud family. And yet, at first glance, Freud endorses them completely.

Rebecca

Let us approach this from the other side. The second son, the one who died, is named on the statue. But is Rebecca, the father's second wife, of whom one never speaks and about whom Freud is supposed to know nothing, inscribed there too?

The reader who is informed about biblical history will perhaps already be a step ahead of us. The name *Rebecca* also makes a bridge between Rome and Vienna, as that of *Jacob* did earlier. Hidden wife of Jakob Freud, Rebecca has a much more explicit place in the Bible. She is actually the mother of the patriarch Jacob.

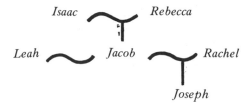

In the Bible, Jacob has two wives, Leah and Rachel, and a mother, Rebecca. In the Freud family, Jakob officially has two wives, Sally and Amalie, and a hidden wife, Rebecca. How can Sigmund Freud manage to represent the hidden wife of his father, about whom he is supposed to know nothing, as if he has "felt" her existence despite everything? Does he share this illicit knowledge with others in order to suffer from it no longer, as psychoanalytic theory itself explains? The Scriptures, which have already furnished him with his role as interpreter of dreams as we shall see, provides Freud with a possible symbolization of a link between a Rebecca and a Jacob, not as a conjugal couple but as a mother-son couple. The hidden fault of the father can be allegorically represented as a union between mother and son; it is thus incestuous. Is this not exactly what Freud has retained from Sophocles? Is this not precisely the central theory of Freud, that of the Oedipal complex?

These coincidences are interesting, but what do they have to do with Freud? He is not a pious Jew, even if he is well versed in the Bible. How can we know if the connection between his father and the patriarch Jacob was really important? If it was not, the other connection, that between the two Rebeccas, would be simply a play on words.

We can verify this connection quite simply. If Jakob Freud does correspond with the biblical Jacob in Freud's mind, this transposition would give to Sigmund Freud himself a place in the patriarchal lineage. Something in his life should resemble the life of the son of Jacob to whom he would correspond. Freud is officially the eldest son of the second wife of Jakob Freud. He therefore finds a parallel with the eldest son of Rachel, the second wife of Jacob. Now the eldest son of Rachel is named Joseph, who is particularly famous as an interpreter of dreams. The resemblance with Sigmund Freud, whose major work, *The Interpretation of Dreams,* had just appeared in 1900, needs no commentary.

Freud's Roman enigma is not confined, as he thinks, only to the statue of Moses. The tomb of the pope, in its entirety, confronts him with what he could not symbolize: the existence of Rebecca, wife of his father. Without being named, the patriarch Jacob and his mother, Rebecca, appear through the presence of the statues of Leah and Rachel. The dead pope, the dead father, is the link between Jacob and Freud's father, who is also dead. The name of this pope presents the name of the dead child, the second Freud son. The existence of Rebecca, mother of Jacob, offers

Freud the possibility of symbolizing the unnamable, the unnamed relation, between his father and Rebecca, his second wife.

Hypothesis

If we really have arrived before the tragic destiny of a lineage, we
cannot avoid linking the death of the second child, Julius, with the disappearance of the second wife, Rebecca. For what reason was the existence
of this wife hidden? According to the logic of ancient tragedy, whereby
one death leads to another death, the decease of the second child could
perhaps be the punishment for the murder of the second wife. But this
seems indeed an audacious idea to apply to Jakob Freud. Of course,
the Bible itself, with the story of David and Bathsheba, presents similar
situations (their first child dies in expiation of the murder of Bathsheba's
first husband). Where should one stop in putting into question a family
history when one has already found two lies?

We cannot go any further in this direction by interpretation. Keeping in mind that this tomb might represent for Freud, eventually, the
faults of his father, faults that concern his relations with women and
whose consequences we have for a moment imagined might be fatal, let
us return to Saint Peter's.

Freud before Moses

From this vantage point in the story, we understand better why the
work of Michelangelo could be so enigmatic for Freud, since it contains
the signs of what had not been signified to him. The monument provides
him with a secret representation of the secret past of his father. Jakob
Freud is represented there allegorically as someone whose sexual life
involves something hidden and perhaps tragic.

Such a suggestion returns us to Don Juan. A sexual fault of the
father is implicit in this monument, and in the midst of all these signs is
Moses, the legislator, the one who handed down the law by which faults
are defined. Moses, here on the tomb of the dead father, is the pope. Is
not the statue of the Commander also erected on the tomb of a dead
father?

Under what identity could Freud endure what this strange spectacle
provoked in him? Having lost his father's name, in whose place did he
put himself to withstand the sight of what would certainly be unbearable
for him had not the truth been transposed, indeed, veiled? From whom
will he borrow an identity to appear, in spite of everything, before this
judge of faults?

In a letter to Fliess, Freud, listing his works, identifies himself with Leporello, Don Juan's valet. Several months earlier, the sculptor Tilgner had died as if struck down by the statue of Mozart's Commander, revealing that he, too, in some mysterious way, was Don Juan. Freud had consequently experienced an intense death anxiety. There again, it is possible that he is identifying with Leporello: indeed, what anxiety the valet experiences as he looks on, powerless, at the encounter between the retributive statue and the seducer, the infidel! The latter's death is all the more terrifying since Don Juan is not annihilated but seized alive, snatched up in the infernal torments that already draw terrible cries from him.

What does Freud say of his feelings in the face of Moses-the Commander? We will resume the paragraph cited above, which presents the "Moses" as a fragment from the papal tomb (the German words that seem particularly ambiguous to us are given in a note so as not to impede the reading).

> It always delights me to read an appreciative sentence about this statue, such as that it is "the crown of modern sculpture" (Grimm). For no piece of statuary ever made a stronger impression on me than this. How often have I mounted the steep steps from the unlovely Corso Cavour to the lonely piazza where the deserted church stands, and have essayed to support the angry scorn of the hero's glance![15]

We note the two adjectives *lonely* and *deserted.* Is it, in fact, such a deserted place? The text continues with the following sentences, whose double meaning becomes apparent as we read further:

> Sometimes I have crept cautiously out of the half-gloom of the interior as though I myself belonged to the mob upon whom his eye is turned—the mob which can hold fast no conviction, which has neither faith nor patience, and which rejoices when it has regained its illusory idols.[16]

Who is speaking here? Freud before Moses, or Leporello before the Commander? Leporello also goes to the cemetery, a solitary and abandoned place, and meets the incensed and scornful gaze of the statue. He tries to stand up under this gaze, but he then slips prudently out of the shadow, on the order of his master. Leporello represents the domestic and the mob—the same word in German—by being employed as a domestic, and finding himself confused with the infidel mob which in fact is his master, Don Juan, the scoundrel who celebrates when his illusory idols—women—are rendered up to him.

Don Juan, like the Hebrew people, betrays his alliance. We can trace the parallel, practically term for term, between Moses before his people and the Commander before Don Juan—two divine messengers before infidels. We have seen this parallel play itself out for Freud, who situates himself before Moses as Leporello before the Commander.

Another infidel's (Jakob Freud's) son fears the glance of another statue, to which he imparts life—he calls it "the hero," as if he himself were in the mob that had unleashed the Judge's anger. This son is Sigmund Freud. But is he still the son of Jakob, the one who, before Moses, loses the name of his father? Freud continues:

> But why do I call this statue inscrutable? There is not the slightest doubt that it represents Moses, the Law-giver of the Jews, holding the tablet of the Ten Commandments. That much is certain, but that is all.[17]

Our reading overturns this certainty. Is it really Moses and only he? Having posed as clear what is precisely the ambiguous point, Freud can indeed be astonished not to know why this statue appears so enigmatic to him. It is true that the statue has elicited opposing judgments, but only from specialists in art. How can we clarify it for him? Only by trying to decipher his emotions, which are the real enigma.

From Leporello to Joseph

Can chance really reunite so many significant elements, belonging at once to three worlds as different as biblical history, the opera of Mozart, and the Freud family? Saint Peter's is really the crossroads for Freud of three meanings whose mysterious conjunction leads him to the fascinating point where the truth shows itself without being said. Here it appears, but as an enigma, that Jakob Freud, the Don Juan threatened with divine punishment, and Jakob Freud, the husband-son of Rebecca. are, in the unconscious heart of Sigmund Freud, one and the same person. Is Freud the valet rather than the son? It is true that until his trip to Rome, Freud conducted himself in society with a resignation that would later seem suspect to him, not daring to do what was necessary to be named professor, which is, basically, master of medicine. This attitude also illuminates his fear of going to Rome, which no longer surprises us; it is now more surprising to us that he finally went.

We have, however, already found the key to this change. In 1900 Freud brought out *The Interpretation of Dreams.* By this book, the master-piece of his life, he became Joseph, son of Jacob. Freud is Joseph—he knows it, writes it here and there in his book. But he ignores that this Joseph has taken upon himself the faults of the father since his death. The enormous work that Freud took upon himself for several years is perhaps not the pure work of research that he seems officially to present to us. Signs in the margins permit us to see him as a son burdened with the hidden faults of his father, blindly carrying out a mysterious expiation.

For the moment, in Rome, Leporello has become Joseph in inventing a science that he uses to interpret the intentions of a statue. From that position he can confront the enigma. Freud has not been able, however, to efface in himself the traces of the valet. We can verify this.

Moses Rises

If Freud had indeed been Leporello—and this identification, doubtless unconscious, cannot for this reason have disappeared—he could only expect one thing: that the statue of Moses, like that of the Commander, would come to life, rise to its feet to punish the guilty. This unconscious expectation would partially, if not totally, explain Freud's fear of going to Rome. Once he had become the interpreter of dreams, he could henceforth face Moses in another way, as interpreter of his thought and no longer as a valet-son who feared the punishment that the master-father deserved.

In fact, the enigma that Freud tackles is clearly the question of which movement Moses has made, which movement he is going to make, and of the profound feelings that would be at the origin of these supposed movements.

Other commentators have suggested that Michelangelo represented the great man at his descent from Sinai, bearer of the Tablets of the Law, as he discovers the idolatrous Hebrews before the Golden Calf; he is about to rise up, to break the tablets, to let loose his anger. According to Freud, however, this does not correspond to the artist's intention; Freud devotes the whole article to proving it. Michelangelo wanted to represent an emotion coming to an end, a mastered anger. Besides, since Moses was supposed to be in the company of other seated statues, "it would create a very bad effect to give us the illusion that [Moses] was going to leave [his] place and [his] companions, in fact to abandon [his] role in the general scheme." Michelangelo could never have committed such a gross error, and the author of the article manages to convince us, to convince himself, of the peaceful intentions of this statue in terms that take on a new meaning for us:

> The figure of Moses, therefore, cannot be supposed to be springing to his feet; he must be allowed to remain as he is in sublime repose like the other figures and like the proposed statue of the Pope (which was not, however, executed by Michelangelo himself).[18]

In German *cannot be* and *must be* do not exist. Moses is the subject of both sentences. Let us develop it literally: Moses cannot, does not, have the

right to spring forward. He must—necessarily—be able to persevere in a
sublime tranquility, and the adjective *sublime* (*hehr*) repeats *Herr,* which
we have already encountered. Thus Moses must remain calm; it is not
possible that he start to leap up. He must remain tranquil like the pope
himself.

Does that mean there is no connection between Moses-the Commander and the father? Freud constructs an argument that tends to dis-
sociate Moses from the furious judge. He bases his argument in favor of a
peaceful Moses upon the presence of the other characters who are beside
Moses, namely the pope and the women. Is this not the opposite of his
unformulated fears, if he is indeed, as we suppose, tormented by anxiety
concerning the judgment of his Don Juan father, and of its consequences
for him? (In *Don Giovanni,* on the contrary, the presence of Don Juan in
the midst of so many women causes the statue of the Commander to come
alive for the vengeance of heaven and of himself.) The text continues,
and it is only after having assured us that Moses must not move, cannot
move, that Freud shares his expectation with us. The sentences are
amazing to us now that we have in mind the image of the Commander
walking on his pedestal to strike down Don Juan. This is what Freud
imagined before Moses.

> And, indeed, I can recollect my own disillusionment when, during
> my first visits to San Pietro in Vincoli, I used to sit down in front of
> the statue in the expectation that I should now see how it would start
> up on its raised foot, dash the Tables of the Law to the ground and
> let fly its wrath. Nothing of this kind happened. Instead, the stone
> image became more and more transfixed, an almost oppressively
> solemn calm emanated from it, and I was obliged to realize that
> something was represented here that could stay without change: that
> this Moses would remain sitting like this in his wrath forever.[18]

It seems as if our research leads us repeatedly to turn our questions
around. We were asking ourselves what happened in Rome that was so
decisive. Now we ask how Freud could have lived in Vienna, with the
vision in his depths of this eternally irritated Moses, with the forbidden
knowledge of his father's fault, in the ambiguous position he occupied in
the eternal confrontation between the judge and the one at fault.

We still are not clear about the fault, and only a patient reconstitu-
tion of it will permit us to guess its nature. The only thing we are certain
of for the moment is that the tomb of Julius II, in which the Moses of
Michelangelo is located, enigmatically puts Freud in the grips of the
hidden fault concerning his father's second wife and perhaps his brother's
death. A fear had long kept Freud far from Rome, far from the tomb and
from what it represents. Freud is in the position of Leporello, valet of
the guilty person. He then becomes Joseph, the interpreter of dreams.

He makes a "discovery," and is in the position of Joseph, the worthy son of a faultless Jacob.

What have we learned that would permit us to orient ourselves for what is to come? On a biographical level we have discovered Freud on vacation—the forests, the journeys—outside Vienna, passionate about his mushroom "hunts" and fascinated by statues. Utilizing his method and our rereading of *Oedipus Rex,* we have opened up the question of symptoms to the point where it crosses the border of the individual psyche and confronts successive generations. Then, carrying over the same myth to the generation preceding Sigmund Freud, we began to see the outlines of the figure of Don Juan in the portrait of the father. Freud himself was not Don Juan, but his witness and his heir. Having identified with his father, he had contracted by this identification the secret debt of his father as a consequence of his fault; a fault of which we know nothing but its mask: the disappearance of a woman and the changing of a birth date.

We have seen how Freud, in his spare time, tried to master this cursed and repressed inheritance by pursuing mushrooms and antiquities, substitutes for Moses-the Commander, by picking them, eating them, buying them, and inviting them to dinner. How could it be possible for such a repressed guilt—all the more inaccessible in that it originated in the fault of another, a guilt that weighed so heavily on the free time of Freud—to stop affecting his daily life in Vienna? According to what he has taught us himself, a forgotten fault leads those who carry it to expiatory rites and sacrifices. Where has the fault moved to then? It has not been recognized, so Freud is not free from it. What remains of it? The repetition, the representation (artistic, pseudoscientific), the expiation, the reparation . . .

A word leads us to the Viennese Freud, toward his conjuring liturgy, the name of the only object that figures in the tomb of Julius II and of which we have not yet spoken: the tablets. Moses actually holds the Tablets of the Law, upon which are inscribed the law given by God to the Hebrew people. The same word, *tablet,* takes us to the house of Sigmund and Martha Freud, at their dining table during dinner.[20]

The Liturgy of the Table

Anyone who cares to observe his fellow men while they are at table will be able to observe the neatest and most instructive symptomatic acts.

Freud, *The Psychopathology of Everyday Life*

What their son Martin tells us about meals at the Freud house merits our attention. The hour of this meal and its ceremony was, according to him, ruled by a strict discipline. He presents us with the daily unfolding of events as if he were opening the mechanism of a clock: "There was never any waiting for meals: at the stroke of one everybody in the household was seated at the long diningroom table and at the same moment one door opened to let the maid enter with the soup while another door opened to allow my father to walk in from his study to take his place at the head of the table facing my mother at the other end."[21] Freud's "favorite dish," boiled beef, was eaten three or four times a week. Here again, as with the mushrooms, the frequency suggests some kind of ritual and not just a taste or inclination. Jones describes the family lunch as "the only time when the whole family would usually be together. . . . [Freud] enjoyed his food and would concentrate on it. He was very taciturn during meals, which would sometimes be a source of embarassment to strange visitors who had to carry on a conversation alone with the family. Freud, however, never missed a word of the family intercourse and daily news."[22] What does this incomprehensible silence at the table signify? Why is it so absolute that it is maintained in the presence of guests, even if these guests are disciple psychoanalysts? Martin Freud's account agrees with that of Jones. He remembers Jung, who, unlike the other guests, "never made the slightest attempt to make polite conversation with mother or us children but pursued the debate which had been interrupted by the call to dinner. Jung on these occasions did all the talking and father, with unconcealed delight, did all the listening."[23]

Another enigma: Why does Freud become silent as a tomb when he is at the table? Is it the same unconscious, internal question that pursues him from Rome to Vienna? The method that permitted us to open a path of interpretation for the "Moses" will serve us again. Let us try to see the whole picture. Who are the people around the table? Martin has forgotten to mention someone who lived with them ever since he was old enough to notice. So that the reader might find his or her bearing, we must ask a little more patience and briefly take up the facts concerning this forgotten person.

The first time that Freud saw Martha Bernays, his future wife, was when she "and probably her sister Minna were visiting the Freud family."[24] The two sisters were no doubt very close, as the following incident informs us. After one of her first meetings with Freud, Martha told her younger sister, Minna, about the conversation she had had with him and about the numerous questions he had asked her. "What do you make of it?" Martha asked. As Jones indicates, the answer was rather deceptive: "It is very kind of Herr Doctor to take so much interest in *us*." Further on, the biographer writes of Minna: "She and Freud got on excellently together. There was no sexual attraction on either side, but he found her a stimulating and amusing companion and would occasionally make short holiday excursions with her when his wife was not free to travel."[25]

At the end of 1896, by which time all of the children had been born, Minna Bernays, whose fiancé had long since died, moved into the Freud household and never left it. How can one fail to notice that Minna's arrival follows very closely upon the death of the father; that it is at this time that Freud begins to collect statues;[26] that he never has any more children (Anna was born in 1895); and that only a year later he renounces his first theory of the guilty father and "discovers" the Oedipus complex?

Let us return to Vienna, to the Freud home, at the dinner hour, and, more precisely still, to one of the numerous times when, having bought a new statuette, he invites it to dinner and places it before him. Is the scene of Saint Peter's reconstituted here? At one o'clock Freud enters the dining room where the mother, her sister, and the children are already seated around the long table.

He arrives with the newly purchased statuette, puts it down, and seats himself. What does he have before him? A *table,* a *statue,* a *group* of children *seated* before him whose initials spell the name of *Moses,* and two women, *two sisters,* living with *the same man,* Martha and Minna with Freud (Martha and Mary in the evangelical stories, Leah and Rachel in the Bible with Jacob). The eldest is active; she manages the household, has numerous children. The second one is rather contemplative, shares Freud's research and ideas. He takes her and not Martha to Rome before writing *The Moses of Michelangelo.* He will only return to Rome one more time, with his daughter Anna, at the point when he has discovered he has cancer.

With what amazing exactitude Freud reproduces the tomb of Julius II in his daily life, at the exact moment when his father dies! It is probably only through the unconscious or in the sacred that one can reunite contradictions in this way. For Freud manages to be both the Biblical Jacob and Jakob Freud *at the same time,* in the same scene—both the anti-Don Juan and Don Juan at once.

Like the patriarch Jacob, he lives with two sisters. In nineteenth-century Europe this could be considered a fault, but no doubt he is equally chaste with both of them, in this way placing them in the same class as companions, not wives.[27] Imitating his biblical father, he atones for his progenitor. The entire situation for infidelity is in place; it seems, however, that it was never carried out. A possible fault is there, or at least represented; at the same time, it is atoned for every day, every night. Moses can indeed see that Freud has succeeded in being Jakob without being Don Juan. However, just as the fault of the father is secret, secret also is the expiation. Nothing is recognized. The scene must always be replayed, the ritual reenacted. Does Freud know what he is replaying there? Who will ever know? His silence at the table cannot be attributed to a particular love of gastronomy. The extreme monotony of the menus hardly suggests this about this always thin and, for his time, rather athletic intellectual. But if, in his heart, he is before Moses, then the silence becomes understandable.

And yet, through his exemplary virtue, Freud, without understanding what he is doing, at once represents and atones for the dissolute life of his father by identifying him with his biblical homonym. In the same scene in which he atones for the fault he repeats it, reenacts it himself. Freud himself is a Don Juan, in spite of his strict family life. He collects conquests—not women, but statues of pagan gods.[28] Like the Hebrew people, he is an infidel, but to his god, not to his wife. The fault, so rigorously expiated in the flesh, is reenacted in the spirit.

The infidel Freud, son of an infidel, succeeds, through the same obscure ceremony, in repairing the paternal fault under Moses' eyes. He repeats it, however, by multiplying idolatrous acts right before Moses himself. What a triumph of wit it is to repeat the fault before the very person who will judge it! The unconscious has these ironic successes. Freud will later acclaim them himself.[29]

Freud claims to be agnostic, and we are willing to believe it, for he is a truthful man. But does he not see what he writes through his geographical travels, through his physical acts and gestures, through his begetting a family? A name is written in Freud's unconscious heart: Moses. He considers himself a free thinker. Who is ever one? We have seen a little of his life; before so many ritual constraints, so many expiations and atonements, one concludes that the strictest Judaism would not finally have been more onerous for Freud the man than this hidden, unconscious, archaic, circular religion without progression. Religion, such as he will describe it in his antireligious books, is precisely his own religion: the hidden murder, the forgotten fault, then the totem, the expiatory sacrifice in which the fault is symbolically reenacted.

Perhaps he never heard the second commandment inscribed on the Tablets of the Law that Moses brought to the infidel Hebrew people, and that constitute the oracle of his hidden life: "You shall not make a carved image . . . for I . . . am a jealous god. I punish the children for the sins of their father," but which ends thus: "I keep faith with thousands, with those who love me and keep my commandments."[30]

CHAPTER 4

REBECCA

In our exploration of the foundations of psychoanalysis we now find ourselves facing a name — Rebecca — and a mystery — the fate of Jakob Freud's second wife. We have met this Rebecca in Freud's life in two ways, in two places: inscribed in a census register in Freiberg as the wife of Jakob Freud — although Freud is not supposed to know about that; and, implicitly, as Jacob's mother in the monument of Julius II in Rome, which Freud contemplates, fascinated, but without discovering her there.

Slender thread of Ariadne. Will we ever know what happened and what Freud knew about it? Can we leave this path, however scattered its traces may be, without looking to see if there is not some vestige of it buried in Freud's own writings? If we were to find some allusion to any Rebecca, we could study it carefully to see what it might tell us.

FIRST APPEARANCE: THE LETTER TO FLIESS

We have already seen that on a very important day in his life Freud wrote to Fliess, "I no longer believe in my *neurotica*," that is, in the theory that he had elaborated of the seduction of hysterics by their fathers. In this letter, where he explains his numerous reasons for no longer "believing," he renounces his first discovery, for which he had waited so long:

> The hope of eternal fame was so beautiful, and so was that of certain wealth, complete independence, travel, and removing the children from the sphere of worries which spoiled my youth. All that depended on whether hysteria succeeded or not. Now I can be quiet and modest again and go on worrying and saving, and one of the

stories from my collection occurs to me: "Rebecca, you can take off your wedding-gown, you're not a bride any longer!"[1]

Thus, at one point Freud had found something that should have assured the realization of all his dreams. Then one fine day he no longer *believes* it. The verb is astonishing in a man of science. How does this termination of belief present itself? "Let me tell you straight away the great secret which has been slowly dawning on me in recent months. I no longer believe in my *neurotica.*"

At what point in Freud's life do these "recent months" occur? Once again, we come back to the same period. The letter is dated September 21, 1897, which is eleven months after the father's death. During these "recent months" a "great secret . . . has been slowly dawning on me. . . . I no longer believe . . ." The commentator in the French edition notes: "One could easily conclude that it was the self-analysis over the summer that permitted Freud to take the decisive step, which was to reject the hypothesis of seduction."

Let us accept this informed opinion. But what, in fact, did Freud do during this summer of 1897? "In the middle of July he met his sister-in-law Minna in Salzburg and they made a short walking tour together to Untersberg and Heilbrunn. Then after a visit to her mother in Reichenhall he returned to Vienna where he had to make the arrangements for his father's gravestone. This was just when he was beginning his self-analysis."[2] We retain the association Jones makes between the gravestone and the beginning of the self-analysis. Freud spends the following month of August with his family and then takes a fifteen-day trip to Italy with his brother and a student-patient. He travels many kilometers, visits a number of cities in the north, among them Pisa (and its tower), which Jones faithfully records. We are told one striking thing: Freud visits Orvieto, where he is particularly pleased by the frescos of Signorelli, and goes into an Etruscan tomb that still contains a skeleton.[3] The name of the painter, Signorelli, is known not only to amateurs of painting but to psychoanalysts as well, because Freud could not remember this name a year later in the course of a conversation he had in a train. This was the first incident of forgetfulness that Freud analyzed in *The Psychopathology of Everyday Life.* The subject of these frescos now appears particularly significant to us: the Last Judgment.

This is all we know about that summer: a trip to Salzburg with Minna, a walk with her, Untersberg, Heilbrunn, Vienna, the father's gravestone, Orvieto, and the "Last Judgment" of Lucca Signorelli.

Let us associate the words and the things: a trip with a woman who is not his wife in the city of Mozart, cities whose names evoke the infernal regions,[4] the gravestone of the father, dead the year before, and the Last Judgment. Lucca, the surname of Signorelli, is also the name of Freud's favorite singer in *Don Giovanni,* Pauline Lucca. Does not all of this speak of the dead father, Don Juan, and of the divine judgment that awaits him? In the analysis Freud makes the following year of his having forgotten the name Signorelli, he finds the word *Herr,* the German equivalent of the Italian *Signor.* This famous lapse might well allow Freud to be led back to the Lord, the judge of his Don Juan father. In his analysis it is a question of sexuality, of death and suicide, the suicide of one of his patients. There again, however, he stops at his own guilt.[5]

The components are now increasing, and we cannot put them all together at once. Let us return first of all to Rebecca and to the famous letter in which Freud begins by renouncing a theory that made the father guilty of provoking symptoms in his daughter. Freud accepts all the consequences of this renunciation and says that he is astonished that he does not feel depressed. Freud expresses this in a very ambiguous way, however, in this sentence: "I have a feeling more of triumph than of defeat (which cannot be right)."[6]

Because of Rebecca, the hidden wife whose disappearance must constitute a fault for the father, Freud, at the moment just before the anniversary of Jakob's death, cannot persevere in the fundamental discovery he has just made. This discovery would in effect reveal the father's fault and would condemn him before his Judge. To speak of Rebecca, however, at the very moment that he refuses to denounce the father is to do the opposite of what he says.

We know—clinical experience shows us even after the old popular liturgies have become silent—how important this first return of a date of mourning is. Is Freud here not similar to the hero of antiquity, Aeneas, who organizes sacrifices and funeral games on the anniversary of the death of Anchises before he leaves, led by the virgin Sybil (Minna for Freud?), to see the beloved father in the underworld? Would not the self-analysis also be this journey to the underworld? There is, in this connection, a strange sentence taken precisely from the *Aeneid* that Freud inscribed at the beginning and at the end of *The Interpretation of Dreams.* For the moment we only want to indicate it; we intend to return to it when the time comes.

If Freud really knew nothing about Rebecca, we would think that her name would not appear as it does, through an association of ideas, at the very moment that Freud renounces revealing the fault of the fathers. If Freud really knew nothing, the theme of Don Juan and the figure of Moses would not call up these symptoms, these rituals, these expiatory liturgies at the same time they set up the transgressions, which in Sigmund's mind, are symbolically equivalent to those of Jakob.

We hypothesize that the name of Rebecca, if it appears again in other writings by Freud, must have found itself there no more through chance than it did in the famous letter to Fliess. Not only does the first name *Rebecca* interest us but also the woman who is loved second and who disappears. Freud's prodigious culture can furnish him with the materials necessary for the disguised representation of this repressed knowledge, and the extent of his work will offer him the occasion for its return.

Rebecca. Our means of investigation are immediately limited, since the first name does not appear in the indexes to either the English or the German editions. And how can one keep in mind the more than twenty volumes of Freud's work?

We have found a Rebecca in one place only: an article entitled *Some Character-Types Met with in Psycho-Analytic Work.* The first name appears in the second part of this work, and our readers will perhaps share our astonishment at the title of this second part: "Those Wrecked by Success."

We have just seen Freud "wrecked by success" as he renounced the discovery on which he based all his hopes: fame, fortune, independence, traveling, and the well-being of his children; and it was then that the name Rebecca came to his mind. Now (this article was written in 1915, but is not the unconscious atemporal?) this name again appears in the very place where Freud describes, without knowing it, the mechanism that played a role in his own life nearly eighteen years earlier.

Freud speaks then of a Rebecca in the second part of this article, which has three parts. The second wife, the second Rome, the second son . . . Instructed by our experience of the tomb of Julius II and of dinner at the Freud home, we check the movement of our curiosity, which led directly to the second part, and ask, Who is this Rebecca? Perhaps the context will once again be revealed as decisive for a new interpretation of the text.

We are going to treat it as we did *The Moses of Michelangelo,* that is, by listening for what Freud might say, in spite of himself, about himself, for a possible representation of what he had to repress of his family's history. We keep in mind our hypothesis, which is being refined as we go along: in spite of himself and probably without knowing that he knew it (because he could not speak of it in his family), Freud knew of a hidden episode in his father's life, an episode that doubtless entailed a serious fault of the same order as Laius's fault regarding Chrysippus. Some traces in Freud's life tend to reveal that he felt himself mysteriously burdened with this hidden fault, which he blindly had to expiate in diverse ways, of which the most interesting to us is his renunciation of his first discovery. This expiation does not, however, prevent Freud from believing himself free of the Jewish law in which he was inscribed and which he specifically transgresses in a way that is also related to the hidden fault (unfaithful to his God, collecting idols).

SECOND APPEARANCE:
"THOSE WRECKED BY SUCCESS"

Let us consider Freud's article carefully. The first part is entitled "The Exceptions." Freud speaks of people who, thinking they have succumbed to serious privations, regard themselves from then on as having dispensed with the exigencies and sacrifices that life in society imposes upon every human being; they are, according to themselves, "exceptions," and they intend to remain so. They therefore offer strong resistance to analysis, to the point where one can discover the origin of this feeling of privilege. This is how Freud formulates it.

> Their neuroses were connected with some experience or suffering to which they had been subjected in their earliest childhood, one in respect of which they knew themselves to be guiltless, and which they could look upon as an unjust disadvantage imposed upon them.[7]

Freud illustrates his remark with a Shakespearean hero, Richard III, who, although he is a villain, commands our sympathy through the suffering that his deformity imposes upon him. We feel within us, says Freud, that,

> Richard is an enormous magnification of something we find in ourselves as well. We all think we have reason to reproach Nature and our destiny for congenital and infantile disadvantages. . . . Why did not Nature give us the golden curls of Balder or the strength of Siegfried or the lofty brow of genius or the noble profile of aristocracy? Why were we born in a middle-class home instead of in a royal palace?

Thus, according to Freud, each of us may have, more or less, the feeling that we have suffered an injustice. Because it is the case for all of the examples Freud cites, we add that each of us may suffer from heredity or family inheritance. Although Freud does not use the word *fault*, we find that it is evoked in his clinical examples. He mentions two patients, a man and a woman, who have rebelled, not against their unhappiness in itself, but because this unhappiness resulted from the neglect of an adult who was responsible for them in their earliest childhood, or from a hereditary defect.

Let us reexamine Freud's terms. "Their neuroses were connected with some experience or suffering to which they had been subjected *in their earliest childhood,* one in respect of which *they knew themselves to be guiltless*" (our emphasis). What can one know oneself to be innocent of if not a fault and only a fault? Yet Freud nowhere speaks directly of a fault. The idea of the fault is implicit, negatively, in this feeling of innocence. Freud's expression is "unjust disadvantage." Let us try to reread at the same time what it seems he says positively and what he suggests without quite understanding it. We all believe ourselves exceptions since we have all suffered in our earliest childhood an incident or an injury of which we think ourselves innocent, although to varying degrees. The injury that we suffered seems linked to a failure, indeed, to a fault of our parents or their substitutes.

Once again we are facing the transmission of the fault. Freud first presents it to us as a trait of the exceptional character, then more generally, as feeling oneself the victim of an iniquitous injury committed on one's person at the very beginning of one's life. What does this tell us about Freud himself? What he explains in this first part is immediately applicable to his own history if the father's hidden fault, in fact, constitutes the event or the suffering that he experienced in his earliest childhood, like a hereditary defect. After this ambiguous exposé of a sort of original injury done to an innocent, Freud offers a second part, four times longer than the first, that he calls "Those Wrecked by Success."

Apparently without any link to what went before, Freud now discusses those who fall ill, not when an internal conflict prevents the satisfaction of their desires, as in ordinary neuroses, but when, on the contrary, nothing is any longer an obstacle to their fulfillment. In this context, Freud discusses a mistress about to be lawfully married, who suddenly neglects her duties and falls mentally ill; a professor who, chosen to succeed his master, declines the offer that he had so ardently awaited and has to cease all activity for several years.

> Analytic work has no difficulty in showing us that it is forces of conscience which forbid the subject to gain the long hoped-for advantage from the fortunate change in reality. It is a difficult task, however, to discover the essence and origin of these judging and punishing trends, which so often surprise us by their existence where we do not expect to find them.[8]

We no longer share Freud's surprise; we are familiar with the idea of a jealous god who punishes the children for the iniquity of the fathers. That in our time this jealous god is more often called the unconscious seems to change nothing regarding the question of transmission across generations.

We now come to Freud's literary examples, since he does not, "for the usual reasons," want to "discuss what we know or conjecture on the point in relation to cases of clinical observation." These "usual reasons" surprise us because Freud does not elsewhere abstain from presenting clinical cases in support of his hypotheses. Things become clearer for us when he names his first example: Lady Macbeth. Freud, then, wants to speak of successes won through criminal acts. He does not say in his examples, however, that the success attained by the two characters (the mistress about to be married and the professor about to be promoted to the master's place) had been reached through guilty maneuvers. His choice of Lady Macbeth is not, therefore, in continuity with medical observations since this choice introduces an element apparently absent from the former: crime.

Would the "usual reasons" finally hide what Freud represses? Only imaginary characters could be guilty, while real people would be only patients, innocents, and neurotics. To understand neurosis itself, however, one would say that Freud feels the need to speak of faults, of dissimulated crimes. He then has recourse to Shakespeare, Sophocles, Ibsen, the great masters of the hidden fault, which is ineluctably revealed in the course of the drama. The works Freud cites most are the Bible, *Faust*, *Hamlet*, *Oedipus the King*, *Macbeth*. All these texts share a central point: the question of good and evil, of the fault, of the fault's expiation and redemption.

Freud is caught in a contradiction that we can formulate thus: It is not necessary to speak of the faults of parents, nor even of anyone living; and yet, it is impossible to continue research on the neuroses without speaking of the fault, because neurotics behave as if they were punishing themselves even though they are innocent.

It seems to us that if we suppress the preliminary data implicit in Freud's work (he must not speak of the faults of parents), we then liberate his work entirely from its yoke. The logical jump between the clinical examples that Freud offers—about incoherent but innocent victims—and the major literary examples—the guilty ones—becomes clearer to us: Freud indeed feels that there is a fault somewhere. Contrary to the majority of his contemporaries, he does not decide to attribute the fault to the hysterics themselves; he refuses to regard them as liars, but he also no longer believes, after his father's death, that he can reveal the fault to be inherited from preceding generations.

Nevertheless, his repression is not total and, at least twice, the name of Rebecca comes to his mind—concerning the renunciation of his first theory, then, eighteen years later, as an explication of this mechanism of renunciation. "Those Wrecked by Success" offers us two literary examples: Shakespeare's Lady Macbeth and Ibsen's Rebecca West, a character in his play, *Rosmersholm*.

The Second Wife

The two women drive someone either to murder or to suicide in order to seize a coveted position. In both cases, sterility is the cause.

Freud hesitates for a long time in his interpretation of Lady Macbeth: "We must, I think, give up any hope of penetrating the triple layer of obscurity into which the bad preservation of the text, the unknown intention of the dramatist, and the hidden purport of the legend have become condensed."[9] Scarcely has he written that when he begins the following paragraph by saying, "One is so unwilling to dismiss a problem like that of *Macbeth* as insoluble." He then offers a way open to a study of Shakespeare in which Macbeth and his wife are really only one person. Freud finds justification for this hypothesis in Lady Macbeth's long sufferings of evils which are first made manifest in her husband (anxiety, hallucinations, insomnia): "Thus what he feared in his pangs of conscience is fulfilled in her." (This is yet another formulation of what we proposed in a preceding chapter: The dominated carries out the repression of the dominating.)

Stating that he could not understand why Lady Macbeth "should collapse after her success"—he never utters the word "suicide"—Freud offers us another literary figure: Rebecca West. She is a "fearless, free" woman who plays the role of governess in the home of the pastor, Johannes Rosmer. The pastor's wife, Beata, sickly and childless, has been dead "[f]or more than a year." A "purely intellectual and ideal friendship" unites Johannes Rosmer and Rebecca, at least in the mind of the former. The scandal, however, overtakes them all the more bitterly since the pastor is in the process of abandoning his former beliefs. The spectator of this drama, in which hidden evil comes to light little by little, as in Sophocles' works, learns that, in fact, Beata has not drowned herself from despair due to her sterility but as the result of an infernal machination. Through allusions, through making books available to this effect, through ambiguous statements, Rebecca had led Beata to question the validity of her sterile marriage, leaving the poor woman to suspect that her husband was about to abandon his faith in order to adopt progressive ideas and that soon Rebecca would necessarily have to leave the house—all this in order to dissimulate the consequences of an illicit affair, in which Rebecca allows Beata to believe without clearly telling her. Beata therefore kills herself in order not to bar her beloved husband from the road to happiness.

The whole play takes place after Beata's death. What interests Freud is Rebecca's refusal to become Rosmer's second wife. Rosmer proposes to her before everything is revealed and in order that scandal be silenced. Rebecca loves Rosmer; she had done everything, including a crime, to have him. And yet she speaks of killing herself like Beata when Rosmer asks why she refuses his proposal of marriage.

She will end by confessing everything when a third person, Beata's brother, comes to tell her that she, Rebecca, is not the adopted daughter but the illegitimate daughter of the man who raised her, Dr. West. Freud then gives a psychoanalytic explanation: Rebecca was surely the mistress of her adoptive father but was unaware that he was her real father. It is for this reason that she breaks down afterward and confesses to everything regarding the murder of Beata. Freud tells us that she reveals one secret (Beata's murder) only to keep another (incest with her father) in silence.

Ibsen's play abounds in ambiguous phrases and situations, and through them the play derives its force. We are surprised, however, after rereading the play, at Freud's definitive tone regarding Rebecca.

> But now we understand, of course, that this past must seem to her the more serious obstacle to their union—the more serious crime.
>
> After she has learnt that she has been the mistress of her own father, she surrenders herself wholly to her now overmastering sense of guilt. She makes the confession to Rosmer and Kroll [Beata's brother] which stamps her as a murderess; she rejects for ever the happiness to which she has paved the way by crime, and prepares for departure.[10]

What Freud recounts here is the end of the act, but not the end of the play. This is odd. He so much admired the implacable unfolding of this play; why, then, does he say nothing of its denouement? We had already noticed that Freud does not mention Lady Macbeth's final suicide. Here again, suicide—a double suicide—is passed over in silence. A final interview between Rebecca and Rosmer takes place at the moment she is prepared to leave Rosmersholm. He would like her to stay, but how will he ever be able to believe her now after so many lies? In a moment of bewilderment and confusion, he lets some words escape that show Rebecca the way: He can only believe her through an action—suicide—that will prove she loves him as much as Beata had. Rebecca accepts; Rosmer, seeing that from now on he can no longer erase what he has said, also chooses to die; arm in arm they throw themselves into the millrace. Rebecca kills herself, therefore, on the basis of a wish hardly formulated by Rosmer (as she had killed Beata perhaps on a wish even less clearly formulated. Does not the double suicide speak of a crime they had also committed together?).

Freud says nothing about all that. Instead, he affirms a criminal act in Rebecca's past, her incest with her father, that is not pointed out by any indisputable traces in the text. Freud's explication evidently conforms to the theory of the Oedipus complex. The domain of Rosmersholm would be for Rebecca the place of repetition. "Everything that happened to her at Rosmersholm, her falling in love with Rosmer and her hostility to his wife, was from the first a consequence of the Oedipus complex—an inevitable replica of her relations with her mother and Dr. West."[11] Is it not curious that when incest concerns imaginary characters, Freud vigorously affirms that it has really taken place, and that the father was then indeed his daughter's seducer, whereas since 1897 he has affirmed, to the contrary, that he has overcome this error? Although he "renounced" the theory of seduction for living beings, his writings are engulfed in it when they concern imaginary characters. We have now discovered a new archaeological site; let us see how the traces we located fit together.

A COMPOSITE PORTRAIT OF REBECCA

— If Lady Macbeth and Macbeth are only one person, then in the play she is the second king. She is childless and will kill herself after having committed her crimes.

— Rebecca is close to being Rosmer's second wife; she also will kill herself without having a child. Freud suspects a crime: incest with the father.

— Freud writes to Fliess, "Rebecca, you can take off your wedding-gown, you're not a bride any longer" when he, also, fails before success, when he refuses to denounce the father.

— In the Bible Rebecca was the mother of Jacob, who had two wives. She is virtually present in the pope's tomb—an allegory of incest?

— Finally, Rebecca Freud, second wife of Jakob Freud, who pretends to have had only two wives, disappears without leaving either a trace or a child.

Do all these different Rebeccas—secret or recognized—who mark Freud's life, together form a secret text in which one could read the mysterious destiny of Rebecca Freud? We can only offer here some hypotheses, but they seem to us to be useful; if after more than a century we cannot establish any facts, due to a lack of evidence that might support these traces in Freud's life and writings, can we not at least try to evaluate the order of magnitude of the hidden fault in Freud's mind? What we regard as Freud's too peremptory affirmation of Rebecca West's incest reenforces our hypothesis; the hidden union of Jakob Freud and Rebecca could also be regarded by Freud, via the Bible, as incest. For Freud, what is hidden is sexual, and particularly hidden is the sexual crime par excellence, incest. What he does not mention about Rebecca West, however, is her suicide; he only speaks of her having caused Beata's suicide.

We recall the formulation that he provides concerning Rebecca West: "Hence it is open to us to suppose that her explanation of her renunciation exposes one motive only to conceal another."[12] What Freud says here can be applied to him in his turn. Just as when he speaks of Rebecca West he implies incest — hypothetically — but does not say a word about suicide, so likewise we can suggest a hypothesis: Does Freud advance the theory of the Oedipus complex in order to disguise a fact that could well be of the same order, that is, yet another suicide?

Let us compare the composite portrait of Rebecca that we have just made with what little we have known for a few years of Jakob Freud's second wife. Our Rebecca, reconstituted by superimposing destinies, is the second wife; she is sterile; she is repudiated; she commits suicide. The Rebecca of the Freiberg register is Jakob's second wife. She disappears without having born a child. The third wife, Amalie Freud, is doubtless pregnant at the time of her marriage. The newlyweds will hide this pregnancy through a lie about the date of birth.

Does Ibsen's play give us the key to this mystery? The fiction has shifted a notch in relation to history. We have seen — and Freud strongly emphasizes — that Rebecca West succeeds in causing Beata's suicide by letting her understand that she, Rebecca, is pregnant with Rosmer's child. Let us transpose this to the Freud family. After the disappearance of his first wife, Sally (this is all we can say about her since no record of her death has been found at Freiberg), Jakob Freud is living with Rebecca in 1852. Then in 1855 he marries a pregnant Amalie. Did Rebecca Freud die as Beata had?

Must we read into Freud's writings that a childless Rebecca Freud committed suicide at age thirty-five, that Jakob then made pregnant a girl age twenty, Amalie, whom he must consequently marry? There is still a troubling detail: Rebecca West gives a false birth date, and yes, she does so to hide the fault of her illegitimate conception.

If . . .

If what we have just supposed corresponds to whatever facts there may be about what occurred before Freud's birth, it then becomes understandable in what way Freud himself would be an "exception." Before even coming into the world, he would have been the cause of a death of which he was innocent. His life would be marked by this stain from the beginning; his false birth date would lead him to question the dates and what they concealed. That would explain the seduction that Fliess, the great decipherer, carried out on Freud. Freud would, therefore, indeed have labored under "an unjust disadvantage" while he was innocent.

This disadvantage would not take the form of an injury to his body but the inheritance of guilt. One would better understand why he could not see clearly into the origin of the curse that weighed upon Oedipus.

One could inquire differently, in passing, into the interpretation of the character of Rebecca West. If Rebecca is really Dr. West's daughter, she is perhaps the heiress of a murderer. Could it be that in killing the wife, Rebecca repeats a murder from the preceding generation, which was also the husband's (indirect) murder of his wife? Freud says that she renounces happiness by confessing to a crime only in order to conceal another crime. He says that she confesses to murder to hide incest. Why would the reverse not be the case? Does Freud himself confess in his work that he carries out incest in his dreams in order to conceal a murder carried out before his birth? Or if not directly a murder, then a suicide, for which his parents would be responsible? In what way was his conception linked to Rebecca's disappearance? A new character would here be introduced into the history of the fault; if that is the case, the father would no longer be the only guilty party, even if he remained, by his infidelity, the probable cause of feminine despair. At his side is another woman, ready to marry him, perhaps even ready to execute not only her own desires to occupy the place of the wife but also, perhaps, the desire of the man himself to do away with the first wife in order to live with the second—or the second in order to live with the third, who knows?

Freud would then have chosen a literary example with an extraordinary irony. In Ibsen, Rebecca is the name of a murderess, but at the same time she is in the same place—that of the second wife—as the victim of the same name in the Freud family. That Rebecca West ends by being the victim in her turn is precisely what Freud does not mention. Like Oedipus, Freud only sees the guilt of the dominated, not that of the dominating who led or wanted to lead the former to death.

Criminals from a Sense of Guilt

As we make our way, we have perhaps forgotten our point of departure; we will return to it. Looking for the name of Rebecca in Freud's work, we have seen that it appeared in an article entitled *Some Character-Types Met with in Psychoanalytic Work*. The first part of the article concerned the "exceptions": those who feel they have the right to privileges in compensation for a serious disadvantage caused by an adult in their earliest childhood. Freud, who was perhaps the cause of a death without being its perpetrator, could himself be one of these "exceptions."

The second part of the text presents us with the story of a Rebecca, one of Ibsen's characters, who occupies precisely the place of the second wife—as Macbeth was the second king—and dies childless, by suicide. Indeed, Freud does not mention her death but concludes with the incest of Rebecca and her father as the true cause of the former's failure. How can we avoid thinking that Freud has found there a representation of his own family's secrets? Something of Rebecca Freud's destiny could indeed be shown there—still more in what is not discussed than in what is interpreted. As Wittgenstein said, "What we cannot speak about we must pass over in silence." We understand here that what we cannot speak about (by saying it) it is necessary to say (by silencing it). Does Freud speak about Rebecca Freud's suicide by mentioning everything except Rebecca West's suicide?

We come to the third, very brief, part of the article, "Criminals from a Sense of Guilt." Freud tells us of an adult patient who commits misdeeds during psychoanalytic treatment. Intrigued, he tries to understand and discovers with surprise that

> such deeds were done principally because they were forbidden, and because their execution was accompanied by mental relief for the doer. He was suffering from an oppressive feeling of guilt, of which he did not know the origin, and after he had committed a misdeed this oppression was mitigated. His sense of guilt was at least attached to something.
>
> Paradoxical as it may sound, I must maintain that the sense of guilt was present before the misdeed, that it did not arise from it, but conversely—the misdeed arose from the sense of guilt.[13]

Freud then evidently sees the origin of this preliminary, ordinary guilt in, once more, the Oedipus complex.

The third part of the article suits us just fine, but in a different way than Freud. What we find there is the idea of a fault preexistent to the subject, for which he feels himself dimly guilty, although he is innocent: a fault that he is led to repeat in order to justify in his own eyes the feeling of guilt. This idea agrees with what we had been led to think by applying the first two parts of the text to Freud himself. This time Freud speaks openly of the fault. Has he, in fact, really spoken of anything else in the course of the article? Here again, the Oedipus complex is the answer to everything; it is the universal hiding place. We think the hiding place reveals the paternal fault. Thus, this article turns around upon itself; for us, the three parts now follow each other perfectly. It is not a question of numerical order, as Freud's titles can make one believe, but of a truly associative chain, which reveals a latent, unconscious text. We can try to formulate it for ourselves: Freud would be the innocent heir of a fault, which would lead him to consider himself an exception and to refuse to submit to Mosaic law; it would require him to fail before success; and in order to relieve his mind of this feeling of preexistent guilt in everything he does, the misdeeds can symbolize the original fault of which he is the heir, in spite of himself. This fault is an infidelity that led a childless woman to suicide. By collecting statues, Freud will also be an infidel, this time toward Moses. He will be relieved each time he commits an infidelity, and at the end, after many hesitations indeed, he will be the murderer of Moses himself.

Once again we come upon what is for us the great question: What is the role of all this in Freud's scientific work? Is his work an allegory of the hidden fault? Its redemption? Its repetition? The question is too vast; we must find another, more restricted. For example: When does Freud inherit the hidden fault? At his birth? If so, why does it seem to weigh upon his destiny only at the moment of his father's death, that is to say when, in effect, he inherits from him?

If we want to research the impact on Freud's work of all that went before we could try to rediscover some trace of this fault in the work that Freud is writing at the moment of his father's death. Freud himself indicates this to us in the preface to *The Interpretation of Dreams.*

> For this book has a further subjective significance for me per-
> sonally—a significance which I only grasped after I had completed
> it. It was, I found, a portion of my own self-analysis, my reaction to
> my father's death—that is to say, to the most important event, the
> most poignant loss, of a man's life. Having discovered that this was
> so, I felt unable to obliterate the traces of the experience. To my
> readers, however, it will be a matter of indifference upon what par-
> ticular material they learn to appreciate the importance of dreams
> and how to interpret them.[14]

"FLECTERE SI NEQUEO SUPEROS, ACHERONTA MOVEBO"

It seems that with this work we run into a major obstacle in our way. This book is the magisterial account of an always guilty dreamer who is surrounded by people who are always innocent. No other work by Freud shows us in a more masterly way that Oedipus alone is at the origin of all misfortune. Nowhere else does Freud signify more vigorously that he has (apparently) given up chastising the father. Where could we find the sign of a link between this work and the concealed fault that preceded it?

Poor humans that we are, hypnotized by ideas and not believing our own eyes; the trace, sought in vain, tranquilly awaits us, veiled by its very obviousness, like Edgar Allan Poe's purloined letter, on the first page.

We mentioned not long ago the hero of the ancient world, Aeneas, celebrating the anniversary of Anchises' death with a sacrifice on his tomb, and we alluded to a strange sentence taken from Virgil's *Aeneid* which appears twice in *The Interpretation of Dreams*. We customarily say that the verse, "If I cannot bend the Higher Powers, I will move the Infernal Regions" (*Aeneid* 7. 312), is the epigraph to the book, but this is not exact. The reader can see for himself. In the first edition (1900), the sentence appears on the first page, below the title and the author's name; it is inscribed rather as a subtitle, although it does not appear beneath the title itself.

We want also to point out that, contrary to custom and contrary to what he himself will do in his next book, Freud here makes no reference to the work or to the author after the Latin citation. Had he wanted to erase a trail, or, once again, to speak by keeping silent, he would not have acted otherwise.

The sentence itself is a little surprising. One can, of course, see in it an allusion to conscious and unconscious forces. We feel, however, that Freud could have found a much better one, and indeed some commentators have been carried away with conjectures on this subject. Freud was himself hardly explicit. Rather than invent a new explication for this enigmatic epigraph, we prefer, as is our habit, to refer to the context from which it was drawn. It is the goddess Juno who speaks: "If my deity is not great enough, I will not assuredly falter to seek succour where it may be found; if I cannot bend the gods, I will stir up Acheron. It may not be to debar him of a Latin realm; be it so; and Lavinia is destined his bride unalterably. But it may be yet to draw out and breed delay in these high affairs; but it may be yet to waste away the nation of either king."[15] What has happened for the goddess to give vent to such anger? Aeneas, in flight after the fall of Troy, wanders with his fleet in the Mediterranean. With him are his father, Anchises, and his son, Iulus (who will found the *gens Julia*, the family of the Caesars); Aeneas's wife disappeared from the world of the living at the moment when they hurriedly fled the city. Aeneas arrives in Carthage, a city protected by Juno, who wants to establish its domination over the rest of the world. Aeneas and his party are received by Dido, the queen of Carthage. Aeneas seduces her, and they spend a night of love together, a sort of secret marriage. But Aeneas's destiny is to go forth and found Rome; the gods remind him of it. He then precipitously leaves Carthage. Dido, in despair, takes her own life. Aeneas finally arrives on Italian soil, meets there with the king and, thanks to the preparatory oracles, immediately concludes an alliance with the king and his daughter, Lavinia. It is at this point that Juno, who will do anything to prevent the establishment of another Mediterranean empire, bursts into imprecations: if she cannot move the gods above, she will move the gods of the underworld.

DIE

TRAUMDEUTUNG

VON

DR. SIGM. FREUD.

»FLECTERE SI NEQUEO SUPEROS, ACHERONTA MOVEBO.«

———◄)(►———

LEIPZIG UND WIEN.

F R A N Z   D E U T I C K E.

1900.

There are still many more elements in *Aeneid* that one could relate to the destiny of the Freud family. We will confine ourselves, however, to the imprecations of Juno that we find in the subtitle of the book on dreams.

This is the context: Aeneas, widower of a first wife, is briefly united in secret nuptials with a second wife, Dido; then he abandons her to rush to another union, which is to enable the foundation of Rome. Dido commits suicide. Aeneas will marry a third time and will have children from this third marriage, which is officially the second. What do we recognize here? This is the story of Jakob Freud, again with the insistent presence of a second wife, a furtive, short-lived, secret presence; and a union ending not in childbirth but in suicide. "Take off your wedding-gown, Dido, you are no longer married." Rebecca Freud's place is once again occupied by someone who is abandoned and who takes her own life.

The Interpretation of Dreams is the result of Freud's refusal to reprove the father. Yet he has scarcely put the title in place when the sentence about Juno's curse against Aeneas, before his third nuptials, comes to his mind. This first page of Freud's masterpiece therefore presents the same contradiction that we saw in the famous letter of September 1897: Freud now wishes to tell us that there is no real fault of the father; there is only the imaginary fault of the son (in dreams). But at the same time, like Juno, he calls on the lower gods if he cannot bend the gods above, all in connection with the guilty Jakob-Aeneas, murderer of the second wife. You will notice again the presence of the first name Iulus, Julius; Aeneas and Jakob Freud have another point of resemblance: they both have a son named Julius.

This then is the illuminating context of this famous epigraph. We find that Freud has penned the same sentence two more times. He returns to it at the end of the same work, in the chapter entitled "The Primary and Secondary Processes." Dreams are the manifestations of repressed material which, through the subterfuge of the formation of compromises, force their way into consciousness; this is what Freud says just before he again cites Virgil's verse, "*Flectere si nequeo. . . .*"[16]

What value should be given to this coincidence? Through the door of dreams Aeneas proceeds into the underworld to see his father, who has been dead for a year.

Freud and the Judgment of the Father

The third time Freud cites this passage from *The Aeneid* is chronologically the first. It appears in his correspondence with Fliess. We think that little commentary will be necessary on the juncture between this enigmatic verse, the concealed fault, and the question of judgment for. the guilty. Jakob Freud died on October 23, 1896; this is what Freud wrote to his friend:

> *Letter 49* (October 26, 1896): The old man died on the night of the 23rd, and we buried him yesterday. He bore himself bravely up to the end, like the remarkable man he was.
>
> *Letter 50* (November 2, 1896): By one of the obscure routes behind the official consciousness the old man's death affected me deeply. I valued him highly and understood him very well indeed, and with his peculiar mixture of deep wisdom and imaginative light-heartedness he meant a great deal in my life. By the time he died his life had long been over, but at a death the whole past stirs within one.
>
> I feel now as if I had been torn up by the roots. . . .
>
> I must tell you about a very pretty dream I had on the night after the funeral. I found myself in a shop where there was a notice saying: "You are requested to close the eyes." I recognized the place as the barber's to which I go every day. On the day of the funeral I was kept waiting, and therefore arrived at the house of mourning rather late.[17]

What the translator gives us as a "notice" is in German a *Tafel:* 'tablet', 'tablet' (of the law), 'table' (for dinner). The "barber's," which Freud calls *Friseurladen,* is surely for men and thus is a *Herrenfriseur,* so that the word *Herr* would also appear again here. Could not this dream then be interpreted as emanating from Freud's desire to make the Lord, the *Herr,* listen to an injunction (a tablet of the law) to close his eyes (in German, one says "to close an eye") on the faults of the deceased who is about to appear before Him?

In *The Interpretation of Dreams* Freud returns to this dream and, curiously, the barber's has become a railway station.

> During the night before my father's funeral I had a dream of a printed notice, placard or poster—rather like the notices forbidding one to smoke in railway waiting rooms—on which appeared either "'You are requested to close the eyes' or 'You are requested to close the eye.'"[18]

Without reinterpreting the whole dream, we can bring the following elements to the reader's attention:

> *Letter 77* (December 3, 1897): At the age of three I passed through the station when we moved from Freiburg to Leipzig, and the gas jets, which were the first I had seen, reminded me of souls burning in hell.[19]

For a long time Freud had a phobia about train travel; he never traveled in the same train with his children when they took vacations.[20]

And finally, the letter to Fliess in which Freud first cites *Aeneid* (7. 312):

> *Letter 51* (December 4, 1896): Apart from that the world is full of the most amazing things, as well as stupid ones—human beings are generally responsible for the latter. The first thing I shall disclose to you about my works are the introductory quotations. My psychology of hysteria will be preceded by the proud words: *Introite et hic dii sunt* [Enter, for here too are gods]; the chapter on summation by:
> *Sie treiben's toll, ich furcht' es breche,*
> *Nicht jeden Wochenschluss macht Gott die Zeche*
> [They are exceeding all bounds, I fear a breakdown;
> God does not present a reckoning at the end of every week]; the symptom-formation by:
> *Flectere si nequeo superos Acheronta movebo;* and resistance by:
> *Mach es kurz!*
> *Am jungsten Tag ist' nur ein . . .*
> [Cut it short!
> On doomsday it won't be worth a . . .]
> I send my heartiest greetings to you and your little family and look forward to *res novae* about them and your work.
>
> Your
Sigm.[21]

CHAPTER 5

FREUD'S
FIRST DISCOVERY I

Many traces still remain to be deciphered in the life of the founder of psychoanalysis, and we do not pretend to give an exhaustive account. Undoubtedly we can say nothing of traces that we did not know how to find because they were outside our field of vision. As for those details we deliberately have left aside, we believe that the reader who has willingly followed our reasoning would find in them nothing new and that the reader who has reluctantly accompanied us would not be more convinced.

That Freud detested the radio and the telephone—voice without a body—will not surprise the first reader nor will it unsettle the second. The list of oddities seems long enough; it has already enabled us to open up a new path. We pause here in our inquiry, which is something of a detective story, to orient ourselves toward what we have caught a glimpse of several times, that is, the juncture between Freud's life and work in light of what we have found.

But before we get to that, a remark about the analytic method, of which we have not ceased to avail ourselves. Was not Freud's great desire to make manifest, readable, conscious, what was latent, unreadable, unconscious? In this sense he is indeed the inspired discoverer, whose discovery has already been effectively transmitted across several generations and down to us. This method works so well that it seems to permit us even to break through the wall of psychoanalytic theory itself. In other words, a certain psychoanalytic procedure would enable one to put in question what, according to Freud himself, is the most superficial part of his work, that is, his theory of mental life. Would not putting it in the service of the truth be the best proof of the excellence of this method of interpretation?

Having said that, we will as certainly disappoint the Freudians, for whom everything in Freud's work is acceptable, as we will the anti-Freudians, for whom everything has to be rejected. Faithfulness to a master has nothing to do with idolatry. At the opposite extreme, one is not better protected against his errors by rejecting everything he produced.

In one of those books that are so penetrating that we forget them even as they nourish us, Eliane Amado-Levi-Valensi applies to analysts what is said in the Talmud—there are four sorts of disciples: the sponges who retain the good and the bad, the funnels who, on the contrary, let everything pass through, the sieves who only retain what is bad, and the filters who retain only the good.[1] We strive to be filters.

WHO INVENTED PSYCHOANALYSIS?

On numerous occasions we have mentioned Freud's first theory, the famous theory of seduction that he renounced for his discovery: the theory of the Oedipus complex. Our research has led us to reverse this proposition: he renounced the discovery—the theory only came later, like a wall that conceals, but on which are painted signs that tell what the wall hides.

What was Freud's first discovery? Where did it come from? How did he establish and formulate it? How did he finally come to abandon it? Once again, in order to be able to advance, we must return to Jones and present a new character, Dr. Joseph Breuer.

Joseph Breuer and Bertha Pappenheim (Anna O.)

When Freud, age twenty-four, met him in 1880, Breuer was fourteen years older and already renowned. A friendship joined them to the extent that they held "all their scientific interests" in common. For several years, Breuer helped his young friend financially. Freud named his eldest daughter after Mrs. Breuer and gave his two other daughters the first names of members of the Hammerschlag family, which was related by marriage to the Breuers. (Old Professor Hammerschlag had formerly taught Hebrew and the Scriptures to Freud.) The friendship of Breuer and Freud lasted many years and ending through a progressive falling-out, which came to a head in 1896. Fliess then took Breuer's place in Freud's good graces.

Freud had expressly declared on several occasions that psychoanalysis had been invented, not by himself, but by Breuer. Jones believes that in doing so Freud "was for some reason modestly transferring that title from himself."[2]

Psychoanalysis in fact was born of a therapeutic method developed in the treatment of hysterics. Where did this first method come from? From an inspired patient and a frank and attentive physician. This physician was not Freud but Breuer. In the *Studies on Hysteria* the patient is called "Anna O." Her real name was Bertha Pappenheim. Deeply hysterical, she lived in a single day in two distinct states of consciousness (what was called "a splitting of the personality"): the one "normal," the other childish and agitated. Moreover, she suffered motor and sensory troubles so diverse and numerous that life became nearly impossible for her. Breuer treated her, according to the style of his epoch, through hypnosis, and tried to make her speak. In her normal state—the phase in which Breuer visited her—the patient

> got into the habit of relating to him the disagreeable events of the day, including terrifying hallucinations, after which she felt relief. On one occasion she related the details of the first appearance of a particular symptom and to Breuer's great astonishment, this resulted in its complete disappearance. Perceiving the value of doing so, the patient continued with one symptom after another, terming the procedure "the talking cure" or "chimney sweeping."[3]

This astonishing occasion for Dr. Breuer is therefore a date in the prehistory of psychoanalysis, since it establishes the link between the narration of an event and the disappearance of a disorder. The reestablishment of the symbol is, for the first time, directly recognized as therapeutic. Here is Breuer's own account of this founding discovery in the book he published with Freud, *Studies on Hysteria:*

> When this happened for the first time—when, as a result of an accidental and spontaneous utterance of this kind, during the evening hypnosis, a disturbance which had persisted for a considerable time vanished—I was greatly surprised. It was in the summer during a period of extreme heat, and the patient was suffering very badly from the thirst; for, without being able to account for it in any way, she suddenly found it impossible to drink. She would take up the glass of water she longed for, but as soon as it touched her lips she would push it away like someone suffering from hydrophobia. As she did this, she was obviously in an *absence* for a couple of seconds. She lived only on fruit, such as melons, etc., so as to lessen her tormenting thirst. This had lasted for some six weeks, when one day during hypnosis she grumbled about her English lady-companion whom she did not care for, and went on to describe, with every sign of disgust, how she had gone to that lady's room and how her little dog—horrid creature!—had drunk out of a glass there. The patient had said nothing, as she had wanted to be polite. After giving further energetic expression to the anger she had held back, she asked for

something to drink, drank a large quantity of water without any
difficulty and woke from her hypnosis with the glass at her lips; and
thereupon the disturbance vanished, never to return.[4]

The "glass at her lips" enacts the passage between the hypnotic state and
waking. What Bertha Pappenheim (Anna O.) said under hypnosis remains, by virtue of the gesture that concludes at the moment she wakes
up. Breuer reports that he and his patient saw a "number of extremely
obstinate whims" disappear after the account of the incident that had
caused them. Then more important symptoms were done away with in
the same way. Breuer continues:

> These findings—that in the case of this patient the hysterical
> phenomena disappeared as soon as the event which had given rise
> to them was reproduced in her hypnosis—made it possible to arrive
> at a therapeutic technical procedure which left nothing to be desired
> in its logical consistency and systematic application.

To this method, Bertha Pappenheim gives, in English (the only
language she could speak during her attacks), the name of "chimney
sweeping" and "talking cure." For his part, Breuer gives this process a
more scholarly name. We return to Jones's commentary:

> In those days, to devote hours every day for more than a year to a
> single patient, and an hysteric at that, signified very special qualities
> of patience, interest, and insight. But the psychotherapeutic arma-
> mentarium was thereby enriched with the method, associated with
> his name, which he called "catharsis," and which is still extensively
> used.[5]

Catharsis: purification. Of what must the human soul purify itself to be
cured if not impurities? Yet the episode at the origin of this discovery
(the patient's incomprehensible horror of a glass of water, her account of
the dog and the companion, and the cure that follows), this trivial episode
says nothing of an impurity of which the patient is herself the author, but
of which a person to whom she should have shown politeness was guilty,
and of which she, the patient, found herself a witness by chance, unable
to express the disgust that this (in her eyes) revolting spectacle provoked
in her.

One will readily raise the question that the disgust aroused by the
scene and its consequences can only be explained if this scene is referred
back to other, more significant scenes (sexual scenes, for example). We
quite agree. If more serious events are concealed behind this scene, how
can we avoid thinking that they doubtless also present the same structure:
that is, that the patient would also describe as disgusting an act before
which she had been the petrified witness?

A little fact like this seems very important to us. On the one hand, it is the occasion and the very basis of the discovery as it was recounted to us. On the other hand, the adult who is the cause of all this is one of the people employed by the patient's parents. Her role in the origin of this symptom and the "fault" that she commits can be expressed, recognized, published.

One conjectures that this was not the case when the perpetrator of the fault was one of the patient's parents: that is, one of the people whom the patient held in respect ("honor your father and mother") and from whom, besides, the physician received his fees. Perhaps here science pays its tribute to the social inequalities of the time. A doctor who does research into one's mental life can indeed denounce the instructive misdeeds of the employees. Can he as freely testify against the employers by whom he is paid? We will rediscover this question, even more acutely, in some of Freud's own pages.

The Cathartic Method

In this epoch there were no doubt somewhere in the world, other similar procedures to liberate the soul, to permit the inner being to develop. In certain religious orders, for example, one finds that the novice is advised to tell the master everything that troubles him. But then it is a question of spiritual direction, whereas for Joseph Breuer and Bertha Pappenheim the objective of this verbal communication was therapeutic, a question of releasing the patient from his psychical and physical disorders. The Viennese doctor and his clairvoyant patient, respectively student and teacher, had not only found a simple, curative method. Through empirical means, and without, it seems, a preexistent theory, they shattered the beautiful, aseptic laity in which nineteenth-century science had evolved. Perhaps that was the end of the modern era insofar as it concerned the medical science of the mind. Have we not here returned, and without yet realizing it very well, to the Middle Ages when one sought evil in illness, the devil in the hysteric? If the fault can lead to a physical and mental breakdown, then is it virtually the end of a science of the mind that would not take moral and religious laws into account? In that case, the patient ("The Ratman") who wanted, in vain, to make Freud understand that the unconscious was a question of good and evil, was right.[6] And Lacan was also right when he dared to teach that the status of the unconscious was ethical.[7]

The "diabolic," divisive effect of the fault. But here, an immense step is silently taken, and Freud will in time devote all his energy to maintain that, unlike in the Middle Ages, it is not a question of the fault of the hysteric herself. The "devil" is not, at first, in her; it is introduced through her relation to another. The hysteric only represents another's evil act, which she has directly witnessed. In saying that, we are scarcely going beyond what Freud himself stated.

Bertha Pappenheim can no longer drink water from a glass. She unceasingly repeats her reaction to this act. What her female companion should not have made her disgusting dog do, Bertha herself does not do. Mute reproach, mimed denunciation. A young woman of twenty-one subjected by her parents to the English companion, Bertha cannot denounce the act that this woman has just committed and that is repugnant to what she has been taught.

The story recalls that of the city of Thebes, where everything is sterile. What the dominating has transgressed, the dominated reveres. Everything then changes, however, since the apparent author of the act is not its sovereign author. This act is in him like the act of another; he bears it passively, that is, like someone who suffers from it. *The patient does not suffer from his own faults but from those of the dominating if he cannot denounce them.* We interpret the joint discovery of Joseph Breuer and Bertha Pappenheim in the same way, although they did not.

The cathartic method, so promising, did not at first lead anywhere. Once the way was opened, Breuer soon closed it. As Freud says elsewhere, it was not enough to invoke the spirits; must one not still take refuge when they arrive? But can we reproach the first one who speaks the truth with having been himself so frightened by it that he fled?

Here is how our faithful Jones relates what he learned from Freud about the fate of Bertha Pappenheim and of her physician:

> It would seem that Breuer had developed what we should nowadays call a strong counter-transference to his interesting patient. At all events he was so engrossed that his wife became bored at listening to no other topic, and before long jealous. She did not display this openly, but became unhappy and morose. It was a long time before Breuer, with his thoughts elsewhere, divined the meaning of her state of mind. It provoked a violent reaction in him, perhaps compounded of guilt and love, and he decided to bring the treatment to an end. He announced this to Anna O., who was by now much better, and bade her good-by. But that evening he was fetched back to find her in a greatly excited state, apparently as ill as ever. The patient, who according to him had appeared to be an asexual being and had never made any allusion to such a forbidden topic throughout her treatment, was now in the throws of an hysterical childbirth (pseudocyesis), the logical termination of a phantom pregnancy that had been invisibly developing in response to Breuer's ministrations. Though profoundly shocked, he managed

to calm her down by hypnotizing her, and then fled the house in a cold sweat.[8]

Let us allow Dr. Breuer to compose himself by taking his wife to Venice the following day. After that, Bertha Pappenheim had to go through difficult years during which she had several relapses, suffered a great deal, and had to resort to morphine. Then her condition improved, leaving her free during the day if only to be led again at dusk to a hallucinatory condition. After having served as a "mother" of an orphanage, she later became the first German social worker, founded a periodical and several institutes to train students, and fought for the emancipation of women. Jones tells us that she never ceased working for children and many times went to other countries "to rescue children whose parents had perished in pogroms," and he adds, "She never married, and she remained very devoted to God."[9]

Breuer spoke to Freud of this case, with which he had been occupied from December 1880 to June 1882, several months after the end of the treatment. Freud was very impressed by it. When he went to Paris to study at the Salpêtrière, Freud spoke of it to Charcot. "He told him about the remarkable discovery, but as he remarked to me, 'Charcot's thoughts seemed to be elsewhere,' and he quite failed to arouse his interest. This seems for a time to have damped his own enthusiasm about the discovery."[10]

A difficult beginning for this method; Breuer fears the effects that it produces; Freud doubtless seeks a master to support him, but the master literally cannot understand it.

Where then does this accursed discovery, which had so deeply agitated its first inventor, lead? Freud indeed feels that there is something new and decisive there, but Charcot's reticent attitude dissuades him from continuing in this direction. He renounces the new procedure and turns toward electrical treatment, and then toward hypnosis. Freud wrote much later that, thanks to hypnosis and Breuer's cathartic method, he was able to make therapeutic advances and to discover the genesis of the symptom. Jones relates this to us but is skeptical regarding Freud's debt to Breuer.[11]

Freud Takes up the Torch

The book published with Breuer in 1895, *Studies on Hysteria,* which includes the case of Anna O., directs us precisely to this subject; Freud moves from hypnosis to psychoanalysis with the first case he imparts to us—that of Mrs. Emmy von N., whom he treated in 1892. Breuer's cathartic method was at that point linked to hypnosis. It was thanks to the technique of hypnosis that one managed to make the patient express traumatic memories, to which, it was believed, she did not have access in her waking state.

Having ascertained, however, that many patients were either scarcely hypnotizable or not at all, Freud decided to employ Breuer's method without recourse to hypnosis. Freud had seen French physicians demand of a subject after hypnosis that he recall everything that had happened during the session, of which he was supposed to be unaware. The supposed, experimental amnesia was then removed, provided that the hypnotist insisted energetically. Freud had the boldness to believe that he could demand that his patients remember events of which their bodies spoke but of which they pretended at first to have no recollection.

The cathartic method went on, little by little, to become the method of "free association." It then lost its meaning of "purification" and became a "purified," scientific method. Is it not there, however, that, by no longer recognizing its relation to impurity, it departed from science in order to enter the world of myth?

Freud's method still, it seems, was superior to Breuer's; the amorous outbursts unleashed in his patients did not prevent him, in the majority of cases, from pursuing either the treatment or his research. Giving the outbursts the technical name of "transference," he succeeded in including them in the method, and continued on his way.

In three of the four cases of hysteria presented by Freud in *Studies on Hysteria*, it would perhaps be possible to read in the filigree the fault of which the patient has been either the victim or the witness. To do so, however, we would have to make some important extrapolations, which would considerably weaken the force of our research. Too many elements are missing here. Either Freud, not looking for anything in this direction, found nothing there, or he has indeed erased its traces. We here present to the reader the reason why we lean in favor of the second hypothesis.

The three cases are taken from his Viennese clientele: two well-to-do women and a delicate Englishwoman, governess of the children of a rich industrialist. Only one of the four cases is outside the usual frame of those who consulted him, outside the nobility or the respectable bourgeoisie of Vienna; she is the young daughter of an innkeeper, whom Freud met by chance in the mountains. It will indeed be interesting for us to see if in this case, situated outside medical deontology and outside his social class, Freud will give hysteria an origin different from the blurred and multiform one that he indicated in the other cases.

Freud and Katharina

We are not disappointed. Whereas the subjects in the lives of the three women are only innocent fathers, an employer entirely above suspicion, and older brothers who are sometimes violent but excusable, things are completely different for Katharina, who is a daughter of the masses. Freud devotes only ten pages to her;[12] it is necessary for him to recount only the one conversation he had with this eighteen-year-old girl.

During his vacation, Freud takes an excursion "so that for a while I might forget medicine and more particularly the neuroses." He climbs a mountain, stops at a refuge, has a meal and then, refreshed and rested, he contemplates the view. The girl, who served him lunch with a sulky expression, begins by asking him if he is not the doctor whose name she had seen written in the register at the inn. Her nerves are bad and could he help her. . . . Freud, who "was interested to find that neuroses could flourish in this way at a heights of over 6,000 feet," begins to ask her questions. A masterly consultation follows, without an office, without fees.

Katharina suffered from shortness of breath; she would then see "an awful face"; it seems to her that she is going to die and that someone is going to leap from behind and seize her. Her troubles began two years ago; and she does not know where they come from.

Then Freud surprises us. He already has an idea prepared on this case, and he goes straight to the point:

> "If you don't know, I'll tell you how *I* think you got your attacks. At that time, two years ago, you must have seen or heard something that very much embarrassed you, and that you'd much rather not have seen."
>
> "Heavens, yes!" she replied, "that was when I caught my uncle with the girl, with Franziska, my cousin."

Freud asks her to tell him what happened. Then, formulating for herself the fundamental rule of psychoanalysis, which is usually in the form of an authorization—one has the right to tell a doctor everything—Katharina begins to talk. First, she accuses herself; it is her fault that her uncle and aunt are divorced, for it was through her that his relations with Franziska became known. Yes, she surprised them by chance one day when, some guests having arrived and her aunt being absent, she went to look for them and found them together in a room. It was then that her troubles began. She was ill at once; then, several days later, she was seized by fits of vomiting. She had been disgusted, but by what? She did not know. Freud tries to relate this story to the awful face that pursued Katharina. No, it does not belong to this scene; the thread is broken. Freud writes, "I told her to go on and tell me whatever occurred to her, in the confident expectation that she would think of precisely what I needed to explain the case." Katharina proceeds with the story. She at last told everything to her aunt, who found her changed. There were scenes between the aunt and uncle; the couple was separated. The aunt left with her children and Katharina to take over the present inn, leaving the uncle with Franziska, who had become pregnant. "After this, however, to my astonishment she dropped these threads and began to tell me two sets of older stories, which went back two or three years earlier than the traumatic moment." One night the uncle wanted to join Katharina in bed. She jumped out of the bed and reproached him.

> "What are you up to, Uncle? Why don't you stay in your bed?" He tried to pacify her: "Go on, you silly girl, keep still. You don't know how nice it is."—"I don't like your 'nice' things; you don't even let one sleep in peace." She remained standing by the door, ready to take refuge outside in the passage, till at last he gave up and went to sleep himself.

Freud asks her if she knew then what the uncle desired of her: "'Not at the time.' It had become clear to her much later on, she said." She recounts still other similar facts concerning her uncle's attempts upon her, then another group of memories concerning the uncle and Franziska.

Katharina then stops talking, and Freud sees that she appears transformed: her sulky expression has disappeared; she is restored. Freud explains to us:

> She had carried about with her two sets of experiences which she remembered but did not understand, and from which she drew no inferences. When she caught sight of the couple in intercourse, she at once established a connection between the new impression and these two sets of recollections.

The symbol is now realized; or, to return to the etymological meaning of the word, the two pieces are rejoined.

> So when she had finished her confession I said to her: "I know now what it was you thought when you looked into the room. You thought: 'Now he's doing with her what he wanted to do with me that night and those other times.' That was what you were disgusted at, because you remembered the feeling when you woke up in the night and felt his body."

This time, everything is said, everything is recognized. Katharina can then rediscover in the awful face that pursues her that of her uncle when she spoke to her aunt about Franziska. He came after Katharina, furious when he realized what was up, and repeating that she was the cause of everything. The girl later told her aunt about the scenes that involved her. Then her aunt said, "'We'll keep that in reserve. If he causes trouble in the Court, we'll say that too.'" (And Katharina does in effect "keep that in reserve," since she retains the memory as a symptom.)

Obviously, this is a story of a fault; a story almost clarified before the intervention of Freud, whose arrival indeed assured the reestablishment of the last symbolic bridge, this time, without leaving anything "in reserve." Freud does a critical analysis of this case according to his theory at the time.

> In every analysis of a case of hysteria based on sexual traumas we find that impressions from the presexual period which produced no effect on the child attain traumatic power at a later date as memories, when the girl or married woman has acquired an understanding of sexual life.

Freud regards Katharina's case typical from this point of view. Moreover, when she has ended her account, Freud observes, "I owed her a debt of gratitude for having made it so much easier for me to talk to her than to the prudish ladies of my city practice, who regard whatever is natural as shameful."

We are also grateful to Freud for having spoken more frankly than usual, without a doubt. Frankly? No, not even this time. A footnote awaits us at the end of the case history.

> (*Footnote added* 1924) I venture after the lapse of so many years to lift the veil and reveal that Katharina was not the niece but the daughter of the landlady. The girl fell ill, therefore, as a result of sexual attempts on the part of her own father. Distortions like the one which I introduced in the present instance should be altogether avoided in reporting a case history. From the point of view of understanding the case, a distortion of this kind is not, of course, a matter of such indifference as would be shifting the scene from one mountain to another.

This masking—and this unmasking—of the truth allows us to suspect many others, probably even more deeply concealed when it is a question of preserving the secrets of his Viennese clientele. Whatever the case may be elsewhere, we learn that in 1895 it was not possible for Freud to discuss the attempted seduction of a daughter by her father. How then are we to understand his "discovery" two years later, that the pretended sexual traumas were in fact only hysterical phantasms?

The Father Who Cries

We find yet another particularly striking case in *Studies in Hysteria.* This time it is no longer in the margins of his consultations but in the margin of his book—in a long footnote—that Freud tells us about this case,[13] which is still more incontestable since this time the father is present and therefore will be on hand to invalidate or to confirm what his ill daughter has to say.

In this case Freud's interest is not in the origin of the hysteria, but in the effect upon a young patient of a particularly stupid posthypnotic suggestion made by Freud himself. The patient succeeded in seeing to it that Freud's prediction was realized (he had said that her umbrella will break in her hands) in order, it seems, to save her doctor's reputation. At the end of this note, however, after having told us that the young patient suffered from difficulties in walking—from whence the need for the umbrella—and that her father, a physician, accompanied her and assisted at the hypnotic sessions, Freud writes,

> Since her condition was not improved by assurances, commands and treatment under hypnosis, I turned to psychical analysis and requested her to tell me what emotion had preceded the onset of her illness. She answered (under hypnosis but without any signs of feeling) that a short time previously a young relative of hers had died to whom she had for many years considered herself engaged. This piece of information, however, produced no alteration whatever in her condition. Accordingly, during her next hypnosis, I told her I was quite convinced that her cousin's death had nothing to do with her state, but that something else had happened which she had not mentioned. At this she gave way to the extent of letting fall a single significant phrase; but she had hardly said a word before she stopped, and her old father, who was sitting behind her, began to sob bitterly.

Can one doubt after such a case that the fault of the dominating is at the origin of hysteria? This time Freud has all the elements that comprise the explicit, if not verbal, recognition of the guilty one. Unlike Breuer, Freud does not flee in the face of this incontestable clinical fact; that is hardly possible, since the scene unfolds right before him. But the result is the same: the treatment is broken off. He adds only a sentence: "Naturally I pressed my investigation no further; but I never saw the patient again." In our eyes, however, only one thing here is evident and "natural" (he uses the word *naturlich*): and that is that Freud cannot face up to what all his research leads him to: the fault of the father.

Victim and Still Guilty

This young patient, so obedient to Freud as a subject of hypnosis, ceases being so when he approaches the origin of her difficulties; for in this domain, her father is implicated. One can imagine that she obeys

Freud when he is her only master but no longer obeys him when she already has another master. She tries to defend each of them: she enacts Freud's stupid command in order, as she herself says, "to save" him. In this way, he will not be at fault. She also conceals for as long as she can her own father's fault. The symptom alone denounces the guilty one, while the patient does everything to hide the fault.

The same goes for Katharina. At first it is *her* fault, she accuses herself for the divorce of her parents. Only after having expressed and recognized her father's fault does she cease taking the fault upon herself. Then she recalls that *he*, her father, *said that it was her fault.* We find the same phenomenon in Freud's life: unable to express the fault of the dominating, the dominated subject finds himself at fault; nevertheless, his symptom silently exclaims the truth.

Neurosis is like a clock whose mechanism has been shaken up: the hands go around without ringing the hours. What can one who wants to make it work again conclude when, reading ten o'clock on the dial, he hears the clock ring only eight times? But the specialists of our mental life are, in this sense, more fortunate than the clockmakers: whereas the latter cannot tell the hour when the pendulum is out of order, the psycho-analysts know that if the pendulum does not ring correctly it still shows the right time: the body of the liar does not lie.

FREUD'S LECTURE

In spite of his reservations and his fear of the impurities to which the cathartic method could one day lead, Freud courageously accepts the lesson of the facts. He follows its course from 1892 to 1896. Yet the book on hysteria was poorly received in medical circles, and Breuer, little by little, by fits and starts, begins to grow distant. He still defends Freud, and publicly declares that he shares Freud's opinions regarding the sexual aetiology of the neuroses. "When Freud thanked him for this afterwards, however, he turned away with the words: 'I don't believe a word of it.'"[14] Breuer had, in addition, expressed his reservations in their joint work: for him, hysteria did not have its origin only in sexual trauma, even if, more frequently than one wanted to admit, this was the case.

After the hesitation one perceives in his clinical practice, Freud comes to believe that every hysteric finds herself confronted with sexual trauma. Of what sort? He principally takes two paths between which he seems to oscillate: either he thinks that patients are subjected to one sexual trauma or another; or he considers that the state of sexual continence in which hysterics generally live is itself the generator of anxiety and symptoms.

In our opinion, the two arguments do not enter into competition with one another since one can issue from the other. Sexual continence can indeed be the consequence of a sexual trauma, that is, of another's sexual trauma which was imposed upon the subject himself. We have already seen—in relation to Freud—how the subject who is heir to the fault has a tendency to atone for it, and, in this specific domain of sexuality, to abstain where the guilty parent had sinned by excess. In this case, continence is only an effect of anxiety and not its origin.

Freud, however, publicly makes a choice. We have an explicit trace of it. In May 1896, he delivered a lecture before the Vienna Psychiatric Society, which remains famous in the annals of psychoanalysis. One of the most famous psychiatrists of the time, Krafft-Ebing, who presided at the session, said at the end of Freud's lecture, "This is like a scientific fairy tale." The reception was glacial. But Freud, at this time, was convinced of the accuracy of his theory, convinced of his discovery, which he compared in importance to the discovery of the sources of the Nile.

We must closely examine this text, entitled "The Aetiology of Hysteria." It interests us in several respects. Freud clearly explains his theory of seduction. He also presents us with two clinical examples that have a very special status in his work because he confesses, a few lines later, that *he invented them*—in spite of the profusion of real cases at his disposal. It is indeed possible that these unexpected inventions will again teach us a little more about the "Freud in the shadows" whom we already met in the preceding chapters. He finally uses a comparison that seems to us rich and illuminating for our interpretation of the rest of his text. It appears at the beginning; let us consider it immediately.

The Stones Speak

At first Freud presents the question very simply: How can we discover the origin of hysterical symptoms? What patients (or those near them) have to say should be subjected to a critical examination; they do not ordinarily have an understanding of their condition. What is operating here? An emotion experienced in the past? Heredity? We should, says Freud, "have a second method of arriving at the aetiology of hysteria; one in which we should feel less dependent on the assertions of the patients themselves."[15] In order to present this other method and to oppose it to the former, Freud uses a comparison; and, for good reason, he talks to us about archaeology.

> Imagine that an explorer arrives in a little-known region where his interest is aroused by an expanse of ruins, with remains of walls, fragments of columns, and tablets with half-effaced and unreadable inscriptions.

Two methods are available to him; the first is to examine what lies exposed and to question the present inhabitants about what has been transmitted to them through tradition regarding "the history and meaning of these archaeological remains."

> But he may act differently. He may have brought picks, shovels and spades with him, and he may set the inhabitants to work with these implements. Together with them he may start upon the ruins, clear away the rubbish, and, beginning from the visible remains, uncover what is buried. If his work is crowned with success, the discoveries are self-explanatory.

The walls of a palace, the columns of a temple appear.

> The numerous inscriptions, which, by good luck, may be bilingual, reveal an alphabet and a language, and, when they have been deciphered and translated, yield undreamed-of information about the remote past, to commemorate which the monuments were built. *Saxa loquuntur!*

The stones speak! Before allowing this phrase to awaken its echoes, we turn our attention to another of Freud's expressions in this paragraph. At first he tells us about effaced and unreadable characters found on "tablets" (again the word *Tafel,* which he used for Moses). Then, when the ruins are cleared, bringing to light was was buried, one finds numerous inscriptions "which, by good luck, may be *bilingual*" (our emphasis). The reader will see Freud present to us, just a few pages later, the text of his own "archaeology": the fabricated clinical example. Freud finds this example justifiably dual, and the idea that he gives us about bilingualism will permit us to do exactly what he indicates here: a decipherment and a translation that yield unhoped-for information.

But first, in order to neglect nothing, let us return to the Latin phrase, *saxa loquuntur!* 'the stones speak'. Freud himself gives no reference for it and neither, it appears, have Freudian exegetes been able to trace this exclamation to a Latin author. Of what, indeed, do the stones speak? In the Bible they are not satisfied with speaking, they cry out. At first we are taken to the curses of the prophet Habakkuk. He hurls five imprecations against him whose soul is not righteous. The phrase we are seeking is in the second curse.

> Woe betide you who seek unjust gain for your house to build your nest on a height, to save yourself from the grasp of wicked men! Your schemes to overthrow mighty nations will bring dishonor to your house and put your own life in jeopardy. The very stones will cry out from the wall, and from the timbers a beam will answer them.[16]

This text has a resonance with the phrase Freud took from the *Aeneid* for *The Interpretation of Dreams* ("If I cannot bend the Higher Powers, I will move the Infernal Regions"). Like the goddess, the prophet calls upon another kingdom to punish the evildoer; in her case the underworld, in his, inanimate matter, is summoned to oppose the guilty one.

Before leaving the prophet Habakkuk, we note that the last imprecation, the fifth, is directed to the idolater, he who makes an idol of the artist's sculpture and speaks to this carved image:

> Woe betide him who says to the wood, "Wake up," to the dead stone, "Bestir yourself!"

The idolater is reminded that "the Lord is in his holy temple; let all the earth be hushed in his presence."[17] (This calls to mind Freud himself sitting before his statues like an idolater, but still respectful of the Biblical commandment since he does not speak to them during the meal.)

Under the pen of Luke the Evangelist, the stones cry out again. The context is totally different. Jesus of Nazareth makes a solemn entrance into Jerusalem amidst a crowd. Some Pharisees intervene with him so that he will stop the acclamations of his disciples. But he replies to them: "I tell you, if my disciples keep silence the stones will shout aloud."[18]

In the two cases, the stones cry out when men are prevented from saying the truth, whether it concerns the denunciation of murder and the injustice of men, or the revelation and recognition of the holiness of God's messenger.

Let us return to hysteria. Freud now explains his metaphor.

> If we try, in an approximately similar way, to induce the symptoms of a hysteria to make themselves heard as witnesses to the history of the origin of the illness, we must take our start from Josef Breuer's momentous discovery: *the symptoms of hysteria . . . are determined by certain experiences of the patient's which have operated in a traumatic fashion and which are being reproduced in his psychical life in the form of mnemic symbols.*

In the field of ruins that is the body of the hysteric, symptoms are the stones that speak. These stones do not speak only of a former state, but also of a cataclysm that put an end to that state. The stone-symptoms speak of a wrong that was done to the city-body. At least this is how we understand what Freud writes here. According to him, Breuer's method is adapted to his own research. It is the shovel, the pickaxe of his archaeology. What does he find when he uses this tool?

> For let us be clear on this point. Tracing a hysterical symptom back to a traumatic scene assists our understanding only if the scene satisfies two conditions; if it possesses the relevant *suitability to serve as*

a determinant and if it recognizably possesses the necessary *traumatic force.*

This vocabulary seems theoretical indeed for Freud, and scarcely made to arouse the interest of his hard-to-please medical audience. And without continuing any further, Freud, as he often does in similar situations, gives an example.

The Double Fabrication

Freud proceeds here as he would in an analysis. First, a memory is presented, about which he makes a theoretical comment; then he exhumes a second, older series, through which a signifying chain appears between the recent memory, which has unleashed the symptom, and the older memory, which had, in its own time, led to nothing. This would not perhaps have held our attention if it were not that, a few moments later, Freud confessed to his audience that these examples were contrived. This is sufficiently odd for us again to take up our investigative attitude toward Freud's personal life. We are ready to leave this attitude behind when we began part of a work that, at first sight, seemed purely theoretical. The two things remain constantly mixed together.

> Let us suppose that the symptom under consideration is hysterical vomiting; in that case we shall feel that we have been able to understand its causation (except for a certain residue) if the analysis traces the symptom back to an experience which justifiably produced a high amount of disgust—for instance, the sight of a decomposing dead body. But if, instead of this, the analysis shows us that the vomiting arose from a great fright, e.g. from a railway accident, we shall feel dissatisfied and will have to ask ourselves how it is that the derivation lacks *suitability as a determinant.*

We are already struck by the first part of the example. We realize that here Freud is inventing; in other words, he is "associating" more or less freely. The example that comes to his mind to give to this audience—the psychiatrists of Vienna—concerns a train and a cadaver. Symptoms, like stones, speak. But then of what do invented clinical examples speak? We know that under Freud's personal ruins there is a well-concealed trauma. Let us proceed.

To this example of an intense trauma (a frightening railway accident), which unleashes a symptom that does not fit it (disgust, vomiting), Freud adds another example, which illustrates the complementary difficulty: when disgust is closely linked to a disgusting event even though the scene that is then evoked seems too weak in intensity to have been able to cause the symptom. "We shall have another instance of an insufficient explanation if the vomiting is supposed to have arisen from, let us say, eating a fruit which had partly gone bad." In the first example, the event was unsuitable as a determinant, while in the second the event lacks traumatic force.

This first disappointment is Freud's way of maintaining suspense in his "fairy tale."

> Moreover, Gentlemen, this first disappointment we meet with in following Breuer's method is immediately succeeded by another, and one which must be especially painful to us as physicians. . . . The patient retains his symptoms unaltered, in spite of the initial result yielded by the analysis. You can understand how great the temptation is at this point to proceed no further with what is in any case a laborious piece of work.

But then Freud says:

> It may be that we ought to pursue the same path a little further; perhaps behind the first traumatic scene there may be concealed a second, which satisfies our requirements better and whose reproduction has a greater therapeutic effect. . . . This supposition is correct.

A few lines before he confesses that he made it up, Freud is still pursuing his simulacrum of an analytic case.

> For example, let us take once again the case of hysterical vomiting which I selected before, and in which the analysis first led back to a fright from a railway accident—a scene which lacked suitability as a determinant. Further analysis showed that this accident, which, it is true, he had not himself experienced but which had been the occasion of his having a ghastly and revolting sight of a dead body. It is as though the combined operation of the two scenes made the fulfillment of our postulates possible, the one experience supplying, through fright, the traumatic force and the other, from its content, the determining effect.

So for the first example of vomiting the hidden scene was a train accident, which the (so-called) patient did not experience himself but which provided the occasion of seeing a corpse (in German, *eine Leiche*). The sentence is somewhat ambiguous. The least that can be said about it is that the contrived example is far from being inconspicuous or harmless. Let us see how Freud concludes the other example he just cited, that of the rotten fruit.

> The other case, in which the vomiting was traced back to eating an apple which had partly gone bad, was amplified by the analysis somewhat in the following way. The bad apple reminded the patient of an earlier experience: while he was picking up windfalls in an orchard he had accidentally come upon a dead animal in a revolting state.

> I shall not return any further to those examples, for I have to con-
> fess that they are not derived from any case in my experience but are
> inventions of mine. Most probably, too, they are bad inventions. I
> even regard such solutions of hysterical symptoms as impossible.

Without letting Freud lead us into the "several reasons" that justify his
strange conduct (of which he, in fact, will only give one: according to
him, it is because real cases are excessively complex), let us return to
what he just said here about the two apparently separate series of examples.

That a train accident is associated with a corpse is likely enough;
but that the example of the rotten apple also refers back to a dead body
seems to us a little forced. At least the dead body establishes a secret link
between the two examples. We have the following sequences:

First sequence: vomiting, train accident experienced by the subject,
train accident not experienced by the subject, cadaver.

Second sequence: vomiting, consumption of a partially rotten fruit,
fallen apples in an orchard, cadaver of an animal. Let us relate these two
series together, as if, according to what Freud just suggested to us in
evoking the bilingual inscriptions, they were a single text in two different languages.

What do we find? The same structure in both chains: the symptom,
an event directly concerning the subject, an event which he did not see, a
dead body. If it is indeed one text in two different languages, then these
two clinical examples are attributable to the same patient. Here is what
happened: he had a train accident and ate a partially rotten apple. Afterward, he did not see the other train accident, and, likewise, he did not see
apples fall—they are already on the ground in the orchard. Then, in
both cases, follows the discovery of a cadaver. That of the animal corresponds to the apple—two natural things. That of the human being corresponds to the machine—two things of the world of men.

In order to decipher the unconscious text from which both sequences emerged, and without at first being preoccupied with meaning,
let us now attempt to read these two sequences together. The patient
suffers following a train accident where he ate a partially rotten apple—and as the result of another train accident where an apple fell, but
neither of which he saw. Finally, he has the occasion to see a cadaver. Let
us move up a notch in the readability of the text: the subject is involved
with something rotten concerning the subject of a train accident; someone
fell from a train; he had nothing to do with that; then there is a cadaver.
It is interesting to hear the German words reverberate: *Fall* a "case" (but
also a "fall"), *faul* 'rotten' (but also "ambiguous" or "doubtful," as in the
expression *a doubtful story*).

Amusing as it is, this exercise in decoding seems to us at first totally hypothetical and empty, much like doing crossword puzzles.[19] If we have correctly sketched its meaning, what can this enigmatic text signify for Freud himself?

At the moment when we are about to push these word games aside in order to resume an apparently more serious effort, we are struck by a detail in Freud's life that we have already encountered but without having fathomed it. Every analyst knows this detail, and Jones himself makes something of it. It is a neurotic symptom which Freud suffered for a long time: his phobia of trains, his fear of being late, of not being able to get on the train.[20] He already suffered from it in 1890: he had an anxiety attack in the station where he left Fliess, with whom he came to have the first of those meetings he called their "congresses" (this first one took place in Salzburg). Only in 1897 would he say he had conquered his phobia.[21] But did he understand it? His children have remarked that he did not travel with them when they left on vacation by train. Is this a simple desire for comfort and solitude, or is it Freud's desire that his family not witness his anxiety, which never completely disappeared? Freud himself linked his symptoms to his having seen his mother nude in a train when he was four years old, and also, a year earlier, to the flames of the gas jets which reminded him of souls burning in hell.

We cannot, therefore, separate our decoding from the two invented examples, since the words that compose it also speak of a train and death. We can only go forward with the hypotheses and try to link things together. A train, the father's wife (the mother), souls of the dead in hell. A train, someone who falls—is not eating an apple the prototype of the fault in the Bible?[22] Moreover, its inclusion of a rotten part, a questionable part, leads in the same direction. Will our Ariadne's thread lead us once again to a fault regarding the father's wife whose death he caused?

If Rebecca Freud committed suicide and there is not trace of her death in Freiberg, is it because she died elsewhere? Could she be the fallen apple, at whose fall Freud the patient was not present? Had she fallen from the train? Had she become a horrible cadaver when she was discovered? Is she at the origin of Freud's railway phobia? Is his fear of not being able to get on the train a revelation, a reparation of the death of Rebecca, who would have descended from the train so violently? In the play by Ibsen that Freud studies, the heroine, Rebecca West, also plunges to her death from a height—into a millrace below. If Rebecca Freud committed suicide by jumping off a train, how did word of it reach Freud? Through whom? When did the incident occur—before or after his birth?

Questions multiply as we advance on this path. We will not resolve this mystery—only the associations of Freud himself (and not ours) could resolve it. These hypotheses only constitute a plausible explication of Rebecca's mysterious end, only a possible interpretation of Freud's phobia and of this astonishing series of invented examples. A little later in the course of his lecture, he will say that he has analyzed eighteen cases of hysteria that all corroborate his discovery. He was not, therefore, in want of clinical material.

Freud expresses a judgment on these examples of his own making. "Most probably, too, they are bad inventions. I even regard such solutions of hysterical symptoms as impossible." Then, we would ask him, why did you choose them in the first place? Could worse examples be imagined? They are "bad," "impossible," and, to end the arguments against them, we will add that they do not in any was correspond to the theory that Freud now goes on to expound to his audience.

All the symptoms in these two examples originate in *death*, while, in the beautiful theoretical edifice that he begins to build, everything originates in *sexuality*. Even if we believe him when he refers to the excessive complexity of real cases in order to justify his fabrication, could he not at least have fabricated something which illustrates his own hypothesis, his "discovery"? What he presents to his auditory is that every hysteric, at a tender, "presexual" age—that is, before puberty—was subjected to a trauma, the sexual meaning of which the patient did not then understand and of which he has lost conscious memory. This unconscious memory will become manifest through a symptom when a second, sexual episode will have later taken place, which then brings along with it the meaning of the first episode. It is in order to defend oneself against this undesirable, intolerable representation that repression will intervene to prevent the junction of the two series, and thus the symptom will appear.

The "bilingual" example that Freud invented does not correspond to the theory with regard to the content of the trauma. On the other hand, the example can be validly interpreted by the method he proposes to us. Our work has effectively consisted in bringing together two series that repression had separated, the second, less significant one bringing along the meaning of the first.

Had he not invented his example, Freud would have been able to find a more appropriate illustration of what he claimed to want to demonstrate. On the other hand, was it so difficult to present a clinical case? The account of Katharina's case did not take a third of the pages that are necessary to transcribe this lecture; how can he tell his audience that the communication of a single case "would occupy the whole period of this lecture"? It does indeed seem that something else intervenes here. Since Freud is under no external constraints, it can only be from the interior.

It is now 1896. The elderly Jakob Freud is declining. He will be dead in six months. If there is indeed a secret Rebecca, which Freud has repressed, is it not inevitable that it haunts him according to what he himself has discovered concerning the way hysterics suffer from memories? When the hour to inherit from a secretly guilty man approaches, the stones begin to speak. Freud knows a lot about the mechanisms of the mind. But Habakkuk sees perhaps further when he reveals what sets them in motion.

It is not insignificant that this revealing fabrication comes to Freud's mind during a conference where the psychiatrists of his city are assembled. Apart from his father, are they not the only ones whom he would recognize as his masters? If he needs to free himself from a shameful inheritance, upon whom would he call if not them? If he feels that his family withheld the truth from him, how can he reestablish it if not by seeking it in the only domain where the right to know is assured, where the search for the truth is also a duty: science?

If we compare Oedipus and Freud once again, or rather, what we have been able to understand anew concerning them both, we find the same phenomenon in the mythic life of the one and in the mythic theory of the other: the sexual fault conceals murder. Oedipus is guilty of incest, and this knowledge will be transmitted all the way to us. But his father is guilty of murder, which is scarcely known at all—in any case, Freud's silence on this subject is total. His theory speaks of sexual trauma, but his examples speak of a cadaver. Must we read the one in terms of the other? So often called the "new Oedipus," is Freud also someone who, even when he has recognized the sexual fault, will ignore to the end that he is heir to a murderer? Chrysippus's suicide—and perhaps Rebecca's—takes place within a sexual context, about which psychoanalysis has much to say. Psychoanalysis dissimulates that the suicide is a murder, that its perpetrator is the seducer, and that the one who commits suicide is the victim.

SEXUAL TRAUMA OR SEXUAL FAULT?

Freud, who speaks of death when he is fabricating, speaks of sexuality when he reflects and expounds. Even then he does not refer to sexual fault but to trauma: a medical discourse, without moral coloration. Yet the idea of the fault is not far off, since he has the courage to name the perpetrators of these sexual "traumas," from which hysterics and children have suffered. Few acts are more odious to civilized men than this abuse by the adult of a child's "innocence"—at least in principle. The doctor, however, should speak the language of science, free of moral evaluation.

The real, however, is not ruled by our little scripts, nor does it submit to our assumptions. For centuries we have made science morally neuter. What if neurosis is not neuter? If it is not, then every honest researcher will unceasingly stumble on this moral, ethical origin, which he will still be unable to recognize. In our opinion, what happens to Freud in this conference at the beginning of his career is already a manifest example of it. Let us follow it then to the end.

Freud arranges the sexual traumas experienced by children who will become hysterics into three categories, according to the personality of the seducer: (1) a stranger: an adult outside the child's family; (2) an adult in the household: parent, servant, etc.; and (3) another child. This last category is, for Freud, only the consequence of the first two; he postulates in effect that "children cannot find their way to acts of sexual aggression unless they have been seduced previously" by an adult. However, two objections come to Freud's mind. He communicates them to us honestly. First, many adults who have not become hysterics remember sexual scenes during their childhood. So much for the individual.

Freud then considers the objection "that in the lower strata of the population hysteria is certainly no more common than in the highest ones, whereas everything goes to show that the injunction for the sexual safeguarding of childhood is far more frequently transgressed in the case of the children of the proletariat." So much for society.

These two questions, perfectly posed, lead to two responses that are doubtless not unrelated to one another since they trigger the same reaction in him: flight. Here is his response to the objection concerning the appearance of hysteria according to social class.

> I then put forward the view that the outbreak of hysteria may almost invariably be traced to a *psychical conflict* arising through an incompatible idea setting in action a *defense* on the part of the ego and calling up a demand for repression. . . . Since the ego's efforts at defense depend upon the subject's total moral and intellectual development, the fact that hysteria is so much rarer in the lower classes than its specific aetiology would warrant is no longer entirely incomprehensible.

How can one better express that the traumatic character of a scene is a function of the laws—in the largest sense of the word—in which the child is brought up? We have just seen Bertha Pappenheim's disgust before the dog who drank from a glass. The same scene would probably not have provoked the same reaction in a girl like Katharina, who did not have an English lady companion.

Is Freud going to continue in this direction and study the question of "moral and intellectual development" or the relation between law, morality, and illness? To the contrary, he immediately turns in another direction: "Let us return once again, Gentlemen, to the last group of objections, the answering of which had led us such a long way." We note this stopping point and set out again with him.

To the other objection—about the adults who remember sexual scenes without becoming hysterics—Freud notices that hysteric patients have absolutely no conscious memory of these scenes.

> From this you will see that the matter is not merely one of the existence of the sexual experiences, but that a psychological precondition enters in as well. The scenes must be present as *unconscious memories.*

He then gets to the question of consciousness and the unconscious:

> But what decides whether those experiences produce conscious or unconscious memories—whether that is conditioned by the content of the experiences, or by the time at which they occur, or by later influences—that is a fresh problem, which we shall prudently avoid.

Again, Freud turns away.

Whether he wants to advance into the social question or the individual question, Freud finds himself confronted with something that turns him aside. Are the questions about moral and intellectual development and about consciousness really two different questions? This "fresh problem" that he "prudently" avoids—is it not the same one that had just "led us such a long way"?

On his quest for the truth about neurosis, Freud is led, in spite of himself, beyond the trauma, and to a point that each time provokes the same withdrawal on his part. We cannot yet circle this point except through a few phrases: a concealed murder, or rape, that is, secret faults—and consciousness of the fault, therefore of laws and interdictions. The first sexual theory that Freud constructs reveals one of the forms of the fault,[23] but it conceals the most serious form. Because of that, it will be possible for Freud to repress his first vision.

Sexual violence is accomplished without a witness and in most cases leaves no traces; one can always say that the victim was dreaming. That is not possible in front of a cadaver. Freud has indicated the way to us in his fabricated double example, even though he does not believe that it is drawn from his own experience. He teaches us when he believes that he is not teaching us. But even elsewhere, in the repressive scientific discourse, he cannot avoid—no matter what he does to flee from it—the oldest human question: the question of good and evil.

CHAPTER 6

FREUD'S
FIRST DISCOVERY II

We just saw Freud officially present his discovery to the medical world in 1896. Step by step, it had taken him several years to get there. If we now want to understand the upheaval of this first explanation of neurosis in its most intimate relation to Freud's personal life, and in order to follow its interment later, we must return to the letters to his friend Fliess.

THE DISCOVERY DAY BY DAY

A Burning Heart

Freud had for a long time thought that sexuality is at the origin of the neuroses. In 1894, he writes to his friend,

> Your acceptance of the theory of obsessional ideas did me good, because I miss you all the time while doing that sort of work. . . . I have something else *in petto* that is just dawning on me.[1]

Besides his ideas, Freud has feelings as well. And at this precise moment they are causing him the sharpest anxiety. He stops smoking, as Fliess advises him to do. But his troubles are getting worse.

> I had violent arrhythmia, with constant tension, pressure, and burning in the region of the heart, burning pains down the left arm . . . all occurring in two or three attacks extending continuously throughout part of the day, and accompanied by a depression of spirits which expressed itself in visions of death and departure.[2]

It is difficult not to notice the numbers Freud gives: two or three, and their conjunction with ideas of death and departure. A clear diagnosis could never be made of Freud's cardiac episode. We can only notice that in the next letter, a month later, there are no longer any health problems.

> I am pretty well alone here in tackling the neuroses. They regard me rather as a monomaniac, while I have the distinct feeling that I have touched on one of the great secrets of nature.[3]

This is surely what makes Freud's heart beat.

The Great Secret: The Sexual Origin

At this moment, Freud is thinking of neurosis in terms of sexual dissatisfaction, the causes of which would be continence or traumatizing contraceptive practices (*coitus interruptus*). Sexual tension is transformed into anxiety: Freud writes that it does not go through the psychical elaboration that would transform it into affect.[4]

Freud is, at this point, more involved in the description of neurotic problems concerning sexuality than with a veritable theory on the origin of neuroses. He finds that continence causes anxiety; but what causes continence (as a symptom), if not anxiety? Heredity, which had been medicine's great answer, also returns to Freud's mind in the course of one case or another. He does not as yet dismiss any possibility. He considers all directions: neurology, psychology, sexology. From these groping efforts can be found passages like the following: "The question deserves to be raised of why anaesthesia is so predominantly a characteristic of *women*. This arises from the passive part played by women. An anaesthetic man will soon cease to undertake sexual intercourse, but women have no choice."[5]

Regarding paranoia, Freud already formulates his ideas clearly. Siding with the profaners against the psychiatrists, he acknowledges that if obsessions issue from affective disorders (conflicts), then madness must be attributed to psychical shock; and to this effect he cites Lessing's play *Emilia Galotti:* "A man who does not lose his reason over certain things can have none to lose." In a gesture that the antipsychiatrists would not disavow, Freud writes, "People become paranoiac about things that they cannot tolerate." But he immediately adds, " — provided always that they have a particular psychical disposition."[6]

It is only October 1895 when he writes to Fliess:

> Note that among other things I suspect the following: that hysteria is conditioned by a primary sexual experience (before puberty) accompanied by revulsion and fright; and that obsessional neurosis is conditioned by the same accompanied by pleasure.[7]

The whole first theory is already here in this passage. Freud is working very hard, in his own fashion ("I do not want to read, because it stirs up too many thoughts and stints me of the satisfaction of discovery"). The next letter comes soon after.

> Have I revealed the great clinical secret to you, either in writing or by word of mouth? Hysteria is the consequence of a presexual *sexual shock.* Obsessional neurosis is the consequence of presexual *sexual pleasure* later transformed into guilt.[8]

This discovery is "the great clinical secret" [*das grosse klinische Geheimnis*]; now, when Freud will renounce it, he will use the same expression but in the opposite way: "the great secret" [*das grosse Geheimnis*] will then be his renunciation of his discovery. For the moment, Freud is elated; Fliess approves immediately; everything is in harmony. Clinical experience "has strengthened my confidence in the correctness of my psychological assumptions."[9]

The period that follows is less rich for Freud; he must write up some required work. The excitement slackens. Still his work progresses; and once again he writes to Fliess with this question: "Have I already written and told you that obsessional ideas are invariable *self-reproaches,* while at the root of hysteria there is always *conflict* (sexual pleasure versus an accompanying unpleasure)?"[10] To encourage Fliess in his own re-search—but is he not also talking to himself?—he writes: "We cannot do without men with the courage to think new things before they can prove them." In their primitive state, however, these new ideas sometimes make his patients flee.

We now come to the years 1896-97, which are so decisive for Freud, for psychoanalysis, and perhaps for the Western world.

Attaining Consciousness and Speech

Congratulating Fliess on the progress of his research, Freud writes, "I see that you are using the circuitous route of medicine to attain your first ideal, the physiological understanding of man, while I secretly nurse the hope of arriving by the same route at my own original objective, philosophy. For that was my original ambition, before I knew what I was intended to do in the world."[11] Freud does not progress, however, without symptoms or resistance: "A small voice [*eine feine Stimme*] has warned me again to postpone the description of hysteria." Sometimes he makes an opening toward the interpersonal relation at the origin of neurosis, then he returns to the individual, immerses himself in the study of psychical phenomena, and returns to neurology.

He works on the question of repression: its mechanism, the fate of repressed ideas in the major categories of psychical illness—hysteria, obsessional neurosis, paranoia. He is preoccupied only with what happens within the individual. The phenomena that he strives to understand are intrapsychical. "It is the oldest ideas which are the most useful, as I am belatedly finding out. I hope to be occupied with scientific interests to the end of my life. Apart from them I am scarcely a human being any longer. At 10:30 after my practice I am dead tired."[12] Yet it is at this hour that he pursues his research and his correspondence.

In a letter of May 1896, from the same period as the lecture before the psychiatrists, there is the following interesting theoretical development:

> We must assume three points about consciousness, or rather the process of becoming conscious [*Bewusstwerden*]:
> 1. that, as regards memories, it consists for the most part of the appropriate *verbal* consciousness—that is, of access to the associated verbal images;
> 2. that it is not attached exclusively either to what is known as the "unconscious" sphere or to the "conscious" one, so that these terms should, it seems, be rejected;
> 3. that it is determined by a compromise between the different psychical forces which come into conflict with one another when repressions occur.[13]

The first two points are particularly engaging. Does Freud mean that coming to consciousness is a coming to verbal consciousness? We emphasize precisely *the coming to, the attainment of,* speech. Lacan has appropriately pointed out that the emission of the voice—as in hypnosis—cannot be regarded as verbalization.[14] To have access (as a subject) to verbal representations, to have (independently) the power of speech: this would be to attain consciousness. It is surprising that, having posed this, Freud goes on to think that the terms *conscious* and *unconscious* should be rejected.

Here, perhaps for the first time, we see the veritable change of axis that is going to bring about psychoanalysis—or at least its method. Who says verbalization presupposes someone to whom it is addressed? As soon as Freud is settled in this position, the categories *conscious-unconscious* loose their interest. Access to consciousness is now linked to the two terms *utterable-unutterable*. Let us draw the consequences from this: "becoming conscious" is subordinate to the quality of the relation to the interlocutor and not to the psychical status of the things repressed. It is obviously easier to understand this idea after having read Lacan. But Freud is already beginning to prophesy that we will be able to do without the unconscious, or rather, go beyond it. Having glimpsed the breach, Freud will nevertheless pass it by without venturing to go through it. Year after year, transmitted from one person to another, the metaphor of the unconscious gradually becomes solidified. It became the answer to everything, the type of response that definitively stops the development of what is really at work in every equation. "The lung, the lung, I tell you," retorts the wily servant of Molière's imaginary invalid when, disguised as a doctor, she plans to ridicule the whole profession. Less amusingly, the unconscious, like the lung, is sometimes used to explain everything—that is, it risks preventing a question from making any progress.

From the Sexual Origin of Neurosis to the Denunciation of the Perverse

In June 1896, old Jakob Freud is "in a very shaky condition." Freud writes no more until a few words on October 26, just after his father's death. From these letters concerning the event, one sentence should be noted here because we will rediscover it a year later—but then in a negative form.

> The old man's death affected me deeply. I valued him highly and understood him very well indeed, and with his peculiar mixture of deep wisdom and imaginative light-heartedness he meant a great deal in my life [*er hat viel in meinem Leben gemacht*].[15]

"The whole past stirs within one," as Freud says. In his dreams, in the titles that he dreams for his future works, including the choice of their epigraphs, a stirring up, an agitation becomes evident; and we have already studied it as the coming to light of his preoccupation with the fault and with the question of judgment. Freud is not only a man who works, he is a man who is being worked on. It is not long before the link between the fault of one person and the symptom of another will rise up before him, clear and precise. Here already are its first formulations.

> It seems to me more and more that the essential point of hysteria is that it is a result of perversion on the part of the seducer; and that heredity is seduction by the father. Thus a change occurs between the generations:
> 1st generation: Perversion.
> 2nd generation: Hysteria, and consequent sterility.
> Incidentally there is a metamorphosis within the individual: he is perverse during the age of his strength, and then, after a period of anxiety, becomes hysterical. Thus hysteria is in fact not repudiated *sexuality* but rather repudiated *perversion*.[16]

The direction that Freud takes agrees perfectly with our rereading of the Oedipean myth. Yet, after having glimpsed that, Freud reverts to his habitual explanation, which contradicts what precedes it: the hysterical attack is "a means to reproducing pleasure," such fits "are aimed at *some other person.*"

Who, however, can go forward without taking a step back? Working so hard, Freud becomes hoarse. "Is that strain on the vocal cords or anxiety neurosis?" he asks Fliess in the same letter; and, two sentences later: "I have now adorned my room with plaster casts of the Florentine statues. It was the source of extraordinary refreshment to me." Does he lose the power of speech when he buys the statues in order "to repudiate perversion"? He will not speak in front of them. We recall Habakkuk: the stones speak (the ones that are not carved will destroy whomever does evil to others); but one need not talk to the carved stones (the mute ones in the form of idols).

Cured without Permission

Asking only for "another ten years" in order to complete his work on the neuroses, Freud continues, ready to defy "all the devils in hell." He writes to Fliess, "I have the most solid foundations for which you could ask."[17] Let us consider, from the same letter, something that still today stirs up so many diverse judgments on psychoanalysis.

Having no news of a patient whom he treated for *only* seven months, Freud learns that the patient has returned to his homeland "to check the genuineness of his memories for himself, and that he got the fullest confirmation from his seducer, who is still alive (she was his nurse, now an old woman)." Without raising an eyebrow, Freud writes, "He is said to be feeling very well; he is obviously using this improvement to avoid a radical cure." This sentence leaves us perplexed, as would any practice of analysis based on such a conception. To claim that one is doing very well in order to escape a total cure—we need a Molière again to make us laugh at this. But, more seriously, who can pass judgment on the cure in analysis? The analyst? Or the patient? (We are delighted that most people who undertake a treatment escape a "total" cure. Yet those who do not escape it do not recover either. These are the depressing facts that persuaded us to begin writing.)

A Genealogy of Madness

It is still January 1897:

> I am looking forward to the solution of a case which throws light on two psychoses, that of a seducer and the later illness of a seduced patient.[18]

A week later Freud gives Fliess the follow-up to this double case.

> Now I was able to trace his own seducer, a man of genius who, however, had had attacks of the severest dipsomania [acute alcoholism] from his fiftieth year onwards. These attacks regularly started either with diarrhea or with catarrh and hoarseness (the oral sexual system!)—that is, with a reproduction of his own passive experiences.

From all the evidence, Freud was, therefore, able to understand the seducer himself speak of both the seduction that he committed and that of which he himself was the victim. The fault is here inexorably transmitted across three generations—at least, this is what Freud tells us. He continues:

> This man had been perverse up to the time of his falling ill. . . . Now, scenes took place between this seducer and my patient, at some of which his little sister (under a year old) was present. Later on my patient had relations with her, and at puberty she became psychotic. This will show you how it comes about that a neurosis increases into a psychosis in the following generation (this is what people speak of as "degeneracy") simply because someone of a tenderer age becomes involved. Incidentally, here is the heredity in this case. . . .[19]

What follows is a chart, which the German edition reproduces in Freud's own manuscript copy and which includes arrows to indicate the sexual relations that took place between members of the same family, organized through the lineage of the two brothers. The arrows, which are not reproduced in either the English or French translations, are included here.[20] We learn from this chart that the patient had relationships with his sisters and his young cousin. Did the perverse uncle have a relationship with his own son, the schizophrenic? All the arrows in this chart emanate from the patient. In order to be exact, the arrow that unites the patient and the uncle should proceed from the latter, while another arrow should come from a person above the uncle down to him. One would then get a clear idea of the transmission of trauma across three generations, because the seducer himself had been formerly seduced, and the patient had been, in his turn, the seducer of his two younger sisters. The victim thus becomes perverse in his turn, to the point that he falls ill; the neurosis more or less inhibits his perversity.

How will Freud afterward reach the point of saying (and above all, thinking) that hysterics have invented the scenes of seduction? There would have to be either new and remarkable facts or strong resistances in order to get to the point of forgetting what has been so clearly understood, recorded, and established.

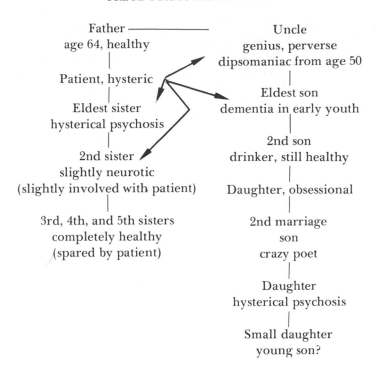

Father ———————— Uncle
age 64, healthy   genius, perverse
                       dipsomaniac from age 50

Patient, hysteric

Eldest sister   Eldest son
hysterical psychosis   dementia in early youth

2nd sister   2nd son
slightly neurotic   drinker, still healthy
(slightly involved with patient)   Daughter, obsessional

3rd, 4th, and 5th sisters   2nd marriage
completely healthy   son
(spared by patient)   crazy poet

                       Daughter
                       hysterical psychosis

                       Small daughter
                       young son?

You can see that I am in the full swing of discovery; otherwise I am feeling very well too.[21]

By the way, what have you got to say to the suggestion that the whole of my brand-new theory of the primary origins of hysteria is already familiar and has been published a hundred times over, though several centuries ago? Do you remember my always saying that the medieval theory of possession, that held by the ecclesiastical courts, was identical with our theory of a foreign body and the splitting of consciousness?[22]

Freud then begins to get interested in books dealing with the devil and sorcery. He sees the great resemblance between possession and neurosis, but he does not truly explain it to himself. "Why were the confessions extracted under torture so very like what my patients tell me under psychological treatment?"[23]

Stories about the devil, the vocabulary of popular swear words, the rhymes and habits of the nursery, are all gaining significance for me. . . .

I am toying with the idea that in the perversions, of which hysteria is the negative, we may have the remnants of a primitive sexual cult.[24]

Freud will maintain this and take it up again years later (*Three Essays on the Theory of Sexuality,* 1905): *"Neuroses are, so to speak, the negative of perversions."* Although the words in this second version are nearly the same, the meaning has completely changed. The first time, it concerns another's perversion, although, as in the preceding example, the victim can, after having been dominated and perverted, become in his turn dominating and perverse. After September 1897 and the abandonment of the theory of seduction, however, perversion and neurosis will be viewed as gathered up together in the interior of the individual psyche; henceforth, the phenomenon of interindividual transmission will, for the most part, be hidden from sight in Freudian theory.

WHAT HAD TO BE PROVEN

The Dream of the Three Addresses

We are now in April 1897. Fliess has left on a trip to Italy. According to Anzieu,

> Freud is without news from Fliess, and is prevented from writing to him because he does not know his address. The address reaches him, probably on the 27th; the same day, Freud thinks of Nuremberg with a friend who lived there [of a place which Freud cannot locate, and regarding which he asks if it is "outside the city"]. The night of the 27th-28th of April he dreams that he receives a telegram which gives Fliess' address.[25]

The text of the telegram can be found in two places; two versions, two transcriptions, two different arrangements.[26] The position of the elements of the text is highly significant. We rely upon the German edition of *The Interpretation of Dreams,* the only text revised by Freud. This is the content of the telegram received in the dream, which bears Fliess's address:

via,
or *Villa,* the second was clear: *Secerno*
or even (*Casa*)

There are three elements; the second is clear. Does this not upset our habitual assumptions? The second element is not supposed to be clear, but troubling for Freud (like the second Rome). Let us continue. What does *Secerno* mean to Freud?

> The second word sounded like some Italian name and reminded me of discussions I had had with my friend on the subject of ety-

mology. It also expressed my anger with him for having kept his address *secret* [*geheimgehalten*] for so long.

In the letter to Fliess where he reports this dream, Freud gives a supplementary indication. Another word, *Venedig* ("Venice"), appears in the second line. In the German edition, *Secerno* is in the first line, *Villa* in the third. The name of the Italian city would not hold any particular interest if one of the three suburbs of Freiberg, Freud's birthplace, were not also named Venedig.

One thing is clear to Freud: the second element of this dream is a secret. Now it is linked to the city where Jakob Freud lived.

The Dream's Associations

Freud tells Fliess the feelings surrounding this dream:

> I felt a sense of irritation with you, as if you were always claiming something special for yourself; I criticized you for taking no pleasure in the Middle Ages, and then . . .

Next, Fliess does not want to help him to prove that the father is responsible for neurosis; Fliess could prove it by correctly analyzing his dreams, by looking into his wife's past.

> As I am still doubtful myself about matters concerned with the father-figure, my touchiness is intelligible. The dream thus collected all the irritation with you that was present in my unconscious.

Let us assemble the associations around this dream: a secret in the second position outside the city; a disliked period (the Middle Ages); all of this linked to a question and a reproach, the father, neurosis. *Via* 'road', 'street'; *villa* and *casa*: house and cottage, toward the country, *outside the city* (suburb?). The second, that of the surroundings, what is not liked, a secret: impossible not to think of Rebecca. In the last chapter we asked, Had she died outside the city of Freiberg? Can we now propose that Freud's dream about Fliess when Freud did not know something about him that he would like to know is the occasion for the return—disguised in the dreamer's mind—of a burning question when he is researching the role of the father in the origin of neurosis?

Freud himself fully authorizes us to do so. As soon as he completes the exposition of this dream in *The Interpretation of Dreams,* Freud, without any transition, follows up with this "chain of thoughts":

> During the night before my father's funeral I had a dream of a printed notice, placard or poster—rather like the notices forbidding one to smoke in railway waiting-rooms—on which appeared either

> "You are requested to close the eyes"
> "You are requested to close an eye."
> or
> I usually write this in the form:
> "You are requested to close the eye(s)."

We have already encountered this dream. It has the same organization as the preceding one:

> one thing
> or a second thing
> a third thing

In the preceding dream (*via, Villa . . . Secerno*), the secret came in the second position. In this dream, its figurative meaning—what one should close an eye (or eyes) to—again occupies the same position. To what then does one close one's eyes if not to faults? The two dreams that Freud associates lead us once more to a secret hiding a fault that cannot be seen in connection with the second position. Freud, who is precisely the one to do everything to open his eyes, calls upon Fliess to help him discover his father's fault; and yet, without understanding it, he accuses his friend of this obscure fault because the secret appears in his friend's address. Jakob Freud, alias Fliess, conceals something from him, and Freud feels provoked by it.

The letter, which began with the account of the dream about the address, remains in suspense. It seems that it was sent off before its author was able to illuminate this story. When he takes it up again, things have been effectively cleared up for him. A patient brings him the answer that he awaited from Fliess (or from his father). It is without a doubt a unique event in Freud's writings that this clinical explanation seems to Freud an unimpeachable proof, since he ends it like a mathematical proof.

Freud's Interpretation: The Father's Fault

The whole passage merits rereading:

> The complete interpretation only occurred to me after a lucky chance this morning brought confirmation of my theory of paternal aetiology. Yesterday I started treatment of a new case, a young woman, whom for lack of time I should have liked to have frightened off. She had a brother who died insane, and her chief symptom—insomnia—dates from the time she heard the carriage driving away from the house taking him to the asylum. Since then she has been terrified of carriage drives and convinced that an accident was going to happen. Years later, while she was out driving, the horses shied

and she took the opportunity to jump from the carriage and break a leg. To-day she came and said she had been thinking over the treatment and had found an obstacle. "What is it?" "I can paint myself as black as necessary, but I must spare other people. You must allow me to mention no names." "Names don't matter. What you mean is your relationship with the people concerned. We can't draw a veil over that." "What I mean is that earlier the treatment would have been easier for me than now. Earlier I didn't suspect it, but now the criminal nature of certain things has become clear to me, and I can't make up my mind to talk about them." "On the contrary, I should say that a mature woman becomes more tolerant in sexual matters." "Yes, there you're right. When I consider that the most excellent and high-principled men are guilty of these things, I'm compelled to think it's an illness, a kind of madness, and I have to excuse them." "Then let us speak plainly. In my analyses I find it's the closest relatives, fathers or brothers, who are the guilty men." "It has nothing to do with my brother." "So it was your father, then."

Then it came out that when she was between the ages of eight and twelve her allegedly otherwise admirable and high-principled father used regularly to take her into his bed and practise external ejaculation (making wet) with her. Even at the time she felt anxiety. A six-year-older sister to whom she talked about it later admitted that she had had the same experiences with her father. A cousin told her that at the age of fifteen she had had to resist the advances of her grandfather. Naturally she did not find it incredible when I told her that similar and worse things must have happened to her in infancy. In other respects hers is a quite ordinary hysteria with usual symptoms.

Quod Erat Demonstrandum[27]

By inscribing at the end of this case the formula that one uses after a mathematical demonstration, Freud clearly thinks he has completed a proof, or rather that he has received one. If Freud founds a theory, it is in the primary meaning of the term *observation.* He accepts what is presented to him and what his interrogation, which is certainly directed and insistent, has aroused in his patient. Credulity, which he will happily retract? Or inspired naiveté, which is content to receive what is presented to it? Who dares to see what she sees?

Freud is there neither Don Juan nor Prometheus, as he will be later when he departs from this simple path. Afterward, he is perhaps in search not so much of the truth as of mastery over his discovery. And yet, because in spite of everything he is a truthful man, he himself will prophesy the failure of his error.

> No critic . . . can see more clearly than I the disproportion there is between the problems and the answers to them, and it will be a fitting punishment for me that none of the unexplored regions of the

mind in which I have been the first mortal to set foot will ever bear my name or submit to my laws.[28]

Who can say *my* laws? Who can bring the mind under subjection?

FREUD: PROPHET OF HIS OWN REPRESSION

Mechanisms and Causes

In the first place I have gained a sure notion of the structure of a hysteria. Everything points to the reproduction of scenes which in some cases can be arrived at directly and in others through a veil of intervening phantasies. The phantasies arise from things *heard* but only understood *later,* and all the material is of course genuine.[29]

Here we are fully in the theory of seduction and yet, at the same time, Freud wants to explore the neuroses from within, in the intrapsychic limits of the individual (drives, defenses, etc.). When do drives lead to neuroses? In order to simplify, let us say it is when they meet an obstacle to their movement. But then, the deviation or the obstruction of the drives explains nothing in itself. The cause of this deviation or obstruction must be found. Freud navigates between two levels of research: (1) finding the causes of psychical disorders, and (2) describing their mechanisms. The first theory is an attempt on the first level (of causes). But the psychoanalytic theory that will follow seems rather to belong to the second level—that is, on the condition that we can no longer accept its recourse to myth (and later to metapsychology) as a causal explanation of neurosis.

It seems that research into causes ineluctably ends in interpersonal relations, while research into mechanisms is limited to the individual's mental life. It is important for our work to distinguish these two levels; in effect, we are soon going to see Freud renounce not only an "error" but also a level of research.

May 1897. Freud is doing well; he is working and making progress. His letters are often accompanied by working notes that he wants to submit to his friend. (They are called *drafts* by the editors and listed alphabetically). We are now at the last days of this mysterious period in Freud's life, when the great reversal is about to occur. We have, for the four remaining months, seven letters and three drafts; in fact, after *Letter 64* (May 31), no draft has reached us, and Freud probably wrote no more. There are no more included in the remaining eighty-eight letters. This change in Freud's way of working and corresponding informs us of an internal upheaval. Something particularly satisfying happens now: Freud affirms his discovery. The recent lecture and the working notes attest to this. Yet we are going to find him more and more paralyzed in his letters as he turns, in his dreams, around the secret, around incest and phantoms. The process of repression has already begun because—perhaps we can formulate it this way—Freud has alone drawn closer to his father's secret. While his dreams recall its existence in what is for him an undecipherable way, while he calls for help from Fliess, who cannot come to his aid, his perceptions are gradually confused (his friend becomes an enemy), his ideas are progressively blocked. Only one liberty remains to him: to theorize. This theorization seems to us like a description and an interpretation of what is underway within him.

We advance in our research like a sailor who catches the wind by pulling the sails to the right and to the left. The reader already possesses numerous components. To these we add some indications about Freud's attitude.

Soon (in September-October), Freud will assert that:

—his father played no role in his neurosis, and moreover, neither probably did other fathers in his patients' neuroses;
—his governess (his nursemaid) was his first seductress;
—the pretended memories of the father that his patients reported to him were in fact phantasms sustained by the incestuous desires of the patients themselves, in their childhood, as in Sophocles' *Oedipus the King*.

These universal desires are the key to neurosis. Having stated this, we are going to reread attentively the correspondence and the working notes addressed to Fliess from May to September 1897.

Draft L*

Architecture of Hysteria

The aim seems to be to hark back to the primal scenes. This is achieved in some cases directly, but in others only in a roundabout way, *via* phantasies. For phantasies are psychical outworks constructed in order to bar the way to these memories, of sublimating them. They are built up out of things that have been heard about and then *subsequently* turned to account; thus they combine things that have

*The subtitles for the drafts are Freud's.

been experienced and things that have been heard about past events (from the history of parents and ancestors) and things seen by the subject himself.[30]

Here, the phantasies are the results of memories and not of desires. They combine the subject's experiences with the stories of his parents' past; the double clinical example Freud invented for his lecture would correspond perfectly to what he now says about the phantasies (an incident that was experienced and an incident that is spoken of).

The Part Played by Servant-Girls

An immense load of self reproaches (e.g., for theft, abortion, etc.) is made possible for a woman by identification with these people of low morals, who are so often remembered by her as worthless women connected sexually with her father or brother. And, as a result of the sublimation of these girls in phantasies, highly improbable charges are made in these same phantasies against other people. Fears of prostitution (fears of walking in the street alone), fears of a man being hidden under the bed, and so on, also point in the direction of servant-girls. There is a tragic justice in the fact that the action of the head of the family in stooping to relations with a servant-girl is atoned for by his daughter's self-abasement.[31]

Freud thinks that the daughter identifies herself with the servant-girl with whom her father or brother have had secret sexual relations. But the feeling of guilt cannot be felt by the servant-girls, since Freud, according to the prejudices of his class and of his time, considers that they are people of "low morals." What he describes there is better explained if one conjectures that the daughter experiences the guilt the father does not feel, and that she atones—or projects on others—the fault she cannot denounce. The "low morals" are therefore those of the head of the family.

Freud is himself also the son of a head of a family whose conduct can doubtless be described as "low." How will he experience it? Exactly as he anticipates it here: through a feeling of guilt, which is of variable intensity, and finally, through "highly improbable charges" against a servant-girl (nursemaid) and through self-disparagement (because of my desires, I am the only one guilty).

Mushrooms

There was a girl last summer who was afraid to pick a flower or *even* a mushroom, because it was against the will of God; for He forbids the destruction of any germs of life. This arose from a memory of religious talks with her mother, who inveighed against taking precautions during intercourse because they meant the destruction of living germs. "Sponges" (Paris "sponges") [*Schwamm* means both "mushroom" and "sponge"] had been especially referred to among possible preventives. Identification with the patient's mother was the chief content of her neurosis.[32]

Freud himself suffers from the inverse symptom: not from the inhibition against picking mushrooms, but the compulsive desire "to hunt" them. Is this through identification with the father? In the case reported here, could the divine precepts have this impact on the girl, if, formulated by the mother, they did not secretly indicate the guilty one? (The father?)

Wrapping-up
Continuation of the mushroom story. The girl insisted that any objects handed to her must be wrapped up. (Condom.)[33]

Is this whim not the transposed repetition of the fault of a man in the family? This leads us to a question: Who played in relation to Freud the role that the mother plays here? Which adult in charge of his education could have transmitted to him a law by the terms of which one of his parents would be found secretly guilty? Would it not be precisely this governess who led him into all the churches and spoke to him of God and hell?

We go on now to the elements of the following draft, which was also written in May 1897. Freud writes, "Inside me there is a seething ferment."[34] The letter accompanying *draft M* begins with the sentence, "I send you herewith *il catalogo delle belle*,"—the list of Freud's works, compared to Don Juan's conquests, read by his valet, Leporello, to the Don's forsaken mistress.

Draft M

Freud again discusses the structure of hysteria. Regarding repressed scenes, he writes,

> Some of the scenes are accessible directly, but others only by way of superimposed phantasies. The scenes are arranged according to increasing resistance. Those which are more slightly repressed come to light only incompletely to begin with, on account of their association with those which are severely repressed. The path followed by [analytic] works proceeds by a series of downward lines: first down to the scenes or to their neighbourhood, then a step further down from one of the symptoms, and then a step further still. Since most of the scenes converge upon only a few symptoms, our path repeatedly follows a line through the background thoughts of the same symptoms. . . .

Repression
It is to be suspected that the essential repressed element is always femininity.[35]

In fact, Freud here wishes to speak about a passive sexual experience for both sexes. It is indeed interesting that he formulates it through the term "feminity" [*das Weibliche*]. The idea obviously corresponds to the ideology of his time. But is also describes—and Freud's use here of the German word *Vermutung* 'suspicion' leads us in this direction—his own family mystery: the repressed element concerns what a woman has passively experienced. After having mentioned the "suspicion" that he has about this subject Freud states his present theory on the transformation of memories into phantasies—and into oblivion—and into unconscious fictions. Keeping in mind that Freud himself is perhaps in the process of taking exactly this same path as he goes from the mystery of the Biblical Jacob-Rebecca to the myth of Oedipus, we turn to the following paragraph:

Phantasies

Phantasies arise from an unconscious combination of things experienced and heard, constructed for particular purposes. These purposes aim at making inaccessible the memory from which symptoms have been generated or might be generated. Phantasies are constructed by a process of fusion and distortion analogous to the decomposition of a chemical body which is combined with another one. For the first kind of distortion consists in a falsification of memory by a process of fragmentation, which involves a disregard of chronological considerations. (Chronological corrections seem to depend precisely on the activity of the system of *consciousness*.) A fragment of a visual scene is then joined up to a fragment of an auditory one and made into a phantasy, while the fragment left over is linked up with something else. This makes it impossible to trace their original connection. As a result of the construction of phantasies of this kind (in periods of excitation) the mnemic symptoms cease. But instead there are now unconscious fictions which have not succumbed to defense. If the intensity of such a phantasy increases to a point at which it would have to force its way into consciousness, it is repressed and a symptom is generated by a backward drive from the phantasy to its constituent memories.[36]

In resumé, one could say that the vanished memory becomes a phantasy. If through its force it risks reaching consciousness, it is repressed and then returns under the form of a symptom; but it can also nourish "unconscious fictions." When a scientist presents ideas and theories that can be neither invalidated nor confirmed, would that be a case of unconscious fictions? Can Freud's skein of symptoms, clinical inventions, curiosities, and ritualizations be unraveled in the light of what he proposes?

Repression in the Unconscious

. . .

One of our brightest hopes is that we may be able to determine the number and species of phantasies as well as we can those of the "scenes." A romance of being a stranger (e.g., in the family) (cf.

paranoia) is found regularly, and serves as a means of bastardizing the relatives in question. Agoraphobia seems to depend on a romance of prostitution, which itself goes back to this same family romance. Thus a woman who will not go out by herself is asserting her mother's unfaithfulness.[37]

Is this family romance purely an invention of the patient, as Freud will soon maintain? Or is it rather the disguised version of the truth, like the play within the play in *Hamlet?* Are phantasies, as he will say later, the origin of false memories, or, as he says here and as our research confirms, are the (vanished) memories at the origin of phantasies?

PARALYSIS

We are now at *Letter 64* (May 31, 1897), the last letter in which Freud is still free to go forward on this path. In this letter, however, Freud is already putting on the brakes.

My dear Wilhelm,

I have not heard from you for a long time. Herewith a few fragments thrown up on the beach by the last surge. . . . I have only had to withdraw the things I wanted to tack on to the system Pcs. [preconscious]. Another presentiment tells me, as if I knew already — though I do not know anything at all — that I am about to discover the source of morality.[38]

We note in passing that the preconscious system in connection with which Freud speaks of renunciation is also the second of three (unconscious, preconscious, conscious).

Two Dreams Joined Together:
Incest, Phantom, Paralysis

Freud prepares to leave Vienna for.a few days and begin his vacation. Yet we are surprised to read: "I do not want to do any more work. I have laid even dreams aside." Even if the first statement is true, at least the second is obviously false; Freud immediately starts to relate one dream, then another.

He "was feeling over-affectionately" for his daughter Mathilde, who in the dream bears the name Hella, the name of Freud's niece living in America. He explains this change of name through the passion that young Mathilde Freud shows for Greek mythology and history, and as an effect of the bitter tears she cries over Greek defeats.

> The dream of course fulfills my wish to pin down a father as the originator of neurosis and put an end to my persistent doubts.[39]

This dream seems to fill an intermediate state between the two Freudian theories: indeed a father is the guilty one. Yet not Freud's father but Freud himself is guilty as a father, or so he thinks.

The letter continues with an account of another dream:

> Another time I dreamt that I was walking up a staircase with very few clothes on. I was walking up very briskly, as was emphasized in the dream (heart not affected!) when I suddenly noticed that a woman was coming up behind me, whereupon I found myself rooted to the spot, unable to move, overcome by that paralysis which is so common in dreams. The accompanying emotion was not anxiety but erotic excitement. So you see how the feeling of paralysis peculiar to sleep can be used for the fulfillment of an exhibitionistic wish.[40]

Here again, in regard to a prohibited sexual act (exhibitionism, like incest in the dream before), and here again, in the manifest, conscious content of the dream, Freud himself is the transgressor. This second dream, which he briefly analyzed in *The Interpretation of Dreams,*[41] leads him—across diverse figures of maids and housekeepers who reproach him for dirtying the house and spitting in the staircase—to recognize the woman who follows him: his Nannie, his governess, who took care of him in Freiberg during his earliest childhood and who reprimanded him when he had not been clean. As we are now accustomed to do, we find in a note the association made by Freud between the verb *to spit* (*spucken*) and the verb *to haunt, to return as a phantom* (*spuken*).[42]

We are all the more inclined to reread these two dreams together, not only because Freud reports them together, but because he himself expresses the idea after his analysis of the second dream:

> Two thoughts which occur in immediate sequence without any apparent connection are in fact part of a single unity which has to be discovered; in just the same way, if I write an *'a'* and a *'b'* in succession, they have to be pronounced as a single syllable *'ab'.*[43]

Once again, by associating these two dreams, Freud has reunited the sexual fault (incest, exhibitionism) and the phantom, as in the explication of his railway phobia (cf. the nude mother, the souls burning in hell). Here the judge appears to be the servant before whom he remains rooted, paralyzed by something erotic. Freud is approaching the center of the mystery. When Fliess or the father was represented or mentioned in the dreams, the fault was hardly evoked (the secret for Fliess, indulgence for the father). Now that everything has been transferred to Freud's ego, it seems that the content of the fault becomes visible, while the perpetrator of this fault becomes more distant. According to the theoretical predictions that he just wrote to Fliess, the connection between the content and the perpetrator is impossible to maintain; the memory has vanished.

Erotic sensation appears in the two dreams which are recounted together. Perhaps it is a bridge of signification (like the cadaver in the double clinical example that Freud presented in his lecture). Concerning this feeling Freud says that he cannot appeal to the maidservant, who is older and far from attractive. It might be, however, that this erotic excitation he displays for the maid is the desire that he felt for Hella, the vanquished. Then one can, thanks to the "bilingual" text, try to reconstitute a lost signification, Freud's missing memory: incest with someone vanquished is disclosed to the maid.

It is not certain that in the first dream Freud is himself the one who commits incest, because his daughter appears there as his niece. He is therefore her uncle. But the uncle is the figure that Freud habitually substitutes for the father when it is a question of denouncing a father's guilty act, as we saw in the case of Katharina.[44] The guilty relation of a father with someone vanquished, an incestuous relation (the Biblical Jacob-Rebecca), is shown to the former governess, a woman from Freiberg. This paralyzes Freud and makes a phantom appear (a ghostly soul from hell, the vanquished Hella).

There are two small details to add: the number three appears in the second dream. Freud writes in *The Interpretation of Dreams* that *"I was going up three steps at a time."* In German, the verb *überspringen* 'to jump over', also means "to omit," "to pass over"—the number three. He has good reason to try to skip the number three, since someone had for good reason omitted to tell him that his father had three wives. So long as he can leap over this question of threes, he can mount the stairs briskly, without cardiac problems. Here, however, he is confronted with what he can no longer omit if he seeks the cause of hysteria, and this brings us to our second detail. In the dream as he reports it to his friend, the maidservant surprises him from behind; but when he writes it up afterward in *The Interpretation of Dreams* he will have her coming to meet him. It is true that the governess, the witness to whom he today shows the mysterious scene that haunts him, will soon be the accused, the seductress who bars his way.

Freud, a new Hamlet, seems charged with an entirely personal mission that he alone perceives, like the Shakespearean hero, without understanding it. Is it not also his mission to rediscover the truth about the disappearance of a person whose place has been usurped? Indeed, but with this difference: he is the son, not of the one who disappeared, but of the guilty one and of the usurper.

There remains a final manuscript for us to go through, which Freud earlier called "a few fragments thrown upon the beach by the last surge."

We are not going to change the subject, although we have transformed the background. Freud's dreams and theoretical preoccupations during this period of his life are completely mixed together.

Draft N

Impulses

Hostile impulses against parents (a wish that they should die) are also an integral part of neuroses. They come to light consciously in the form of obsessional ideas. . . . [In paranoia] they are repressed at periods in which pity for one's parents is active—at times of their illness or death. One of the manifestations of grief is then to reproach oneself for their death (cf. what are described as "melancholias") or to punish oneself in a hyterical way by putting oneself into their position with an idea of retribution. The identification which takes place here is, as we can see, merely a mode of thinking and does not relieve us of the necessity for looking for the motive.

It seems as though in sons this death-wish is directed against their father and in daughters against their mother.[45]

The author of these lines is also a man in mourning, for a year has not yet passed since his father's death. Freud, according to his own ideas, could indeed repress hostile impulses with regard to his own father. It is not by chance that this theory comes to him at precisely this time. It could again be said that the theoretical account is the conscious formulation of phenomena that are at work in him. But he cannot recognize in himself what he has clearly seen, or at least so it appears, in the others.

Freud then alludes to the phantasies that replace certain memories. Then two paragraphs appear which, if our hypotheses are correct, effectively prefigure both Freud's destiny as a scientist and the cause of his destiny. The first is entitled "Transposition of Belief"; and he will very shortly transpose his belief ("I no longer believe in my *neurotica*"). The second analyzes poetic creation, and the chosen example—what can be said of such a coincidence?—is a story of unhappy love and suicide.

Transposition of Belief

Belief (and doubt) is a phenomenon that belongs wholly to the system of the ego (the Cs.), and it has no counterpart in the Ucs. In the neuroses belief is transposed: it is withheld from the *repressed* material if it forces its way to reproduction, and—as a punishment, one might say—is transposed on to the *defensive* material. So Titania, who refused to love her rightful husband Oberon, was obliged instead to shower her love upon Bottom, the ass of her imagination [cf. *A Midsummer Night's Dream*].

Poetry and Fine Frenzy

The mechanism of creative writing is the same as that of hysterical phantasies. Goethe combined in Werther something he had experienced (his love for Lotte Kastner) and something he had heard of (the fate of young Jerusalem, who killed himself). He probably toyed with the idea of killing himself and found a point of contact in this for identifying himself with Jerusalem, whom he provided with a motive from his own love-story. By means of this phantasy he protected himself against the consequences of his experience.

So Shakespeare was right in his juxtaposition of poetry and madness (the fine frenzy).[46]

Freud also transposes his belief: he no longer wants to believe what he has discovered (the transmission of faults, at least, of sexual faults). As he predicts, belief "is withheld from the *repressed* material." He will no longer believe what he first observed with his own eyes, what he heard with his own ears. Since Freud refuses to believe in reality, all that remains to him is myth. Like Titania, who does not want to love her legitimate husband and finds herself compelled to love an "ass of her imagination," Freud, who does not want to recognize reality, finds himself compelled to recognize only the phantastic story of Oedipus. He puts all his faith in this myth, which, moreover, he has misconstrued. Belief "is transposed on to the *defensive* material"; that is, on to the poetic-scientific creation that he constructs in order to protect "himself against the consequences of his own experience." Blending in what he experienced and what he heard, he builds a fiction, which will protect him from the brute return of a nonsymbolizable reality. And indeed, through dreams and during the summer this transposition of belief is carried out for him as well: a night from which he will awaken no longer believing in what he has seen but in an "unconscious fiction." It is then that the myth of Oedipus returns to him; wanting to recognize in it a protective explanation, he restricts its meaning. Yet he is not mistaken, because the myth taken in its entirety is exactly what he is trying to flee. The ass, Bottom, is only Oberon disguised.

Which necessity thus drives him to reveal everything by concealing it, by believing that he hides the father's secret fault? Would he only have a choice between the revelation of the fault and its repetition? Does the noble and respected Freud attempt to escape at the same time from these two dangers, which are, on one side, the revelation of a fault that makes him heir to a criminal (*Verbrecher,* the word that appears in the dream of the uncle with the yellow beard), and on the other side, total silence, which compels him to repeat in his own actions the father's fault? His life and his work would form a compromise: a partial representation in some symptoms (death anxiety, phobias, etc.), a partial repetition through acts of symbolic "donjuanism" (collecting statues, etc.), a partial atonement in the rituals of everyday life (domestic, sexual, alimentary, etc.), and a partial revelation through a partly phantasmatic "scientific" theory.

Hardly has Freud spoken of the transposition of belief, when he, in effect, performs his own transposition:

> ### Motives for the Formation of Symptoms
> Remembering is never a motive, but only a method—a mode. The first motive force, chronologically, for the formation of symptoms is libido. Thus symptoms are *fulfilments of wishes,* just as dreams are.[47]

The swing of the pendulum has already begun. As soon as he speaks of "the motive force" for the formation of symptoms he abandons the field of intersubjective motives and limits himself to intrapsychic mechanisms. The libido explains the phantasies; the symptom is the realization of desire.

Whose desire? And for what? What if the desire in the symptom was to represent the unspeakable, to reestablish the symbol, which joins the one who suffers to the Other. What if the symptom were the demand for recognition? Freud concludes this final draft with this paragraph:

> ### Definition of "Saintliness"
> "Saintliness" is something based on the fact that, for the sake of the larger community, human beings have sacrificed some of their freedom to indulge in sexual perversions. The horror of incest (as something impious) is based on the fact that, as a result of a common sexual life (even in childhood), the members of a family hold together permanently and become incapable of contact with strangers. Thus incest is antisocial and civilization consists in a progressive renunciation of it. Contrariwise the "superman."[48]

Freud No Longer Understands

Freud's first phase is now practically finished. A period of paralysis and depression begins with his letter of June 12, 1897. All summer Freud is intellectually dragging himself along.

> I have never yet imagined anything like my present spell of intellectual paralysis. Every line I write is torture.

He nonetheless prepares his next "congress" with Fliess in August.

> At Aussee I know a wonderful wood full of ferns and mushrooms, where you shall reveal to me the secrets of the world of the lower animals and the world of children.[49]

It is curious that Freud, who is always asking for these meetings, will at the last moment send Fliess a counterorder to tell him not to join him on vacation.

In this same letter Freud presents yet a last case that conforms to the discovery that he is going to bury. One could call this an intermediate case: the father is not the guilty one; he is already dead.

> The latest [case] is a girl of nineteen with almost pure obsessional ideas, who greatly interests me. According to my hypothesis obsessional ideas date back to a later psychical age, and so *a priori* do not point back to the father, who treats the child the more carefully the older it is, but to her slightly older brothers and sisters in whose eyes the child has not become a woman. Now in this case the Almighty was kind enough to remove the father by death before the child was eleven months old, but two brothers, of whom one was three years older then my patient, shot themselves.
>
> Otherwise I am empty and ask your indulgence. I believe I am in a cocoon, and heaven knows what sort of creature will emerge from it.[50]

Sexuality, death (suicide)—with what insistence this double theme returns under Freud's pen in his literary examples, his dreams, his omissions, his phobias, his clinical practice, and soon, but implicitly, in his mythological theorization.

Like all of Freud's biographers, we return again to some lines describing the crisis that he is going through, his inhibition, and the disarray in which he finds himself.

> I still do not know what has been happening to me. Something from the deepest depths of my own neurosis has ranged itself against my taking a further step in understanding of the neuroses, and you have somehow been involved. My inability to write seems to be aimed at hindering our intercourse.[51]

"The chief patient I am busy with is myself,"[52] he writes to Fliess just after having refused to meet with him. There are few letters that summer, but he does occupy himself with excursions (to Salzburg) with his sister-in-law, Minna, making arrangements for his father's headstone, the start of the systematic self-analysis, and a trip to Italy (to Orvieto, Signorelli's frescos of the Last Judgment). Before this trip to Italy, Freud again suffers from his railway phobia. He mentions it in a passage concerning a woman and an accident. This time it concerns his wife.

> Martha is looking forward to the journey, though the daily reports of train accidents do not make the father and mother of a family look forward to travelling with any pleasure. You will laugh—and rightly —but I must confess to new anxieties, which come and go but last for

half a day at a time. Fear of a railway accident deserted me half an
hour ago when it occurred to me that Wilhelm and Ida [Fliess] were
also on the way. That ended the idiocy. This must remain strictly
between us.[53]

The Transference of the Fault

Anzieu has spoken of Freud's "transference neurosis" during the
summer of 1897.[54] This expression seems to us suitable indeed. Freud
plainly transfers to Fliess something that he cannot consciously accept;
he knows only that he is prevented from continuing to write to him. And
when he fears that his wife and he may be victims in a train accident, his
anxiety is dispelled at the thought that Fliess and his wife are themselves
in the train.

How can we reread and rejoin these signs? Freud had had his
falling out with Joseph Breuer the year before. Even the most indulgent
biographers have been distressed at the tone in which Freud spoke of it
in several letters. They even admit that they thought it preferable not to
publish the passages in question. Is there a transference there also? The
aging father is considered a good man, but is this not a case of "transposed
belief"? The truth of the fault, which is refused in regard to Jakob Freud,
is borne for a while by Joseph Breuer. What remains for Freud after he
has ended his relationship with Breuer? The hostile transference with
Breuer was carried out at the moment when Freud's relation to Fliess was
already extremely deep; now, the latter is his "only public." As Freud
approaches his father's fault on his voyage within, he must be able to
transfer this disavowed (unrecognized) fault onto someone else. Fliess is
of course appointed. But that means to lose him as a friend, which Freud
does not want; he would lose at the same time his only witness. He must
then avoid Fliess—not write to him often, not meet him—until he could
divert the transfer of the fault onto someone else.

In effect, Fliess cannot occupy two different positions in relation to
Freud. He cannot be at once the witness who hears everything and
someone who is taken for the guilty party. When Freud imagines him on
the train, in his place, and diverts the anguished expectation of the
accident to him, (which all seems to Freud an "idiocy"), he is actually
showing by what psychic mechanism he tries to master those things that
come from "the deepest depth" of his neurosis. But Fliess is not on that
second level in the position of the analyst. If Freud makes Fliess bear
what he had already placed on Breuer's back, he puts an end to the only
relation in which he ever could hope to understand both himself and his
burdensome unconscious secret. If the other cannot occupy two positions

before him (those of the guilty one and the witness), it is therfore necessary to find someone who can again be charged with the fault. From the isolation in which he finds himself there remain very few possibilities for Freud. If the father is not the perpetrator of his fault; if he is not the one who had a shameful and hidden relationship with a woman whose name, according to the Bible, is that of his own mother; if Jakob Freud, the father who has been dead almost a year, should be considered innocent of what he nonetheless did, then it is indeed necessary to attribute this fault to another.

It is no longer Breuer; and it cannot be Fliess. Placed in the same situation as Oedipus, Freud will discover the same solution: like Oedipus, he will interrogate his mother. Unhappily for us and contrary to his illustrious Greek predecessor, he believes her. A month will be enough to make him forget what he has seen. A month to make him silence a voice, to efface a vision, to construct a wall in defense against the truth.

All this, finally, in order that he himself can cry out, louder than the stones, "I alone am the guilty one."

The unconscious is that part of the concrete discourse, in so far as it is transindividual, that is not at the disposal of the subject in reestablishing the continuity of his conscious discourse. . . .

The unconscious is that chapter of my history that is marked by a blank or occupied by a falsehood: it is the censored chapter. But the truth can be rediscovered; usually it has already been written down elsewhere. Namely:

—in monuments: this is my body. That is to say, the hysterical nucleus of the neurosis in which the hysterical symptom reveals the structure of a language, and is deciphered like an inscription which, once recovered, can without serious loss be destroyed;

—in archival documents: these are my childhood memories, just as impenetrable as are such documents when I do not know their provenance;

—in semantic evolution: this corresponds to the stock of words and acceptations of my own particular vocabulary, as it does to my style of life and to my character;

—in traditions, too, and even in the legends which, in a heroicized form, bear my history;

—and, lastly, in the traces that are inevitably preserved by the distortions necessitated by the linking of the adulterated chapter to the chapters surrounding it, and whose meaning will be reestablished by my exegesis.

Lacan, *Ecrits: A Selection*

CHAPTER 7

THE TRUTH
IS BURIED

In research of this kind the reader must keep in mind all the various elements so that he can judge their suitability for himself. The procedure is burdensome for him and for us. But a scientific theory that has been established for so many years and is securely lodged in so many places in our society cannot be reexamined, questioned, and, *a fortiori*, overturned without a concerted effort.

We now have reached the end of our expedition. With the end of the summer of 1897 comes the time for Freud to abandon the first foundations of his work and to lay down a new base. While the first were established on the bedrock of fact, however, the second rest upon the sands of myth. Psychoanalytic theory is incontestable, which is exactly what makes us doubt that it is scientific. Like myth, it is unquestionable. We had to go into its foundations in order to be able to interrogate it.

There are only two things that remain to be done: to discover the last person whom Freud gave a decisive role to play in his great reversal, and to reread carefully three letters (69, 70, 71), written between September 21 and October 15, 1897. By the time we reach the anniversary of Jakob's death, October 23, by which time the mourning for the father will be ended, Freud will have founded psychoanalysis—but he will have buried his discovery.

We have already mentioned the person whom we now are about to present. Her image arose in Freud's dreams and suggested itself to him at the moment when he wanted to base the truth of the father's role upon his own neurosis, at the moment when he approached "the great secret," "the source of morality," which to us means the hidden fault.

NANNIE (MONIKA ZAJIC)

The Official Version

This is the account Jones gives.

> In the household [of Jakob Freud in Freiberg] there was also a Nannie, old and ugly, with the nurse's normal mixture of affection for children and severity towards their transgressions; she was capable and efficient. Freud several times refers in his writings to what he called "that prehistoric old woman." He was fond of her and used to give her all his pennies, and he refers to the memory of the latter fact as a screen memory; perhaps it got connected with her dismissal for theft later on when he was two and a half years old. She was Czech and they conversed in that language, although Freud forgot it afterwards. More important, she was a Catholic and used to take the young boy to attend the church services. She implanted in him the ideas of Heaven and Hell, and probably also those of salvation and resurrection. After returning from church the boy used to preach a sermon at home and expound God's doings.[1]

We are at first struck by a phrase in Jones's account—Freud's expression in quotation marks: "prehistoric old woman." One could imagine a very old grandmother. What does Freud himself say about this Nannie? In a dream we have already mentioned, Freud climbs the staircase, meets a maid, and finds himself paralyzed.

> The staircase dream to which I have referred was one of a series of dreams; and I understood the interpretation of the other members of the series. Since this particular dream was surrounded by the others it must have dealt with the same subject. Now these other dreams were based on a recollection of a nurse [*Kinderfrau*] in whose charge I had been from some date during my earliest infancy till I was two and a half. I even retain an obscure conscious memory of her. According to what I was told not long ago by my mother, she was old and ugly, but very sharp and efficient. From what I can infer from my own dreams her treatment of me was not always excessive in its amiability and her words could be harsh if I failed to reach the required standard of cleanliness. And thus the maidservant, since she had undertaken the job of carrying on this educational work, acquired the right to be treated in my dream as a reincarnation of the prehistoric old nurse. It is reasonable to suppose that the child loved the old woman [*Erzieherin* 'educator'] who taught him these lessons, in spite of her rough treatment of him.[2]

A note follows, which explains the dream and also completes Freud's portrait of the Nannie:

Here is an "over-interpretation" of the same dream. Since *"spuken"* [haunting] is an activity of *spirits*, *"spucken* [spitting] on the stairs" might be loosely rendered as *"esprit d'escalier."* This last phrase is equivalent to lack of ready repartee [*Schlagfertigkeit*, literally "readiness to strike"]—a failing to which I must in fact plead guilty. Was my nurse, I wonder, equally wanting in *"Schlagfertigkeit"?* [*schlagen* 'to strike or beat'; *Fertigkeit* 'readiness'].[3]

We are moving toward the unofficial version of this little-known person. Freud had already spoken of her to Fliess in one of the famous letters of October 1897, before writing the book on dreams. Hardly has the father been removed as a cause ("my father played no active role") than Freud denounces to his friend someone new upon whom he wants to pin his neurosis:

My "primary originator" [*Urheberin*] [of neurosis] was an ugly, elderly but clever woman who told me a great deal about God and hell, and gave me a high opinion of my own capacities; that later (between the ages of two and two-and-a-half) libido towards *matrem* was aroused; the occasion must have been the journey with her from Leipzig to Vienna, during which we spent a night together and I must have had the opportunity of seeing her *nudam*.[4]

Freud goes on to mention his brother Julius, whose birth must have aroused "ill wishes" in him and whose death left in him "the germ of guilt." He then mentions his nephew (who is one year older due to the difference of generations that resulted from the father's remarriage), and also the cruelty with which they had sometimes treated the latter's young sister. "My nephew and younger brother determined, not only the neurotic side of all my friendships, but also their depth. My anxiety over travel, you have seen yourself in full bloom."

Let us go over the chain of ideas in this paragraph: the father plays no active role; the "primary originator" of neurosis is the old nurse; she speaks to him of God and hell, and of his own capacities; he takes a journey by train where he has occasion to see his mother nude; he feels "ill wishes" against Julius; Julius dies; relations with the nephew ensue; the uncle (Sigmund) and the nephew were cruel to the little sister; he experiences a fear of traveling.

We have then an innocent father and a guilty nurse. Guilty of what? We still do not know. But themes that are knitted together in Freud's life reappear here once again: in front of a witness (the Nannie, Moses, etc.) the themes of sexual transgression, the death of someone innocent, and the female victim pass by one after the other. Among all these themes the railway phobia stands out. Freud continues in *Letter 70.*

I still have not gotten to the scenes which lie at the bottom of all this. If they emerge, and I succeed in resolving my hysteria, I shall

have to thank the memory of the old woman who provided me at
such an early age with the means for living and surviving.

Freud does not express a trivial gratitude toward the old nurse. Thanks
to her he was able to live and survive.

Freud does not send this letter to Fliess right away. He keeps it and
returns to it the next day.

> Oct. 4th. The children have arrived. The fine weather is over. Last
> night's dream produced the following under the most remarkable
> disguises:
> She was my instructress in sexual matters, and chided me for
> being clumsy and not being able to do anything (that is always the
> way with neurotic impotence: anxiety over incapacity at school gets
> its sexual reinforcement in this way). I saw the skull of a small
> animal which I thought of as a "pig" in the dream, though it was
> associated in the dream with your wish of two years ago that I might
> find a skull on the Lido to enlighten me, as Goethe once did. But I
> did not find it. Thus it was "a little *Schafskopf*" [literally "sheep's
> head"; figuratively "blockhead"]. The whole dream was full of the
> most wounding references to my present uselessness as a therapist.
> Perhaps the origin of my tendency to believe in the incurability of
> hysteria should be sought here. Also she washed me in reddish water
> in which she had previously washed herself (not very difficult to
> interpret; I find nothing of the kind in my chain of memories, and so
> I take it for a genuine rediscovery); and she encouraged me to steal
> [*wegnehmen*] "Zehners" (ten-Kreuzer pieces) to give to her. A long
> chain of association connects these first silver Zehners to the heap of
> paper ten-florin notes which I saw in the dream as Martha's house-
> keeping money. The dream can be summed up as "bad treatment."
> Just as the old woman got money from me for her bad treatment of
> me, so do I now get money for the bad treatment of my patients.[5]

In the staircase dream it was Freud who displayed to the Nannie something relating to sexuality. Here, she is his professor in "sexual matters."
He learns poorly. He sees a skull, but it does not clear anything up. Is it a
pig or a sheep? Jakob Freud was a trader in sheep's wool. The Nannie
washes Sigmund in reddish water; is the interpretation so easy? She
shows him something relating to sexuality; he is incapable and stupid, as
one is at school when one understands nothing. It involves an animal's
skull and water mixed with blood. This skull is associated with the Lido,
therefore, once again, with Venice, like the via/villa Secerno dream. Is
Venice a city in Italy or one of the three suburbs of Freiberg?

> A severe critic might say that all this was phantasy projected into
> the past instead of being determined by the past. The *experimenta
> crucis* would decide the matter against him. The reddish water seems
> a point of this kind. Where do all patients derive the horrible perverse

details which are so often as alien to their experience as to their knowledge?[6]

This is the end of *Letter 70,* at least in its published form. The word *cross* returns yet again, in Latin this time (*crucis*), after the *Kreuzers* in the dream; both times this word is associated with the reddish water. Freud is certainly right to say that it is a dream about mistreatment, but who is mistreated, and by whom? Like the fabricated clinical example, there is a dead animal. Could we not say that, in the dream, Freud tries once again to learn something about his Nannie, who had "the spirit of repartee"? But what desire is fulfilled through this dream? It seems that Freud does not even consider the question. Having forgotten his own theory, he tries to learn from the dream something about his past and its secrets. The translators, who know what happens in the following letter, make the idea of a theft already apparent: "She encouraged me to steal." The German text is more vague (*wegnehmen* can mean "to steal," but more often it means "to take away," "to remove," "to carry off"). Jones writes that Freud remembered that he "used to give" all his pennies to the Nannie.

In describing what happened after this dream, Freud writes to Fliess that his self analysis

> suddenly broke down for three days, and I had the feeling of inner binding about which my patients complain so much, and I was inconsolable. . . .
> My practice, uncannily [*unheimlicherweise*], still allows me plenty of time.[7]

The adjective *unheimlich* is known to all analysts. Freud will devote an essay to the notion of *das Unheimliche* [*The Uncanny*], (1919): that which is familiar (*Heim* 'home') becomes most disquieting when this familiarity becomes negative (*unheimlich*) and suddenly appears strange to us. Freud's still sparse practice is somewhat disturbing to him, in the simple sense of its effect on his survival and his future career, but why this idea of the uncanny here? Perhaps it corresponds better with what went before (the three-day breakdown) and with what immediately follows.

> All this is the more valuable from my point of view because I have succeeded in finding a number of real points of reference. I asked my mother whether she remembered my nurse. "Of course," she said, "an elderly woman, very shrewd indeed. She was always taking you to all the churches.[*in alle Kirchen*]. When you came home you used to preach, and tell us all about how God conducted His affairs. At the time I was in bed when Anna was being born" (Anna is two-and-a-half years younger). "She turned out to be a thief, and all the shiny Kreuzers and Zehners and toys that had been given you were

found among her things. Your brother Philipp went himself to get
the policeman, and she got ten months."[8]

The end of Amalie-Jocasta's discourse to Freud-Oedipus. The version
that Freud's mother gives of the story does not conform to what the
dream seemed to mean. Freud, however, continues his letter in these
words:

> Now see how that confirms the conclusions from my dream inter-
> pretation. I have easily been able to explain the one possible mistake.
> I wrote to you that she got me to steal [*stehlen*] Zehners and give
> them to her. The dream really means that she stole herself. For the
> dream-picture was a memory that I took money from a doctor's
> mother, i.e., wrongfully. The real meaning is that the old woman
> stood for me, and that the doctor's mother was my mother. I was so
> far from being aware that the old woman was a thief that my interpre-
> tation went astray.[9]

Such is the weight of his mother's word that he necessarily concedes that
she is right, even if it means contradicting himself. Freud, the grand
master of suspicion, has no doubts here: his mother speaks the truth.

Another Interpretation

In addition to the dissimulation about the father's second marriage
and the son's curious double date of birth (March 6 or May 6, 1856),
regarding which it is difficult not to imagine that Amalie Freud could be
held responsible, we have also discovered that the "prehistoric old
woman," the Nannie, is also a part of the story. In Freiberg the Freuds
lived in the house of a locksmith named Zajic. This is what Anzieu tells
us about the nursemaid: "Single and in her forties, her first name was
Monika and she belonged to the Zajic family; she was therefore on the
same floor with them."[10] According to Josef Sajner, who has investigated
first-hand, Monika Zajic was an employee of Jakob Freud's eldest son
(from his first marriage), which means that she worked for Emanuel and
Maria Freud, whose children, along with little Sigmund, were under
her care.[11]

Monika Zajic is an inhabitant of Freiberg. The Freuds rent from
her family the one room that serves as their lodging on the second floor.
It now seems even more difficult to accept the version of the story given
by Freud's mother. Is it credible that this relative of the landlord, this
shrewd and hard-working middle-aged woman—who is not so old, in
fact, nearly the same age as Jakob—stole the pennies and the toys that
this poor child was able to collect? A poor prize for an intelligent thief. It
hardly seems plausible. We know, finally, only one thing about her: she

spoke a lot to Sigmund about Heaven and hell. Jones adds, "and probably also . . . salvation and resurrection." We could add, atonement for a fault and for a phantom.

We have only a hypothesis to try to make some sense of all this. Monika Zajic is a native of Freiberg. Jakob Freud lived there before his remarriage with Amalie. Monika Zajic was doubtless also in Freiberg then. Things become known in a town of five thousand inhabitants.

What does this Catholic mean by repeatedly leading this Jewish child to church? (There is only one church in Freiberg; the tour of "all the churches" of which Amalie Freud spoke could be done quickly.) Let's try to reposition what Freud tells us about his Nannie within the context of a church. The coins take on a new meaning if they are used to fill the church's collection box; like the one, for example, that can be found near the relics of Saint Urban, which was brought to Rome, so it is said, by a shoemaker from Freiberg.[12] The remains seen in the dream of the animal skull are not far from this context. Freud in fact tells his adult patients to see in the animals in dreams a recollection of young children. As for the water in which she washes him after having washed herself, that can also represent holy water in which the adult dips her hand, and then wets the hand of the child, who is too small to reach the basin, and then she traces the sign of the cross on herself. The two words, *Kreuz* and *crucis*, (the latter is of course Latin), would have their function precisely here.[13] When Freud mentions the reddish water, he adds: "not very difficult to interpret." We have learned from Freud himself that something apparently easy portends nothing other than a resistance against any further interpretation.

Perhaps it actually concerns a woman's blood. But which woman? Is it menstrual blood? In the church the blood that washes clean indeed has a place and a significance. For Catholics, of whom the Nannie is one, is it not in Christ's blood, the blood spilled on the cross, that mankind is cleansed of its faults? In the Mass, does not the priest mix together wine and water before the consecration, which is supposed to make them the blood of the Redeemer?

Might it not be that Freud, who will be particularly interested in Lady Macbeth, dreams that his Nannie makes him atone for a fault through these offerings, that she cleanses him of a sin in holy water? If that is the case, then we would understand completely Freud's curious sentence: "I shall have to thank the memory of the old woman who provided me at such an early age with the means for living and *surviving*" (our emphasis). Is Monika Zajic aware of Rebecca's disappearance? Are her pious or magical practices with the child Sigmund intended, in her mind, to protect him from a destiny similar to his brother's, to protect him from the consequences of some tragic and reprehensible facts? Would this dream be the trace left in the mind of a young Jewish child by the, to him, incomprehensible explanations and gestures of a Catholic Nannie concerning a fault about which he knows nothing and concerning a sacred gesture (making the sign of the cross on one's breast) which he cannot understand?

It seems audacious to conjecture all this. But is it any more unlikely than this bizarre echo in the adult Freud that we find in the notes of Lou Andreas-Salomé, an affectionate disciple, who had also become the confidante of his daughter Anna?

> Listening to Anna talking about her father; about picking mushrooms when they were children. When they went collecting mushrooms he always told them to go into the wood quietly and he still does this; there must be no chattering and they must roll up the bags they have brought under their arms, so that the mushrooms shall not notice; when their father found one he would cover it quickly with his hat, as though it were a butterfly. The little children—and now his grandchildren—used to believe what he said, while the bigger ones smiled at his credulity; even Anna did this, when he told her to put fresh flowers every day at the shrine of the Virgin which was near the wood, so that it might help them in their search. The children were paid in pennies for the mushrooms they had found, while the best mushroom of all (it was always Ernst who found it) got a florin. It was the quality and not the quantity of the mushrooms that mattered.[14]

Let us return to Freiberg. Like many facets of our work, what we have just conjectured is impossible to verify directly. This hypothesis at least enables us to realize that versions other than the official one can be given in a way that is also entirely plausible.

What is the sequel to this story? Officially, the Nannie is discovered as a thief and incarcerated for ten months. Without any apparent link to this event, we learn that, in the following months, the Freud family emigrates from Freiberg; before the Nannie has finished her sentence, they all depart: the elder sons for England, Jakob, Amalie, and their two young children for Leipzig and then Vienna. This is Jones's version. For Sajner, things are much more entangled. According to him, the three most important events in Sigmund's childhood—the birth of his sister Anna on December 31, 1858, the dismissal of the nursemaid, and the departure from Freiberg—follow one another in less than two months.

We do not find that chronology at all unlikely, because, even if we accept Amalie Freud's version, if Monika is indeed a Zajic, her denunciation to the police would, at the very least, have created difficulties in the relations between landlords and tenants.[15] This period of early 1859 is therefore mysterious indeed. We will soon see that the nursemaid's disappearance has left a trace in Freud's memory; he recalls a scene where he screams while looking for his mother, who he fears has disappeared like the nursemaid. Is this disappearance unrelated to the upheaval in the Freud family? What happened then? Was the Nannie a troublesome witness? What did she do or say to little Sigmund to warrant the accusation, forty years later, that she had stolen his coins and toys? The passing of time and the lies have engulfed these events in immeasurable depths.

The reasons that were later advanced to explain the departure from Freiberg, such as antisemitism or economic catastrophe in the textile business, are, after Sajner's work, inadmissable. Although it is difficult to assert that a predominantly Catholic country did not show signs of hostility to a Jewish minority, it is true that Freud himself speaks of a friendly family, the Fluss family, who lived in Freiberg and were wealthy; and they were also Jews who worked in textiles.

It is still true that in 1859 the Nannie disappears and the Freuds leave town. Emanuel and Philipp will settle in Manchester. Officially, everything is fine. how can we fail to understand, however, the protest against the family's unjust destiny contained in this very brief dream noted by Freud, a dream in a series in which he wants to demonstrate the links between the events during wakefulness and the dream itself:

> *A man standing on* A Cliff in the Middle of the Sea, in the Style of Böcklin.
> Source: Dreyfus on Devil's Island; I had had news at the same time from my relatives in England, etc.[16]

Freud speaks of the Nannie as a "prehistoric old woman." Is that to say that his own history begins after her, at least the history that he is permitted to know? After the Nannie's departure, he would have the right to know—since everything that he should be unaware of is from now on well concealed; everything before would be Freud's prehistory, a period that is shipwrecked in his memory and of which only some debris remains. He cannot gather them together; his mother's discourse intervenes in order that the pieces are not recollected into symbols, which would perhaps lead the perspicacious Sigmund Freud to his family's secret dramas.

Prehistory, rupture, history. When therefore does Freud's history begin? At the departure from Freiberg to Vienna, via Leipzig? Jones observes:

> Curiously enough he gives his age then as between two and two and a half, whereas he was in fact four years old on that journey. One must surmise that the memories of two such experiences had got telescoped.[17]

Anzieu, who also notices the error, wonders, "What 'departure' took place at the age of two-and-a-half?"

It is astonishing that Sajner's research in Freiberg reaches the same conclusions as Freud, and that Freud's "error" confirms the findings of the excavation undertaken by Sajner. A mysterious nursemaid joins the mysterious Rebecca. Perhaps they are linked to one another in Freud's prehistory. It is, of course, in prehistory that Freud locates the murder. This time it is the prehistory of humanity, and the murder is of the primordial father, chief of the primitive horde, the prehistoric Don Juan, who possessed all the women. Is *Totem and Taboo* a revengeful myth?

When, in 1911, Freud is engaged in research on this project, he writes:

> I know I am following a crooked way in the order of my works (i.e. "working"), but it is the order of unconscious connections.[18]

A few weeks later, he writes a sentence that, for us, cannot fail to evoke the father's second wife.

> The *Totem* work is a beastly business. . . . I haven't time every evening, and so on. With all that I feel as if I had intended only to start a little liaison and then discovered that at my time of life I have to marry a new wife.[19]

THE BURIED FOUNDATIONS AND THE NEW FOUNDATION OF PSYCHOANALYSIS: AN EFFORT AT RECONSTITUTION

We must now gather all the signs that we have discovered in the first site where Freud had begun to build a theory. Many of them have already been assembled. But we would like to present a general view. What have we unearthed? Let us consider all these vestiges of Freud's life and work in the aggregate and then try, little by little, to see what they indicate.

The First Site

—The name of Laius plays no part in the first site, while in the foundations of the myth of Oedipus it constitutes the center.

—We have found that mushrooms and statues receive curious treatment (the ritual of the mushroom "hunt"; the *Herrenpilze,* which are ritually consumed; the statue collection; the statues invited to dinner).

—Traces of Don Juan appear in several places (an exclusive preference for this opera of Mozart, or for those very much like it; crises of death-anxiety; the Commander's statue; inhibition against going to Rome; the fascination before the statue of Moses; Freud's identification with Don Juan's valet).

—We have seen a repeated interest in the figures of the Judge (Moses) and the Last Judgment (dreams; epigraphs after his father's death; his forgetting the name of Signorelli).

—Rebecca—Regardless how completely it was effaced, a name reappears on several occasions: at first spontaneously in a letter to Fliess (the Jewish story), it later stands out in relief (Ibsen), or appears in a concave recess (the tomb of Pope Julius II) in relation to incest (Rebecca-Jacob), as though in the place of a second wife. Also associated with the appearances of this name are the ideas of repudiation ("Rebecca, take off your wedding gown") and suicide (Ibsen's Rebecca West and Dido in the *Aeneid*); suicide is either inscribed secretly (the subtitle of *The Interpretation of Dreams*, with no reference), or not mentioned at all (Ibsen's Rebecca, Lady Macbeth), or else forgotten (the case of Signorelli).

We observe that:

—Freud's first theoretical foundations (seduction theory) are abruptly abandoned at the time of his mourning for Jakob-Don Juan.

—Nevertheless, they corresponded to the plan that takes shape from all the signs we have retrieved; the theory of seduction corresponds at once to Don Juan and to the incest of the biblical Rebecca-Jacob.

—The question of murder, direct or indirect, remains practically buried beneath the sexual theory. Still, it returns repeatedly (literary examples, Signorelli, the railway phobia, the invented clinical example—the corpse, the train accident and the fallen apples, associations relating to a phantom—the Commander's statue, the souls of the dead, the ghosts in the epigraphs and the dreams).

We have also found a group of theoretical texts written by Freud just before the abandonment of these first foundations (drafts L, M, N), which seem to describe, in advance, the error that Freud the architect is going to commit (mourning that represses hostility toward his parents), how he will conceal it (phantasies), and why he will not be aware of it (transposition of belief: one refuses credence to facts, one accords it to myth.)

Three Letters: The Great Transition

Here we learn how, in less than a month, a truth is buried in three letters. The first anniversary of his father's death is approaching. Freud returns from an uncommonly long vacation, during which he was intellectually paralyzed. He has begun his systematic self-analysis; he went to Salzburg (Don Juan) and to Orvieto (the frescos of the Last Judgment); he saw to his father's headstone. This period conveys an impressive unity of direction. The journeys, the feelings, the letters, the dreams, and the theory: everything seems to converge on the same question, the question of the guilty father, who is the promoter of the neurosis of his child, and the question of the guilt of his own father. During these months he draws ever closer to the mystery. At the moment when he is perhaps about to find the key, the forces of repression rise up in him; forces that he has himself so well described in his premonitory manuscripts. In these three letters we are going to see the fault pass from the father—who should not have to bear it—to the governess, then to Freud himself. The first theory, which we could call that of the transmission of faults (with the sole reservation that, officially, Freud is only concerned with sexual faults), is abandoned on September 21. The "discovery" of Oedipus takes place on October 15.

Are three weeks enough to make a new theory? Or, rather, is it not the same theory that makes its return by another path, which Freud does not recognize? The history that was expelled returns disguised as myth. One will no longer speak of the father, Jakob, who doubtless led his wife Rebecca—his mother, according to the Bible—to death; but one will speak of Oedipus, without saying what his father had done and without making too much of the fact that Oedipus also led his wife—the concealed mother—to a similar death. From now on, the bearer of the fault will no longer be the father but the son; Freud wanted to see Oedipus only as a son and not also as a father who, in his turn, will send those he loves to death.

Since the fault was not recognized, it becomes necessary, as it is for every fault without an author, to find someone who can be charged with it so that the symbolic order can be, if not reestablished, at least filled in. We are therefore entirely within what anthropologists describe to us as the mechanism of the "emissary victim."[20] The phenomenon is sometimes very difficult to notice. Consider a comparison. In the monotheistic religions in which God is an invisible, living being, it is difficult to discover how this same God—the true one according to his believers—can nevertheless become the object of a cult that makes of him a simple idol: the most perverse of idolatries, the idolatry of the true God. Much work, reflection, and time are likewise necessary to discover the emissary victim, the one who must bear the faults that are unrecognized by those who commit them, especially when, in a case like Freud's, the one who points out the process to us is himself its victim—and like him, we ourselves are victims.

Letter 69:
"*I no longer believe in my neurotica. . . . Rebecca, you can take off your wedding-gown, you're not a bride any longer.*"

My dear Wilhelm,

Here I am again—we returned yesterday morning—refreshed, cheerful, impoverished and without work for the time being, and I am writing to you as soon as we have settled in again. Let me tell you straightaway the great secret which has been slowly dawning on me in recent months. I no longer believe in my *neurotica*. That is hardly intelligible without an explanation; you yourself found what I told you credible. So I shall start at the beginning and tell you the whole story of how the reasons for rejecting it arose.[21]

September 21, 1897

Freud gives four motives for his disbelief:

1. "The continual disappointments of my attempts to bring my analyses to a real conclusion."
2. "The astonishing thing that in every case blame was laid on perverse acts by the father, *my own not excluded [mein eigener nicht ausgeschlossen]*, . . . though it was hardly credible that perverted acts against children were so general."[22]
3. "The definite realization that there is no 'indication of reality' in the unconscious, so that it is impossible to distinguish between truth and emotionally-charged fiction."
4. "The consideration that even in the most deep-reaching psychoses the unconscious memory does not break through, so that the secret of infantile experiences is not revealed even in the most confused states of delirium."

In other words, Freud abandons his first theory because:

1. He does not yet know how to terminate an analytic cure.
2. He cannot admit the idea of guilty fathers in the cases of all hysterics.
3. He has no means by which to distinguish truth from fiction in his patients' discourse.
4. He cannot break through to the secret in the most advanced cases of psychosis.

Do any of these four elements constitute a clinical proof or a real argument? No, they are, as Freud himself says, only "factors," which we understand to be his personal motives. Considering it a little more closely, it is somewhat a list of his present powerlessness. Should he be astonished at not yet having overcome all these difficulties? But can he, for all that, justify abandoning a theory?

To him who thus finds several reasons that do not make a proof, Freud will later recount an appropriate sophism:

> A. borrowed a copper kettle from B. and after he had returned it was sued by B. because the kettle now had a big hole in it which made it unusable. His defense was: "First, I never borrowed a kettle from B. at all; secondly, the kettle had a hole in it already when I got it from him; and thirdly, I gave him back the kettle undamaged."[23]

Freud is complaining here that he cannot reach either the end or the secret in his analyses. But at the end, when he finds that the secret of hysteria is the father's hidden fault, he cannot believe it; moreover, he adds that it is unverifiable. The argument could work as well in another direction: Freud would benefit, with his method as it is now, from what could prove nothing against the father in order to abandon his discovery. It is as if his therapeutic incapacity constituted the most certain alibi to be able to say, I have not seen anything.

Hardly has he said that he no longer believes in this genealogical transmission and that he no longer knows where he is, than he reintroduces heredity: "The factor of hereditary predisposition regains a sphere of influence from which I had made it my business to oust it—in the interests of fully explaining neurosis."

The paragraph that follows is characteristic of what happens in the course of an analysis when someone, after a perhaps too rapid advance toward a repressed truth, is seized by a reversal. While the repression is reinforced, thus securing the prohibited site from returning to memory, the individual at first goes through a period of alleviation, which is, nevertheless, secretly accompanied by a mild feeling of hesitation, and more profoundly, by a feeling of inauthenticity:

> Were I depressed, jaded, unclear in my mind, such doubts might be taken for signs of weakness. But as I am in just the opposite state, I must acknowledge them to be the result of honest and effective intellectual labour, and I am proud that after penetrating so far I am still capable of such criticism. Can these doubts be only an episode on the way to further knowledge?
>
> It is curious that I feel not in the least disgraced, though the occasion might seem to require it. Certainly I shall not tell it in Gath, or publish it in the streets of Askalon, in the land of the Philistines[24]—but between ourselves I have a feeling more of triumph than of defeat (which cannot be right).[25]

The style of this passage is that of an impossible compromise between yes and no; the style is echoed elsewhere in Freud's work. The editors of the Freud-Fliess letters link this paragraph—"I have a feeling more of triumph than of defeat (which cannot be right)"—to a note Freud added in 1924 to an article he had written in 1896:

> This section is dominated by an error which I have since repeatedly acknowledged and corrected. At that time I was not yet able to distinguish between my patients' phantasies about their childhood years and their real recollections. As a result, I attributed to the aetiological factor of seduction a significance and universality which it does not possess. When this error had been overcome, it became possible to obtain an insight into the spontaneous manifestations of sexuality of children. . . . Nevertheless, we need not reject everything written in the text above. Seduction retains a certain aetiological importance, and even today I think some of these psychological comments are to the point.[26]

Freud no longer believes in the theory of seduction, and yet it "retains a certain aetiological importance" all through his career. Either seduction is the cause of hysteria or it is not. One cannot attribute a "certain importance" to it without explaining oneself further. That is, however, what Freud will do from 1897 on. If we regarded Freud only as a person like anyone else, who speaks only for himself, this compromise would not bother us; but because he poses as a scientist, as a man who knows all about the others, we can no longer content ourselves with an amiable tolerance to these particular contradictions; we must be more rigorous.

It is in this state of mind—half content, half ill at ease—that Freud urgently asks to see Fliess in this same *Letter 69:*

> If during this slack period I slip into the North-West station on Saturday night I can be with you by Sunday midday and travel back the next night. Can you make the day free for an idyll for two, interrupted by one for three and three-and-a-half?

An idyll for two: Freud and Fliess; an idyll for three, Freud, Fliess, and his wife Ida, the half being the child she is expecting. Again the familiar numbers two and three appear. Fliess apparently no longer bears Jakob's fault, since there is no longer a father's fault to be borne. Freud, who cancelled a meeting with Fliess two months before, can now see him without risk.

> To go on with my letter. I vary Hamlet's remark about "To be in readiness"—cheerfullness is all. I might be feeling very unhappy. The hope of eternal fame was so beautiful, and so was that of certain wealth. . . . All that depended on whether hysteria succeeded or not. Now I can be quiet and modest again . . . and one of the stories from

my collection [of Jewish anecdotes] occurs to me: "Rebecca, you can take off your wedding-gown, you're not a bride any longer!"[27]

The passage in *Hamlet* that Freud approximates, and that actually reads "The readiness is all," appears just before the duel with Laertes, in which Hamlet—and many others—will die; in his presentiment of what is about to happen he declares himself in readiness for death.

What does Freud have left now? He himself says the theory of dreams and psychology; he even speaks of his metapsychology, his fiction of the psychical apparatus that in "Analysis Terminable and Interminable" (1937) he will call "the witch." Only one path remains to him: the appeal to sorcery, to myth. The access to facts, direct access to the facts of his own history, is impossible for him. Sorcery, myth, dreams, and jokes are all indirect paths for the return of the repressed.

Letter 70:
"In my case my father played no active role.... My primary originator was an ugly ... woman who told me a great deal about God and hell."

It is now October 3, 1897; Freud returns from Berlin where he met with Fliess.

> For the last four days my self-analysis, which I regarded as indispensable for clearing up the whole problem, has been making progress in dreams and yielding the most valuable conclusions and evidence. At certain points I have the impression of having come to the end, and so far· I have always known where the next night of dreams would continue. To describe it in writing is more difficult than anything else, and besides it is far too extensive. I can only say that in my case my father played no active role, though I certainly projected on to him an analogy from myself; that my "primary originator" [of neurosis] was an ugly, elderly but clever woman who told me a great deal about God and hell, and gave me a high opinion of my own capacities.[28]

The letter continues with the accounts of the mother seen nude on the train, the dead brother, the nephew with whom he cruelly mistreated the young niece, his fear of journeys, and, once again, his gratitude to the old woman for giving him the means to live and to survive.

Let us stop for a moment at this first part of the letter. Freud's first assertion is, "in my case [the] father played no active role." Our first reaction is laughter; besides all we have deciphered, Freud himself said the contrary a year before (November 2, 1896): "he means a great deal in my life." The present phrase is therefore clearly a negation, that is, an explicit *méconnaissance* of the truth. But one word is unaccounted for, the word *active*. Freud writes, "no active role," which could mean, "my father played a role but not, in my case, an active one." Contrary to what happens in hysteria, Freud's father would have done nothing of which his son Sigmund could have directly been the victim.

The assertion about his "primary originator" of neurosis can be read in two ways: she is actually the victim of the father's active role, perhaps representing Rebecca, if she has in fact also been dismissed (take off your gown, Monika), and all memory of her is buried under a lie—a scandal for the young Freud. Or, by giving young Sigmund the ideas of good and evil, of God and hell, she also gives him the law before which one or both of his parents can stand accused—scandal for the young Freud.

In this way Freud would be right. His father would not have played an active role *toward him,* and little Sigmund would not have been the object of seduction; but he would be the witness of what his father had done: causing a woman's disappearance. The Nannie's disappearance would be a figuration of Rebecca's disappearance.

The first and second propositions of this letter are not to be read separately, but, like all of Freud's double examples, they must be read together as bilingual texts. The origin of Freud's neurosis should be reread thus: It is not my father's relation to me, but my father's relation to a woman who has been dismissed, or has vanished.

The letter continues with an account of the dream where the nurse-maid is his professor of sexuality—the small animal's skull, the reddish water, the ten Kreuzers—all of which we have already studied.

Letter 71:
"I asked my mother what she remembered of the nurse. . . . She turned out to be a thief. . . . The gripping power of Oedipus the King *. . . becomes intelligible."*

This third letter, which resulted from an inner crisis that Freud says he had suffered for three days, begins with some clarifications from Freud's mother. We have already considered this part of the letter. It is his mother's portrait of the Nannie as a thief. Freud ends by saying, "I was so far from being aware that the old woman was a thief that my inter-pretation went astray." He also makes inquiries about the doctor who had attended them in Freiberg, "because I had a dream full of animosity about him." Freud notices that he associates this doctor with a history professor, and then suddenly understands why: they both had only one eye.

The doctor from his childhood toward whom he feels animosity is Dr. Joseph Pur. Sajner tells us that he was also the mayor of the city.[29] Does Freud, in his dream, now resent the history professor for having recounted the story to him with only one eye opened (to close an eye: to be indulgent about faults), as Freud himself had wished would happen when, a year before, the supreme Judge was to have received his father?

On the other hand, it seems impossible for Freud to dare to think that his mother lies. But if, in spite of everything, he does feel that she is lying, who is going to bear the burden of her lie? Is Dr. Joseph Pur available, like the Nannie, to become the guilty party?

> It might be objected that these coincidences are not conclusive, because I might have heard that the nurse was a thief in later childhood and to all appearances forgotten the fact until it emerged in the dream. I think myself that that must have been the case. But I have another unexceptionable and amusing piece of evidence. If the woman disappeared so suddenly, I said to myself, some impressions of the event must have been left inside me. Where was it now? Then a scene occurred to me which for the last twenty-nine years has been turning up from time to time in my conscious memory without my understanding it.[30]

Psychoanalysts are usually interested in the content of this scene when young Freud cries his heart out because he cannot find his mother and asks his brother Philipp to open a cupboard only to find that, of course, his mother is not there; then his mother appears, "slim and beautiful." The interpretations are equally customary: Freud had heard it said that his Nannie was locked up and he fears the same fate for his mother. Another interpretation has it that Freud fears that his mother is pregnant again (that she has a child in the cupboard).

But faithful to our attention to the margins, we look at a very small detail. Why "twenty-nine years"? Freud, who is now forty-one, is precise about the scene having episodically come to his mind for the past twenty-nine years. He would therefore have been twelve years old at the time. What then is the striking event that could provoke in young Freud the return of this scene, which was incomprehensible at the time, this memory, which had been totally blocked during the preceding ten years? (Recall that Freud was two-and-a-half when the Nannie left.) What could have diminished the efficacy of the repression in the year 1868?

There is no choice. In light of Anzieu's detailed biography of the young Freud,[31] only one fact related by Freud could belong to the period in question.

The Father's Hat

In the associations relating to one of the dreams in which Freud sees himself reaching Rome, (which by day he is prevented from doing), Freud gives us the following narrative:

> At that point I was brought up against the event in my youth whose power was still being shown in all these emotions and dreams.

I may have been ten or twelve years old, when my father began to take me with him on his walks and reveal to me in his talk things in the world we live in. Thus it was, on one such occasion, that he told me a story to show me how much better things were now than they had been in his days. "When I was a young man," he said, "I went for a walk one Saturday in the streets of your birthplace; I was well dressed, and had a new fur cap on my head. A Christian came up to me and with a single blow knocked off my cap into the mud and shouted: 'Jew! get off the pavement!'" "And what did you do?" I asked. "I went into the roadway and picked up my cap," was his quiet reply. This struck me as unheroic conduct on the part of the big, strong man who was holding the little boy by the hand. I contrasted this situation with another which fitted my feelings better: the scene in which Hannibal's father, Hamilcar Barca, made his boy swear before the household altar to take vengeance on the Romans.[32]

Jones tells us that after this incident, "his father never regained the place he had held in his esteem."[33] Let us return to our mystery of the scene that rises again to consciousness. If Freud could remember it only since the event we have just cited, then his father had to fall in his esteem in order for him to gain access to that first scene. Would the feeling of deception regarding his father which he experiences here recall another such scene? Can we deduce from it a first scene (the Nannie's disappearance) that would also concern a fault of the father, if in fact with this admission of another fault—without, however, fully recognizing it—the first scene reemerges? This would entirely conform, at least in the mechanism put into operation, with what Freud himself has described as deferred action [*Nachträglichkeit; l'après-coup*].

Oedipus

We at last reach Freud's "discovery" of Oedipus as he continues his letter to Fliess after having reported the cupboard memory. He says he has gotten "much further, but have not yet reached a real resting-place." Many things remain incomplete:

So far I have found nothing completely new, but all the complications to which by now I am used. It is no easy matter. Being entirely honest with oneself is a good exercise. Only one idea of general value has occurred to me. I have found love of the mother and jealousy of the father in my own case too, and now believe it to be a general phenomenon of early childhood. . . . If that is the case, the gripping power of *Oedipus Rex*, in spite of all the rational objections to the inexorable fate that the story presupposes, becomes intelligible. . . . The Greek myth seizes on a compulsion which everyone recognizes because he has felt traces of it in himself. Every member of the

audience was once a budding Oedipus in his phantasy, and this
dream-fulfillment played out in reality causes everyone to recoil in
horror, with the full measure of repression which separates his infantile from his present state.[34]

This is Freud's first explicit reference to the Oedipus complex. In our
phantasies everyone of us is Oedipus. There is nothing from reality
here; no event is at the bottom of all this. With the exception of cases
concerning servants, where reality plays a role, there remains no basis
other than the dream emotions of Sigmund Freud. His mother told
him—and did he not go to her simply to hear it repeated—that the nursemaid was a thief. Everything finally comes from the subject himself and
from his desires. Besides the all too familiar humiliation of a Jewish
father, who is shamefully treated by a Christian, there is no trace of a
fault. From that episode, however, there does remain a trace. The revengeful son will become someone, will go to Rome—while again and
again he puts the father's hat over the mushroom called *Herr*, Sir, like
Herr Jakob Freud.

That is the end of seduction, of the real fault.

And yet . . .

In exactly the same way that the name of Rebecca came to Freud's
mind when he had just abandoned the idea of the father's real fault, the
name of Hamlet appears after he has discovered Oedipus. It is not that
Freud fails to interpret it in a way consistent with his new theory. We are
going to emphasize three words from his remarks on Shakespeare in this
letter:

> I am not thinking of Shakespeare's conscious intentions, but sup-
> posing rather that he was impelled to write it by *a real event* because
> his own unconscious understood that of his hero.

There is nothing then to prevent us any longer from saying that *a real
event* in Freud's life—and not only an incestuous desire—enables him to
understand Oedipus's unconscious and the entire question of the transmission of faults of which Oedipus is the plaything; this real event impels
him to construct the myth, the scientific parable that is the theory of
psychoanalysis. Between the symbol and the *diabolē* 'false evidence' is the
parable (*parabolē* = *para* 'beside' + *ballō* 'to throw').

CONCLUSION

Foul deeds will rise,
Though all the earth o'erwhelm them, to men's eyes.

Shakespeare, *Hamlet*, 1.2.257-58

Take no part in the barren deeds of darkness, but show them up for what
they are. The things they do in secret it would be shameful even to mention.
But everything, when once the light has shown it up, is illumined, and
everything thus illumined is all light.

Paul, *Letter to the Ephesians,* 5:11-13

Our inquiry now draws to a close, even though there are still many
elements to add; the reader who is acquainted with psychoanalysis will
have certainly noted them in passing. We have presented what seemed to
us necessary to mark the way; we chose a certain rhythm in proceeding,
which would not have been possible to maintain if we had wanted to be
encyclopedic. Although the reader must be the judge, we believe that the
new synthesis that we are attempting requires an almost simultaneous
presentation of all its elements.

At the origin of his illness was the governess' unrecognized fault;
Freud saw it and then buried it. If his method, which was developed
through so much work and with so much genius, leads somewhere other
than to his theory, then we should see some effect of that in the field of
psychoanalysis today. We should be able to identify the attempts, fruitful
or not, to pass beyond this theoretical barrier of the Oedipus complex,
which has been made the unquestionable base of the psychoanalytic
edifice.

Is it by chance that psychosis, a domain in which Freud did no
clinical work, now attracts so many psychoanalysts? Is it by chance that

the psychoanalysis of children, a domain in which Freud did practically no work, enjoys the success that we now see?

Is it by chance that the theoretical discourse of psychoanalysis progresses, for the moment, in an ever more hermetic fashion, like a censured discussion that twists and turns past obstacles thanks to its code of habitual artifice? This has been the case to such an extent that a snobbishness concerning the difficult text has been able to develop.

Is it by chance that psychoanalytic societies always maintain a deep silence about suicides, and sometimes even about less tragic deaths, that have taken place within their own ranks? It reaches the point where we might say that these societies do not symbolize death. The silence on this subject has already stirred up questions from outside as well as inside psychoanalysis. One now openly speaks of the suicides in Freud's entourage, in particular, that of Victor Tausk.[1] But it still requires real courage, within certain psychoanalytic milieus, simply to mention the names of the "victims" about whom rumors circulate each year.

Madmen and children: the two free domains where psychoanalytic method has been able to be utilized without the burden of a totalizing, if not totalitarian, theory. What practitioners-researchers have found in these two specific fields has the capacity to subvert Freudian theory and to lead it back to Freud's first intuitions. These analysts have dared to say that, regarding those who have been absolutely dominated — and who is not something of a madman or a child? — a real fault has been committed either against or in front of the patients, and that they had been subjected to traumatizing situations. In the institutions designed for them, it is hoped that the victims will find a place to get out of their systems what they had actually suffered. In order to help them, practitioners would accept momentarily to be taken for the former tyrants, doing their best not to use their power to abuse them as had the actual tyrants, and thus creating a situation which is suitable for an illumination of the past and for a recovery of confidence in human relations.

Do Laing, Neil, Bettelheim, and Mannoni, to mention only the most well known names, place their trust in Freud's second theory or in his first theory, understood in its most complete sense? Do those who create institutions for the insane, for children or for insane children, believe that a phantasm is at the origin of the (false) memory, or rather that the (true) memory manifests itself through phantasms? Do they think that the traumatic scenes and situations that reappear in the course of a cure, or in pedagogic relations, are invented by the patient or the student as a result of repressed desires? Or is it rather that the perverse conduct of an adult is actually at the origin of the problems and the suffering of the madman or the child whom they have taken under treatment?

What sort of things do they organize in their institutions? Sessions in which the upheaval of unconscious sexual desires is possible? Or a life style such that the patient can reestablish, little by little, the confidence with which he expresses to others his corporeal integrity and his freedom of movement and thought? What have these founders created if not a living space where their patients and students will be able to create one basic experience: that in which their rights and their person are respected, even if, as a result of what they went through earlier, they themselves are not yet prepared to respect a person's otherness.

We realize that those who have created institutions and whose books are widely known have gone beyond the official doctrine. Where life and theory are at variance, they have chosen to listen to life, and more particularly, to the wounded life. What they have thereby learned and what they repeat to us returns repeatedly not only to the question of desire but above all to the question of the misfortune and pain visited upon those who are weakest in human society. What the wounded life tells them resembles what it also said to Sigmund Freud in 1896.

Those who have been sexually violated — by seduction — have tried to express — through hysteria, through the negation of sexuality — what they underwent. How would those whose thought and discourse have been violated tell what has been done to them if not through a condition where one no longer has either thought or speech? How would they try to escape if not by making use of a language that could not be understood, but which could also not be taken away from them? And those who, though not killed, had their lives taken from them, how could they fail to see in suicide the only act through which they could, paradoxically, recapture their lives?

Freud at first recognized only sexual violation. Was this not his way of manifesting what he had been deprived of: the knowledge of a sexual fault? How could he find it again?

How can we still ignore that not only sexuality and the interdiction against incest are involved at all levels of mental disorder, but the entire person and every law that affects him?

The distinction between neurosis as a disorder of sexual origin and psychosis as a pregenital disorder certainly indicates something real to us. Is that reality only in the reference to sexuality, or rather in the distinction between what affects a part and what affects a whole — between an attribute of the subject, no matter how important it is, and his life itself?

We have stated that a number of psychoanalysts, whose purpose is above all to help their patients to get out of the impasse in which they find themselves, have for a long time put the theory back in the place from which it should never have left: that of a formulation that can always be revised, even if revisions are late in coming. The analysts' clinical practice is perhaps more closely allied to Freud's first discovery than to the monument he later constructed. They have often initially wanted to apply the theory strictly; then, faced with the suffering that it aroused in their patients, they softened their attitude. It nonetheless remains difficult for an analyst to share with his colleagues those things in his experience that disagree with the reigning theory, the theory around which they are all gathered. Even when theory is not used as a weapon of intellectual terrorism, analysts have difficulty in both clarifying and elaborating the changes in their way of listening because they regard them more or less as failings or transgressions on their own part. It seems to us that their attitude oscillates between two poles: either they accept the theory, reject what they experience, and become embittered workers who haunt psychoanalytic societies, endlessly seeking from a master or a group something that they would be certain not to understand; or they accept what they experience, reject the theory, grow distant from professional groups, and bear in difficult solitude the burden of their calling.

Although our inquiry is over, we still have not quite finished our task; some questions, which were posed at the beginning, await us. They concern Freud, consciousness, and clinical practice. Moreover, a new question has been added on the way, one we did not expect; it consists of a word that until now scarcely belonged to the psychoanalytic world: the word is *fault.*

FREUD: THE ANALYZABLE TEXTS

What is our position now in relation to Freud's work? Would we no longer have any use for it? Quite to the contrary. It begins, or rather, it begins again to reveal to us more riches than we had ever suspected. Yet it does so only on the condition that it be reread not only as a course on the interpretation of the unconscious but as a work that must itself be interpreted.[2]

The texts we have thus far explicitly considered constitute only a small part of Freud's work. The research that remains to be done is immense: clinical texts, theoretical and technical texts, applications of psychoanalysis in diverse fields, Freud's correspondence. All these pages can now be reread in a new optic. We particularly have in mind Freud's five famous case histories. A link between what parents, governesses, and educators did and then concealed, and what the children suffered from, can be established by being attentive to those occasions when Freud, in spite of his convictions, has noted for us enough facts concerning these adults. Freud is on friendly terms with the parents of Dora and little Hans. The facts in these cases are therefore not too defective.

Regarding the Ratman, we now have at our disposal, in a bilingual, French-German edition, the notes that Freud took after the sessions. These are the only clinical notes by Freud to have escaped destruction. Ratman tells Freud—who is not particularly attentive—that his problems began when he learned, through an allusion by his uncle, that his father had deceived his mother. The familiar German expression that signifies adultery (and that corresponds to the French *donner des coups de canif au contrat* 'to be unfaithful to the marriage contract') can literally be translated as "to jump aside" [*Seitensprünge machen*].[3] The words signifying the father's fault extend to the son's symptoms, and even to his preparation for his examinations where he skips "pages" [*Seiten*] (which also means "sides" in German). And the monetary debts that his father neglected to pay are absurdly, repetitively reimbursed by the son.

Although the Ratman case offers us at first glance few facts in the direction of the fault, the case of President Schreber has already been the object of a particularly satisfying study. It is not a question of a cure but of Freud's analysis of a text: the *Memoirs* of a magistrate who was hospitalized for many years as a paranoiac. Freud analyzed this text with customary finesse; but he failed to give any attention to the writings of Schreber's father, a doctor who was well known as the author of several books on "pedagogy." Morton Schatzman, an American psychiatrist, was greatly astonished by that fact: "Freud, an avid reader, neglects—as do his followers—books on child-rearing by a man whose son's childhood experiences Freud is trying to derive."[4] The effects of the father's "pedagogy" can already be read in his children: the eldest son committed suicide, the second son went mad. His "educational methods" cannot be contemplated without a feeling of profound horror, so much do they call to mind a prison for children. Moreover, one can recognize in their author a precursor of Nazism. The educational practices sanctioned by the father can be placed in relation, point for point, with the supposedly delirious ideas of his psychotic son. One can reread the word "father" everywhere that the miserable patient, in the grips of every variety of mental persecution, dared to write only the word "God." Morton Schatzman demonstrates this definitively. He also vigorously denounces Freud's blindness regarding the persecution administered by fathers, be it in mythology (Laius) or in his clinical practice. We must admit that this book did not at first win our interest, so true is it that we avoid being confronted with new information that we could not relate to what we already know—or think we know—and that we are reluctant to share its subversion with anyone else.

Many other of Freud's texts lend themselves to a new reading. We want to take still another example, this time in the domain of art: the study that Freud devoted to a novella that Jung made known to him—Jensen's *Gradiva.* This is what Jones has to say about it:

> The story is of a young archaeologist who falls in love with a bas-relief of a Grecian girl who has a particularly striking gait. His phantasies about her assume a delusional form and he becomes convinced that she perished in the eruption that overwhelmed Pompeii in 79 A.D. He is drawn there and finds the girl, who may be a spirit or a living maiden. She recognizes his mental state and successfully undertakes to cure him, with the inevitable happy result. She then turns out to be a childhood playmate whom the youth had completely forgotten, but who still lived in the same town as himself.[5]

Of this novella Freud makes an analysis of rare elegance: the repressed childhood returns under the form of a very distant and buried past (the Pompeii of the archaeologist). The statue is fascinating only by virtue of its resemblance to a living and forgotten person. In offering to his master a story of a living statue and a woman who disappeared, how close did Jung come to exposing Freud's secrets? This statue has an interesting role in the history of psychoanalysis. Jones explains:

> The relief with which the hero of the story fell in love may be seen in the Vatican Museum, where Freud discovered it that September [1907]. After Freud published his book it became fashionable among analysts to have a copy of the relief on their walls. Freud had one himself in his consulting room.[6]

What Jones says is not quite exact; the reproduction in Freud's office depicts only a third of the bas-relief, the only intact part: a woman, in profile, gracefully walking. In the Vatican Museum the bas-relief includes, by a strange coincidence, three women: on the left is the *Gradiva,* intact; the second is without head or feet; and of the third one sees only the hand [see frontispiece].[7]

Freud's Office

With this bas-relief of three women we again pass from Freud's work to his life. Where in his office did he place this reproduction? From the photographs that were taken in Freud's house—office and residence—in 1938, just before his departure for England, we know that the *Gradiva* was placed on the wall against which rested the famous couch; the bas-relief is in fact at the foot of the couch.[8] Near it was a painting of Oedipus before the Sphinx, and a photograph, which touched the bas-relief: a portrait of Freud's admired friend, Fleischl, who fell seriously ill and whose end Freud involuntarily hastened by giving him cocaine as a harmless substitute—so he believed—for the morphine to which he was addicted.

The friend whose death he caused, the statue of a woman, the only one intact from a group of three of which the two others are not represented, Oedipus before the enigma—this is what we find at the foot of the couch. What then is directly above the couch? A large photograph of the four colossal statues of Rameses II from the temple of Abu Simbel. Only one of these statues is destroyed: the second.

Like his life and that of his family, Freud's work has not yet ceased to excite our interest and our surprise. We should learn from the fact that Freud dedicated his mind to science for reasons other than those he himself gave.

A second question returns to us: an ancient, immense, and human question.

CONSCIOUSNESS/CONSCIENCE

Although we have not perhaps noticed it, a curious phenomenon of language has transpired. We are in the habit of distinguishing psychological consciousness and moral conscience.[9] In the course of our inquiry these two forms of consciousness have become increasingly entangled, since the problems of the (psychological) consciousness of one person were found to be linked to the hidden (moral) faults of another.

Must we establish a new theory of consciousness/conscience in order to account for the transmission of unrecognized faults from generation to generation, through perversion, or through the refusal of this transmission which occurs in illness?

Science without Conscience: The Soul's Ruin

Recall that the son of the civil servant who stole public funds treats his hand as if it had been cut off. It seems that no one in a position of authority around this child-patient recognized the fault that he had heard about by accident. He knows, and he is the only one to know that he knows. Then he forgets all that, while unconsciously this knowledge remains and becomes manifest in the symptom. Psychoanalysis has always held that what has become unconscious is not, however, completely unknown, and that the last word of a cure could well be, "I have always known it."

What then is the difference between what the patient consciously knows and what he knows unconsciously? There is no difference if it is not what distinguishes "he knows" from "he knows that he knows." Science without conscience—how does one know what he knows? In the case of the severed hand, the son knows that the father has stolen, but he is alone in his knowledge. The person or persons who alluded to this theft in front of him have neither clearly testified to the fact before him nor clearly acknowledged that he was informed of it. He knows all alone; he knows as if he did not know. He represses the information that he must carry alone; it becomes inaccessible to him, at least insofar as it is information that is very important to him. He finds only that he begins to treat as equally insignificant the law before which his father's act constituted a fault.

When will all that return to consciousness? When he meets someone—the analyst (here, Lacan)—with whom he can speak about it.[10]

Presented in this way, we are somewhat baffled. Is not that to make Freud's unresolved and arduous question (what is consciousness? what makes memories conscious or unconscious?) into something so simple that it cannot possibly be true? If we push on with our reasoning, we conclude that what one knows with the Other is conscious, and what is known without the Other is unconscious. The son knows about his father's theft, but he does not know it *with* his father. This knowledge then assumes the status of the unconscious.

It is often very disagreeable to find oneself confronted with simple things, above all if this simplicity appears as an answer to a problem that one has long pondered. Passing from "that's idiotic" to "why didn't I think of it earlier" takes a long time, sometimes years. Fortunately, "the facts are stubborn." The idea which was first rejected returns from another side. We find that this distinction between conscious and unconscious, based on the presence or absence of the Other, corresponds exactly to the Latin etymology of the word *conscience*. It derives as much from the substantive *conscientia* as from the adjective *conscius* and also from the Greek verb *sunoida*, from which the two Latin words seem to have been formed.[11] The meanings that are given by the most well known dictionaries are:

1. To know with someone—knowledge shared with someone; suggesting a confidant, an accomplice, a witness.
2. To know in oneself—clear knowledge within; with the meaning, in a moral sense, of the idea of good and evil.

According to the dictionary there are then two meanings of *conscience:* knowledge with another and knowledge with oneself. Does this involve two successive stages of mental development? Would the subject become his own witness, this Other with whom he knows? If we are conscious of what we know with another—even if we ourselves are this Other—and if we are unconscious of what we know without the Other, then the prefix *un* of *unconscious* applies, not to the knowledge, but to the relation to the Other; the unconscious is what we know without the Other.[12]

Psychoanalysis says that repression always goes back to childhood; that seems explicable after what we have just said. Is is not during childhood that the Other takes us under his control? Is it not thus that the internal witness is constituted in us?[13] All this seems simple, in fact, too simple. In La Fontaine's words, is the question of conscience/consciousness a mountain whose rumbling is about to bring forth a mouse? But when one poses a real question, can one say in advance what form the answer will take? We cannot disregard our answer because it leads to another question: the unrecognized fault and its relation to the symptom.

Conscience/Consciousness and the Fault

Symbolic, symptom, consciousness/conscience: with the Greek or Latin prefixes, these words convey the meaning of "reunion."

Diabolic, fault (*diaptoma*), unconscious: these words convey the meaning of "separation."

Recall Lacan's clinical example: what the son knew all alone became strange to him. There was no one around him with whom to know that he knows. What does this knowledge concern? It concerns an unrecognized fault, something that his father concealed from him. His father does not want to share his knowledge of the fault with the son. There is therefore a hole, an obscure zone, in the discourse that they share. It concerns the fault of which the father does not wish to speak, which he does not want his son to know. If the son learns of it, it will be through allusion, that is to say, through a discourse without an author: without an author who can either attest to it or to what someone else had heard about it.

The son knows, without a witness. He represses this knowledge and only rediscovers it when a witness (the analyst) shows up in order to recognize not the fact itself, in which he did not participate, but the knowledge that the patient has of it and of which only the hand speaks. The analyst recognizes that the patient knows about his father's fault. Now he too can know that he knows, and his hand can once again be used as a hand and not as the expression of a wordless language.

What one cannot speak to another about is by no means the fault itself. Does not everyone commit faults everyday which do not lead to illness or symptoms? Reproaches, protestations, and cries tell the one at fault that he is in the process of harming the other. Discussion follows, and finally, little by little, the perceived facts and feelings are shared through words—even if they are violent.

There is, however, a situation outside this scheme in which the dominating one wants to hide something in his life; not only does he want the dominated to ignore it, but, even if the dominated could know it, the dominating would refuse to recognize that the other knows; he would probably say, "You're crazy."

What the dominating does not want to recognize, the dominated cannot know. If the dominated does know, he will know alone, losing the witness who is still necessary to hold his knowledge in consciousness. The fault that the witness refuses to recognize will become, within the other, the word that is lost, buried, unconscious. We have seen this in Lacan's patient, in Oedipus, in Freud himself, and in his patients. In this very place of the hidden fault of the dominating-witness the consciousness of the dominated fails. If he wants to hide his fault, the witness fails to testify as he should.

This is only a sketch, a beginning in order to understand the evidence that psychoanalytic treatment confirms everyday: To become conscious—in order to cure—is to rediscover the witness to what we had known alone. It is to share with another the hitherto disrupted knowledge of something hidden. It is to be recognized as knowing.

CLINICAL PRACTICE: THE TRANSFERENCE OF THE FAULT IN THE PSYCHOANALYTIC CURE

Many paths are again opened here, traces of which we have already found in Freud's life. How can we reorient ourselves toward otherness—an otherness better disposed to understand the buried knowledge of a fault? Is it not by transferring it to someone who will be able to recognize it? The analytic session can be rethought in this sense; the analyst no longer listens only for the patient's repressed desires but for forgotten knowledge, which is at first represented through symptoms, then realized in the transference to the analyst. In this way, two Freudian discoveries are articulated which have never been reunited in theory: the traumatic memory and the transference. When Freud discovered the transference, he had, in effect, abandoned the theory according to which the events causing neurosis were real.

If the analyst does not refuse it he can be taken, in the unconscious transference that his patient makes toward him, for the one at fault whom the patient never dared to denounce and of whose fault he is probably even ignorant, at least as a fault. From this place where the patient puts his analyst, (who accepts without really occupying it), it will be possible for the analyst to seek the meaning with his patient. Because he is taken for an other, the author of an unrecognized fault, the analyst enables his patient to rediscover the trace of that lost knowledge.

The Analyst's Fault

It is necessary that the analyst, now imagined as being at fault, not really appear to be guilty in the eyes of the patient; and, if he is seen as guilty, he must recognize it as such. If not, is this not a simple repetition of the past?

How can we hope for progress in analysis if the analyst conducts himself like a tyrannical parent who fails to recognize his patient's autonomy? The possibility of a transference will not arise if the analyst effectively becomes that for which he is imaginatively taken. Even the conditions for the cure—in particular, the patient's ignorance of the analyst's private life—enable the analyst to occupy the place of "symbolic innocence" which the patient needs in order to transfer the fault he unconsciously carries and to become conscious of it.[14] The conditions of the analytic cure should not be altered in the direction of a reinforcement of power.

What does a human being gain if he passes from familial despotism to analytic despotism and can no more disclose and speak the analyst's fault than he had been able to disclose and speak the fault of those people who raised him? What recourse is there if he is incapable of being analyzed without letting definitively fall again upon him the shadow of the faults whose authors he was unable to recognize? Is it really honest to call the patient of such an analysis an *analysant*?[15] In view of the opposition between the activity explicit in *analysant,* and the passivity of *analysé,* is it not a mockery for the analyst to demand an exorbitant fee for a session whose length, which is arbitrarily fixed by the analyst each time, cannot exceed two minutes? And is not his discourse, which is so rare, more like that of an oracle than an interpreter? If the famous "silence of the analyst" becomes systematic, then does not the analyst risk defeating speech instead of listening to it? In this tyranny exercised over him, and to which he is unfortunately already accustomed, the patient, like President Schreber, is robbed twice: first, of his money; second, of his consciousness of the first theft. We prefer to return to the old term *patient* even if it does not explicitly situate the subject in the active role that is properly his; at least it recognizes his state of suffering without adding the derision of what may be a false acknowledgment.

Likewise, the fault that the analyst commits and that the patient involuntarily witnesses renders the progress of the cure impossible if the patient cannot express his knowledge of it to the analyst. Not everything can be interpreted. When someone relates a fact, there is nothing to interpret; every interpretation of a true discourse is an exercise in misapprehension.

Strictly speaking, nothing in psychoanalytic theory permits the analyst to disagree with the patient who regards his own desires as the cause of his misfortune. Whoever is assigned the task of curing such an emissary victim can only repeat what Freud himself did. How, if not intuitively, can we suspect that this self-accusation — even if it has carried over to the unconscious and to desire — is not the last word of an analysis but the screen with which the patient still protects the witness, who is necessary to him, from speaking about his still impossible fault?

These are only the initial reflections on psychoanalytical clinical practice which occur to us after our investigation; a simple marker for the renovation of the psychoanalytic session.

The question whose end we have not yet reached is also for us the newest one: the fault and its condition *sine qua non,* the law.

THE FAULT AND THE LAW

The idea of the fault was indispensable to us from the start of our research, and we have not abandoned it. That hardly puts everything in order for us; we still have reasons to be suspicious about a notion that accounts for so much abuse, so many false accusations (the scapegoat phenomenon), so many excessive constraints. To place the unrecognized fault at the base of illness could constitute a disturbing regression toward a moralization at once stupid and terrifying, the final consequences of which we have known in the course of history. Is that not to leave "scientific" research for accusation, judgment, and punishment?

What is to be done, however, if we have seen that the origin of neurosis is not sexual desire alone nor even sexual trauma alone, but all the faults committed by the very people who present the law to the child, either directly or indirectly — faults that have not been recognized? What is to be done, if the entire Decalogue now presents itself as the theory of illness?[16] The law of Moses would have an unanticipated continuation (which again agrees with what is written in Genesis): if someone oppresses his fellow man in his physical, psychic, or sexual life, in his speech or his well-being, and that someone does not recognize his act, then those for whom he is the witness will suffer; their bodies will cry out what their mouths cannot say; they will lose control of their acts even to violence — and this will continue until the truth is made known.[17]

Several times Freud cites this phrase from Goethe's *Mephistopheles:*

Das Beste was Du wissen kannst
Darfst Du den Buben doch nicht sagen

[The best that you know
You must not tell to boys][18]

It is true that he does not have the right to tell us the best of what he knows. But even though he warned us about it, did he not let it be known, in spite of himself?

The Interpretation of Dreams, his masterpiece, which should prove "the fundamental idea of psychosexuality dominating every manifestation of mental life," only succeeds in hiding precisely this idea.[19] We have also seen that many of his dreams atone for offenses and humiliations that he underwent, or try to resolve enigmas or to protect himself or someone close to him from divine or social judgment. In doing so, they allude to every kind of fault. Freud explains a strange paradox to us in this paragraph, where his failure to address certain problems is particularly surprising:

> There are special reasons, which may not be what my readers expect, why I have not given any exhaustive treatment to the part played in dreams by the world of sexual ideas and why I have avoided analyzing dreams of obviously sexual content. Nothing could be further from my own views or from the theoretical opinions which I hold in neuropathology than to regard sexual life as a *pudendum* [i.e., something shameful], with which neither a physician nor a scientific research worker has any concern. . . . What governed my decision was simply my seeing that an explanation of sexual dreams would involve me deeply in the still unsolved problems of perversion and bisexuality; and I accordingly reserved [*sparte*] this material for another occasion.[20]

How can we explain that he reserves, that he "lays by" [the German *sparen* means "to save" or "to be thrifty"] precisely what was supposed to form the base of his edifice? Is it because he chose to present to us what was most acceptable? Or is it the silent triumph of the truth?

Is sexual desire really so scandalous? Bourgeois society became well accustomed to this "revolution." Was it really so costly to grant to the domain of sexuality its freedom and its place in the limelight? If one cannot secretly steal, cheat, deceive, exploit, and lie without making one's children bearers of the suffering of these misapprehended faults (unless the children can retransmit them to those who are yet weaker), then there is something that appears to us even more onerous and unacceptable.

A Thousand and Three Questions

There is an immense field open to us if we want to continue on this path. What is the relation between the nature of the hidden fault and the nature of the symptom which represents it? What is the difference in the symptoms of a patient who does not want to recognize a fault and one before whom or upon whom a fault was committed? How can we reconsider the question of "mental structure" and that of whether or not one "chooses to be neurotic"? And what about the mother's fault? We have rarely encountered it except as a lie to cover the father. Without independence or authority can one really commit a fault? Can one who does not transmit the law become the object of scandal? The example Marie Cardinal has discussed clearly reveals that a mother who has become the head of the household can also become, through her fault (in this case, abortion, which is mentioned sarcastically but not recognized as a fault against the child), the generator of symptoms that, in her daughter, tell of the fault (in this case, her daughter's uterine hemorrhage).[21]

And what of psychosis? Can the fault directly committed affect the child's life without any allusion having ever been made to indicate it? Schatzman insists on an important point in this regard: in the case of President Schreber, not only did the father subject his children to persecution, but, in addition, his system of repression was such that the victims had no possibility of noticing it. They were, as we said earlier, doubly robbed: of their autonomy and of their perception of that first theft. We are not used to saying that a father or a mother appropriates desires, sensations, sexuality, and speech from his or her child. It is difficult to pose the problem in these terms because the Decalogue regards the child as being quite a separate being, as being quite apart from his parents.

If this is the parent's conduct, however, then what has the adult himself been unjustly made to bear? Who had alienated him that he now alienates his child? Who still possesses him? Whose faults does he carry? Before this chain of faults and misapprehension which passes from generation to generation, is it possible, just, or useful to believe that one can discover the person who was originally responsible?

The enunciation of the fault is radically different from the denunciation of the one responsible; the effects of the one and the other are totally opposed. Making an accusation, a denunciation, concerns a human being; it identifies him with his fault and leads him to a judgment separated from his proper context. The enunciation concerns the act itself; it reveals the secret that displaces the guilty one from his relational position, and leads him, through recognition, to be reunited with what is properly his own through links that are again symbolizable.

The Displaced Commandment

If the fault of the father or mother is not enunciated by the son or daughter, what becomes of it? Besides repression and symptoms, there is some strange process that we do not yet comprehend: the fault seems to be transferred onto some supreme authority—*whether or not the subject believes in it.* God then becomes the accused. This was as apparent for Freud as it was for President Schreber and for Lacan's patient. In the last case the patient's total disinterest in religious questions enabled Lacan to find the source of the problem.

Are we not witnesses to a curious displacement of the commandments? The Fourth Commandment, "Honor your father and your mother," now appears in first place, precisely in God's place. Where it is written, "You will have no other gods before me," it seems that a note has been added: me, your father. Once the father has attained the place of God, is it not logical that God goes to the place of the father, and that the child, seeking to identify the father as the author of the fault, makes the one who now occupies his place bear it, be it God, Moses, or anyone who has drawn up the supreme law? The father remains idolatrized as the one who cannot be transgressed. His faults, which the child nonetheless perceives, are attributed to the one who will be his judge as long as he has not been lowered to the position of the guilty one.

From the beginning of his work, Freud was aware of the weight that this commandment about parents places upon the human mind, but he did not denounce its displacement to the first line of the law.

An Absurd Dream

Freud devotes a section of *The Interpretation of Dreams* to absurd dreams; he wants to prove that, in fact, they are not at all absurd. These dreams concern the dead father, and Freud's interpretations of them are particularly interesting to us because he uses ingenious methods to avoid posing the question of the father's fault—although to us it is readable indeed. This is certainly the case in the dream in which Freud asks his dead father what happened in 1851; Freud dreams that he has just received a bill from his birthplace for hospital fees and has learned that his father had, before his birth, gotten drunk and been locked up.

> *"So you used to drink as well?" I asked; "did you get married soon after that?" I calculated that, of course, I was born in 1856, which seemed to be the year which immediately followed the year in question.*

Freud then goes on to interpret this dream:

Whereas normally a dream deals with rebellion against someone else, behind whom the dreamer's father is concealed, the opposite was true here. My father was made into a man of straw, in order to screen someone else; and the dream was allowed to handle in this undisguised way a figure who was as a rule treated as sacred, because at the same time I knew with certainty that it was not he who was really meant.[22]

We know now how the manifest text of this dream is related to Jakob's life and to what happened between 1851 and 1856 concerning a marriage. The suppression of these five years in the dream is not at all absurd; without a doubt they correspond to the silence surrounding Rebecca Freud. Freud's interpretation—I know with certainty that it does not concern my father—seems to us like a tricky game of heads and tails: tails I win, heads you lose.

THE PERVERSION OF THE LAW

The authority wielded by a father provokes criticism from his children at an early age, and the severity of the demands he makes upon them leads them, for their own relief, to keep their eyes open to any weakness of their father's; but the filial piety called up in our minds by the figure of the father, particularly after his death tightens the censorship which prohibits any such criticism from being consciously expressed.[23]

This sentence immediately precedes the dream of "1851-56," which, along with Freud's interpretation, is its involuntary but magisterial demonstration.

Earlier in the same book, Freud writes:

We must distinguish between what the cultural standards of filial piety demand of this relation and what everyday observation shows it in fact to be. . . .

Let us consider first the relation between father and son. The sanctity which we attribute to the rules laid down in the Decalogue has, I think, blunted our powers of perceiving the real facts. We seem scarcely to venture to observe that the majority of mankind disobey the Fourth Commandment. Alike in the lowest and in the highest strata of human society filial piety is wont to give way to other interests. The obscure information which is brought to us by mythology and legend from the primeval ages of human society gives an unpleasing picture of the father's despotic power and of the ruthlessness with which he made use of it. Kronos devoured his children just as the wild boar devours the sow's litter; while Zeus emasculated his father and made himself ruler in his place.[24]

Freud, who wants to demonstrate the lack of filial piety, here succumbs without knowing it to his own excessive piety. He commits an error that will be brought to his attention and that he will recognize in his next book, in the chapter where he studies precisely the three errors he committed in his book on dreams. The third of these errors involves Kronos:

> I state that Zeus emasculated his father Kronos and dethroned him. I was, however, erroneously carrying this atrocity a generation forward; according to Greek mythology it was Kronos who committed it on his father Uranus.[25]

Then Freud tries to understand why he erred; he writes that all three "errors are derivations of repressed thoughts connected with my dead father,"[26] and that the third is specifically related to some advice given him by his eldest half-brother, advice that "lingered long" in Freud's memory.

> "One thing," he had said to me, "that you must not forget is that as far as the conduct of your life is concerned you really belong not to the second but to the third generation in relation to your father."

We understand that this was disturbing advice for the young Freud. The passage continues:

> Our father had married again in later life and was therefore much older than his children by his second marriage. I made the error already described [i.e., about Kronos and Zeus] at the exact point in the book at which I was discussing filial piety.[27]

While the English translation faithfully reproduces the German text, the French translation contains yet another interesting error. Granoff has already revealed that Jankelevitch, the translator, mistakenly states that Freud's father married again for the "third" time.[28] In making this error, Jankelevitch, curiously enough, seems to have understood what Freud's half-brother perhaps wanted Freud to understand without actually being able to say it.

Returning again to the commandment concerning parents and to the delusion it arouses when put in the place of the first, we note this observation by Lacan: "I maintain that the real father is excluded from analysis, and that Noah's cloak is most effective when the father is imaginary."[29] Granoff comments on Lacan's observation: "That he wants to get rid of the father there is no doubt. That he fails to do it is more to the point. That one can do it is another matter altogether. That in fact is the Freudian project itself!"[30]

The impossibility of speaking of the father's fault is indeed at the heart of the Freudian enterprise. While his method enables us to rediscover the buried traces of the fault within each of us, Freud's theory seeks to establish that only the desire of each one of us alone is at the origin of mental disorder.

The impossibility of uttering the fault, however, is not without effect. The father, falsely innocent, is misapprehended [*méconnu*]. The child, falsely guilty—at least concerning the father's fault—is no less misapprehended. Finally, the will to conceal has nothing to do with love; it does not lead to either love or tranquility. The displaced, unacknowledged fault will perform its work of separation across generations, separation from others and from oneself. "Neither god nor brothers" are its work. In Freud's words, "Not all men are worthy of love."[31] He realizes that absolute submission to educators makes it impossible for human life to develop fully, but his realization is itself inscribed in divine law:

> So long as a person's early years are influenced not only by a sexual inhibition of thought but also by a religious inhibition and by a loyal inhibition derived from this, we cannot really tell what in fact he is like.[32]

One will not, in effect, be able to know what the person is really like if he has been subjected, body and soul, to another, if he has denied the consciousness that he could have had of the fault. But is an end to this tyranny to be sought, as Freud believed, through an "education freed from the burden of religious doctrines"?[33] We have seen its effects, which Freud could not yet have seen, and we can no longer share his "great expectations" on this point.

Will we know what a person is if, in the place of the mysterious being of which the First Commandment of the Decalogue speaks, we substitute an existing being (in the primary meaning of the word),[34] be it a person, a group, a party, or a church?

Will we know what a person is if we pervert the law, which at once distinguishes him from and unites him to otherness, by displacing its articles, by declaring that we know who occupies the first line? The perversion of the law has two faces: they are both expressions of *certitude*, positive or negative, concerning the *existence* of God.

If the First Commandment ceases to be a mystery, a question, a sacred place that no mortal can occupy, then who or what will be engulfed there? Which law—familial, political, or religious—will then attempt to subjugate man? It must be made clear that this first place, once it is emptied of the mystery occupying it, is never left empty again.

"Modern barbarism began when the intellectual pretended to have done with God—one will think what one wishes of that, but it is a *fact*," writes Michel Le Bris.[35] Religion has finished with God when, like the sciences, it pretends to possess him, making itself an idol; like parents or governesses who have done with God when they usurp his place or pretend that they alone are the guides to the truth. Even for believers, the eternal is not certitude, but rather the being that they can reach only through faith. Proof that for them, God does not exist; he is.

Transmitted secretly and by means of the secret itself, the fault nonetheless emerges in our lives. If perversion reproduces it, illness, on the contrary, attempts both to disclose it and to prevent its transmission. Art represents the fault and, through beauty—the refuge of truth—denounces it through the metamorphoses of its fictions.

Science has for too long helped to conceal the fault. It can be used instead to detect the fault when it is buried in human beings and can no longer be spoken except through the body.

Now, after the Freudian revolution, we pose the same question that Nicolevski and Bukharin posed fifteen years after the Russian Revolution: "Have we reached the point where the commandments of Moses must be rediscovered as a new truth?"[36]

If, in order to keep our idols in place, we pervert the law, we would also gradually destroy our human *conscience*. The fault, the most terrible fault, is, however, only a paltry thing that disappears beneath one's gaze. When recognized, it disappears like a shadow when light appears. The consciousness of human beings, which lives within and between them, through recognition and through symbols, emerges strengthened:

> But everything, when once the light has shown it up, is illumined,
> and everything thus illumined is all light.

NOTES

TRANSLATOR'S INTRODUCTION

1. Gilles Deleuze and Felix Guattari, *Anti-Oedipus: Capitalism and Schizophrenia,* trans. Robert Hurley, Mark Seem, and Helen R. Lane (New York: Viking, 1977), p. 55.

2. Sigmund Freud, *The Origins of Psychoanalysis: Letters to Wilhelm Fliess,* ed. Marie Bonaparte, Anna Freud, and Ernst Kris; trans. Eric Mosbacher and James Strachey (New York: Basic Books, 1977), p. 215 (*Aus den Anfängen der Psychoanalyse: Briefe an Wilhelm Fliess* [Frankfort: S. Fischer, 1975], p. 186).

3. Ernest Jones, *The Life and Work of Sigmund Freud,* 3 vols. (New York: Basic Books, 1953-57), 1:261-67.

4. *The Origins of Psychoanalysis,* p. 219 (*Aus den Anfängen der Psychoanalyse,* p. 189).

5. *The Origins of Psychoanalysis,* p. 218 (*Aus den Anfängen der Psychoanalyse,* p. 188).

6. Freud failed in his efforts to persuade his friend and student, Marie Bonaparte, to return to him the Fliess letters, which she had acquired in December 1936. In a letter to her on January 3, 1937, he wrote, "I don't want any of them to become known to so-called posterity." *The Origins of Psychoanalysis* includes only 168 of the available 284 letters and drafts, and most of the letters that are included have been censored. Following a stipulation first suggested by Bonaparte in response to Freud's consternation, the complete correspondence will not be published until the year 2018, eighty years after Freud's death. As Bonaparte wrote to Freud on January 7, 1937, "Who could be hurt then, even among your own family, by what they contain?" References to the Freud-Bonaparte exchange are from Max Schur, *Freud: Living and Dying* (New York: International Universities Press, 1972), pp. 487-88.

7. Josef Sajner, "Sigmund Freuds Beziehungen zu seinem Geburtsort Freiberg (Pribor) und zu Mähren," *Clio Medica* 3 (1968): 167-80 (Oxford and New York: Pergamon Press). This article has been translated into French by Marie-Josée Amrhein-Locquet as "Les rapports de Sigmund Freud avec sa ville natale Freiberg (Pribor) at avec la Moravie," *Lettres de l'Ecole Freudienne de Paris* 26 (March 1979): 9-23. Renée Gicklhorn, "The Freiberg Period of the Freud Family," *Journal of the History of Medicine* 24 (January 1969), pp. 37-43.

8. Schur, *Freud: Living and Dying,* p. 191.

9. Robert Graves and Raphael Patai give an account of this myth in their *Hebrew Myths: The Book of Genesis* (Garden City, N.Y.: Doubleday, 1964):

> Isaac obeyed and, finding Rebecca's maidenhead broken, sternly asked how this had come about. She answered: "My lord, I was frightened by your appearance [Rebecca had seen Isaac on his way back from Paradise, walking on his hands, as the dead do], and fell to the ground, where the stump of a bush

173

pierced my thighs." "No, but Eliezer [the servant] has defiled you," cried Isaac. Rebecca, swearing by the living-God that no man had touched her, showed him the stump still wet with her virginal blood; and he believed at last (p. 185).

10. *The Origins of Psychoanalysis,* p. 216 (*Aus den Anfängen der Psychoanalyse,* p. 187).

11. Sigmund Freud, *On the History of the Psychoanalytic Movement,* in *The Standard Edition of the Complete Psychological Works of Sigmund Freud,* ed. James Strachey et al., 24 vols. (London: Hogarth Press, 1953-66), 14:15. References to the *Standard Edition* will henceforth be abbreviated as *S.E.*

12. Ronald Clark, *Freud: The Man and the Cause* (New York: Random House, 1980), p. 7.

13. *The Interpretation of Dreams, S.E.* 4:262.

14. *The Origins of Psychoanalysis,* p. 223. Mosbacher freely translates "*ein solcher Ödipus,*" from *Aus den Anfängen der Psychoanalyse,* p. 193.

15. In a note to *The Ego and the Id* (1923) Freud describes the problem of complicity that results from an unconscious identification with another's guilt. What he writes perfectly fits Balmary's hypothesis regarding Freud's unconscious relation to the fault: "One has a special opportunity for influencing it when this *Ucs.* sense of guilt is a 'borrowed' one—when it is the product of an identification with some other person who was the object of an erotic cathexis. A sense of guilt that has been adopted in this way is often the sole remaining trace of the abandoned love relation and not at all easy to recognize as such. (The likeness between this process and what happens in melancholia is unmistakable.)" *S.E.* 19:50, n.1. I apply Freud's suggestion regarding unconscious guilt and melancholy to Freud himself (see below).

Balmary analyzes Freud's symptoms in a way reminiscent of Freud's analysis of the history of religion in *Totem and Taboo:* a forgotten fault leaves behind a residue of guilt which is expiated through symbolic rituals.

16. *The Interpretation of Dreams, S.E.* 5:525. I have cited the more accurate translation of this sentence by Samuel Weber from his "The Divaricator: Remarks on Freud's *Witz,*" in *Glyph 1,* ed. Weber and Henry Sussman (Baltimore: Johns Hopkins University Press, 1977), p. 8.

17. *An Autobiographical Study, S.E.* 20:42.

18. "The phantom is the unconscious work of another's unacknowledged secret (incest, crime, bastardy, etc.). Its law is the demand for complete ignorance," Nicolas Abraham and Maria Torok, *L'Ecorce et le noyau* (Paris: Aubier-Flammarion, 1978), p. 391.

19. *The Origins of Psychoanalysis,* p. 206 (*Aus den Anfängen der Psychoanalyse,* p. 179).

20. Cf. René Girard's *Violence and the Sacred,* trans. Patrick Gregory (Baltimore: Johns Hopkins University Press, 1977).

21. *Mourning and Melancholia, S.E.* 14:248.

22. Ibid., p. 249.

23. *Letter 126, The Origins of Psychoanalysis,* p. 306 (*Aus den Anfängen der Psychoanalyse,* p. 262.

24. Jacques Derrida, *La Carte postale* (Paris: Aubier-Flammarion, 1980), p. 547.

25. *The Interpretation of Dreams, S.E.* 5:608.

26. Sir Stephen King-Hall and Richard K. Ullmann, *German Parliaments: A Study of the Development of Representative Institutions in Germany* (London: Hansard Society, 1954), p. 63.

27. Jones, *The Life and Work of Sigmund Freud,* 1:192.

28. In "Politics and Parricide in Freud's *The Interpretation of Dreams,*" in *Fin-de-Siècle Vienna: Politics and Culture* (New York: Knopf, 1980), Carl Schorske points out that *Aeneid* 7. 312, appears on the title page of Ferdinand Lassalle's *The Italian War and the Task of Prussia*

(Berlin, 1859). Freud knew Lassalle's book and even wrote to Fliess about it (Letter 111, *The Origins of Psychoanalysis*, p. 286 [*Aus den Anfängen der Psychoanalyse*, p. 246]). My effort is to perceive what Schorske calls "the counterpolitical ingredient in the origins of psychoanalysis" from a more encompassing perspective. Freud's knowledge of "Lassalle's Acheron of the angry *Volk*" is only the façade of Freud's more deeply buried "knowledge" that Bismarck's chicanery, Jakob's fault, and the new "science" of psychoanalysis were interchangeable figures.

Schorske also does not notice that Bismarck sought Lassalle's aid during the early 1860s and that Bismarck probably derived his slogan from Lassalle. Jakob must have followed with interest the Jewish Lassalle's negotiations with the father of German unification. Regarding Bismarck's unlikely alliance with a Socialist (whom Marx called "a Jewish nigger"), King-Hall and Ullmann are admirably succinct: "Lassalle confirmed [Bismarck] in his opinion that the masses could be won over by demagogy," (*German Parliaments*, p. 64).

29. King-Hall and Ullmann, *German Parliaments*, p. 64.

30. *The Interpretation of Dreams*, 5:427-28. Freud's often recounted memory in which he looks for his mother (or, as he says in one version, "something nice") also involves a "stool." In the version in *The Interpretation of Dreams* the two- or three-year-old Sigmund uses a stool [*Schemel*] to reach the cupboard (*S.E.* 5:560). When the stool slips and Sigmund falls, he receives a facial scar which remains for life. The scar is mentioned earlier in *The Interpretation of Dreams* in a passage that was later cancelled and in "Screen Memories" (1899). Freud is curiously ambivalent about this incident: he returns to it repeatedly, but he tells only a little at a time and leaves the fragments dispersed, and then, in 1922, he cancels one reference to his scar (*S.E.* 4:17, n. 1) only to include another in "Dreams and Telepathy" (*S.E.* 18:198). (In "Screen Memories" Freud tried to conceal that the patient with the scar was himself.) The physical scar may be the figure for the scar left by his unconscious identification with Jakob. Freud's *Narbe*, his facial scar, becomes a *Spur*, a trace, i.e., the pre-text for more than his beard. The scar of mourning thus differs from the "open wound" of melancholia (*S.E.* 14:253). Freud's fall from the stool and the scar that remains are well described by Abraham and Torok's idea that the phantom is the effect upon the descendant of what had been for the parent "a wounding experience, indeed, a narcissistic catastrophe" (*L'Ecorce et le noyau*, p. 430).

INTRODUCTION

1. A child's response, cited by Françoise Dolto, *Lettres de l'Ecole freudienne de Paris*, no. 22 (1977), p. 292.

2. Henri Ey, *La Conscience* (Paris: Presses Universitaires de France, 1963), p. 413.

3. See Jean-Baptiste Pontalis, *Après Freud* (Paris: Gallimard, 1968), p. 50.

4. Jacques Lacan, *Séminaire I: Les Ecrits techniques de Freud* (Paris: Editions du Seuil, 1975), p. 129.

5. See Jean-Pierre Vernant and Pierre Vidal-Naquet, *Mythe et tragédie en Grèce ancienne* (Paris: Maspero, 1972), especially the chapter titled "Oedipe sans complexe."

6. Martin Freud, *Sigmund Freud: Man and Father* (New York: Vanguard Press, 1958), p. 60.

7. See Jean Delumeau, *Le Christianisme va-t-il mourir?* (Paris: Hachette, 1977). This confusion between what is prescribed and what is experienced does not seem to have been reserved to Christianity alone within this context of the nineteenth-century European bourgeoisie.

8. See François Roustang, *Un Destin si funeste* (Paris: Editions de Minuit, 1976), and, in a different style, Catherine Clément, *Les fils de Freud sont fatigués* (Paris: Grasset, 1978).

9. Maud Mannoni, "Sur la formation des analystes," Conference, Institut Océanographique, December 8, 1977.

10. David Bakan, *Freud and the Jewish Mystical Tradition* (New York: Van Nostrand, 1958).

11. Georges Devereux, "Why Oedipus Killed Laius," *International Journal of Psychoanalysis* 34 (1953):132.

12. Glauco Carloni and Daniela Nobili, *La Mauvaise Mère* (Paris: Payot, 1977).

CHAPTER 1

1. Anatole Bailly, *Dictionnaire grec-français* (Paris: Hachette, 1967).

2. François Grolleron brought this antonym to our attention.

3. Pierre Grimal, *Dictionnaire de la mythologie grecque et romaine* (Paris: Presses Universitaires de France, 1969), s.v. "Laius."

4. Ibid.

5. Ibid., s.v. "Chrysippus."

6. Ibid., s.v. "Oedipe."

7. See chap. 11, "The Structural Study of Myth," in Claude Lévi-Strauss, *Structural Anthropology*, trans. Claire Jacobson and Brooke G. Schoepf (New York: Basic Books, 1963), pp. 206-31.

8. Grimal, *Dictionnaire*, s.v. "Oedipe."

9. Euripides, *The Phoenician Women*, trans. Elizabeth Wyckoff, in *Euripides V*, ed. David Grene and Richard Lattimore (Chicago: University of Chicago Press, 1968), l. 13-20. All subsequent references in the text are to line numbers in this edition.

10. *Introductory Lectures on Psychoanalysis, S.E.* 16:331.

11. Euripides, *Oeuvres*, ed. Henri Gregoire and Léon Mendier (Paris: Les Belles Lettres, Universités de France, 1961), vol. 5.

12. Sophocles, *Oedipus the King*, trans. David Grene in *Sophocles I*, ed. David Grene and Richard Lattimore (New York: Washington Square Press, 1967), l. 23-28. All subsequent references in the text are to line numbers in this edition.

13. *Oedipe Roi*, in Sophocles, *Tragédies*, ed. Alphonse Dain (Paris: Les Belles Lettres, Universités de France, 1972), 2:67.

14. Colette Astier, *Le Mythe d'Oedipe* (Paris: Armand Colin, 1974), p. 21.

15. Karl Reinhardt, *Sophocle* (Paris: Editions de Minuit, 1971), p. 180.

16. Ezekiel 18:2 and Jeremiah 31:29.

17. Jacques Lacan, *Séminaire I* (Paris: Editions du Seuil, 1975), p. 221.

18. Ibid., p. 222.

19. Ibid., p. 223.

CHAPTER 2

1. *Leonardo da Vinci and a Memory of His Childhood, S.E.* 11:63.

2. Josef Sajner, "Sigmund Freud's Beziehungen zu seinem Geburtsort Freiberg (Pribor) und zu Mähren," *Clio Medica* 3 (1968): 167-80.

3. Max Schur, *Freud: Living and Dying* (New York: International Universities Press, 1972); Didier Anzieu, *L'Auto-analyse de Freud*, 2 vols. (Paris: Presses Universitaires de France, 1975); Wladimir Granoff, *Filiations: L'Avenir du complexe d'Oedipe* (Paris: Editions de Minuit), 1975).

4. Ernest Jones, *The Life and Work of Sigmund Freud*, 3 vols. (New York: Basic Books, 1953-57), 2:385.

5. Ibid., 1:150.

6. Ibid., 2:393.

7. Ibid.

8. Granoff, *Filiations*, p. 437.

9. Jones, *Life and Work of Sigmund Freud*, 1:178.

10. Cited by Schur, *Freud: Living and Dying*, p. 97. This letter is not included in Sigmund Freud, *The Origins of Psychoanalysis: Letters to Wilhelm Fliess*, ed. Marie Bonaparte, Anna Freud, and Ernst Kris; trans. Eric Mosbacher and James Strachey (New York: Basic Books, 1977).

11. Schur, *Freud: Living and Dying*, p. 102.

12. Ibid., p. 103.

13. Ibid.

14. Freud, *The Origins of Psychoanalysis*, Letter 63 (May 25, 1897), p. 202.

15. We are aware of the vagueness of the terms *dominated* and *dominating* but we use them, however, for lack of better words.

16. Jones, *The Life and Work of Sigmund Freud*, 1:1-2.

17. Jones's remarks on this problem appear in 1:1. Granoff, in *Filiations*, p. 325, refers to S. Bernfeld and S. C. Bernfeld, "Freud's Early Childhood," in *Freud as We Knew Him*, ed. Hendrik Ruitenbeek (Detroit: Wayne State University Press, 1973). (Translator's note).

18. Granoff, *Filiations*, p. 320.

19. Schur, *Freud: Living and Dying*, p. 21.

20. Jones, *The Life and Work of Sigmund Freud*, 2:127.

21. Martin Freud, *Freud, mon père* (Paris: Denoël, 1975), p. xix.

22. Martin Freud, *Sigmund Freud: Man and Father* (New York: Vanguard Press, 1958), p. 58.

23. Ibid.

24. S. Freud, *The Origins of Psychoanalysis*, Letter 60 (April 28, 1897), p. 196.

25. Jones, *The Life and Work of Sigmund Freud*, 2:366.

26. Exodus 20:3-7.

27. Passing through London, Elisabeth Guyonnet, who wanted to help us in our research, asked Anna Freud for a list of the statues collected by her father. She received a courteous reply: "The statues . . . are not just a few, but there are hundreds of them. It is quite impossible to give you a list.—Anna Freud." We are not far from the "one thousand and three" of Don Juan.

CHAPTER 3

1. Ernest Jones, *The Life and Work of Sigmund Freud*, 3 vols. (New York: Basic Books, 1953-57), 2:16.

2. Ibid.

3. Sigmund Freud, *The Origins of Psychoanalysis: Letters to Wilhelm Fliess*, ed. Marie Bonaparte, Anna Freud, and Ernst Kris; trans. Eric Mosbacher and James Strachey (New York: Basic Books, 1977), pp. 317-19.

4. Ibid., pp. 321-30. The citation in *Letter 139* is from Goethe's *Faust* 2.5. The whole passage concerns Freud very much; here are the verses that surround Freud's epigraph, with the necessary correction ("the air" and not "the world," as Freud writes, a word that is in the preceding verse. This error relates the verse that he does not cite with the one he does cite):

> A man, I used to be, before searching the obscurity,
> Before having, by a sacreligious word, damned myself and the world.
> Now the air is so full of this phantom
> That no one knows how to escape it.
> Even when day smiles upon us, clear and bright,
> Night encloses us within its tissue of dreams.

5. Freud, *The Origins of Psychoanalysis,* pp. 333-34.

6. Jones, *The Life and Work of Sigmund Freud,* 2:20.

7. Freud, *The Origins of Psychoanalysis,* p. 341, *Letter 151,* March 8, 1902.

8. Ibid., pp. 342-44, *Letter 152,* March 11, 1902.

9. Jones, *The Life and Work of Sigmund Freud,* 2:20.

10. Freud, *The Origins of Psychoanalysis,* p. 335-36, *Letter 146,* September 19, 1901.

11. Jones, *The Life and Work of Sigmund Freud,* 2:20.

12. *The Moses of Michelangelo, S.E.* 12:213.

13. Ibid., 13:220.

14. *Ergreifen* means "to seize," but also, for example, "to lay hold of" (an evildoer).

15. *The Moses of Michelangelo, S.E.* 13:213. "It always delights me" renders the German *Ich freue mich,* literally "I rejoice." The verb is *freuen,* of which the substantive is *die Freude.* The translation effaces the proximity of the verb to the name *Freud.*

16. The word *mob* translates *Gesindel,* derived from *Gesinde,* which means "domestics," "servants."

17. *S.E.* 13:213.

18. Ibid., 13:220.

19. Ibid., 13:220-21.

20. The German *Tafel* can designate, as in French and English, at once the "tablets" on which the Mosaic law was inscribed and the "table" set for dinner. The expression *pleasures of the table* is *Tafelfreuden* in German.

21. Martin Freud, *Sigmund Freud: Man and Father* (New York: Vanguard Press, 1958), pp. 32-33.

22. Jones, *The Life and Work of Sigmund Freud,* 2:382.

23. M. Freud, *Man and Father,* p. 108.

24. Jones, *The Life and Work of Sigmund Freud,* 1:103.

25. Ibid. 1:104, 153.

26. Didier Anzieu, *L'Auto-analyse de Freud,* 2 vols. (Paris: Presses Universitaires de France, 1975), 2:769-70.

27. S. Freud, *The Origins of Psychoanalysis, Letter 73,* October 31, 1897: "sexual excitation is of no more use to a person like me" (p. 227).

28. In 1895, therefore probably before beginning to collect the statues and before the father's death, Freud wrote: "If an old maid keeps a dog or an old bachelor collects snuff-boxes, the former is finding a substitute for a companion in marriage and the latter for his need for a multitude of conquests. Every collector is a substitute for Don Juan Tenorio—so too the mountain-climber, the sportsman, and so on" (*The Origins of Psychoanalysis,* "Manuscript H," p. 112).

29. In this sense, see Sigmund Freud's "Delusions and Dreams in Jensen's *Gradiva*": "It is a triumph of ingenuity and wit to be able to express the delusion and the truth in the same turn of words" (*S.E.* 9:84).

30. Exodus, 20:5-7.

CHAPTER 4

1. Sigmund Freud, *The Origins of Psychoanalysis: Letters to Wilhelm Fliess,* ed. Marie Bonaparte, Anna Freud, and Ernst Kris; trans. Eric Mosbacher and James Strachey (New York: Basic Books, 1977), *Letter 69,* September 21, 1897, pp. 217-18.

2. Ernest Jones, *The Life and Work of Sigmund Freud,* 3 vols. (New York: Basic Books, 1953-57), 1:334.

3. Didier Anzieu, *L'Autoanalyse de Freud* (Paris: Presses Universitaires de France, 1975), 2:472.

4. *Unter* 'under', *Berg* 'hill'. Using the French edition of Jones, Balmary writes Heilbrunn (*Heil* 'cure', *Brunnen* 'spa') as Hellbrunn (*hell* 'clear', inferno in English).

5. "I . . . diverted my attention from pursuing thoughts which might have arisen in my mind from the topic of 'death and sexuality'. On this occasion I was still under the influence of a piece of news which had reached me a few weeks before. . . . A patient over whom I had taken a great deal of trouble had put an end to his life on account of an incurable sexual disorder" (*The Psychopathology of Everyday Life, S.E.* 6:3).

6. Freud, *The Origins of Psychoanalysis,* p. 217.

7. *S.E.* 14:312.

8. *S.E.* 14:318.

9. *S.E.* 14:323.

10. *S.E.* 14:328.

11. *S.E.* 14:330.

12. *S.E.* 14:326.

13. *S.E.* 14:332.

14. *S.E.* 4:xxvi.

15. *The Aeneid,* in *Virgil's Works,* trans. J. W. Mackail (New York: Modern Library, 1950), bk. 7, pp. 310-16.

16. *S.E.* 5:608.

17. Freud, *The Origins of Psychoanalysis,* pp. 170-71.

18. *S.E.* 4:317.

19. Freud, *The Origins of Psychoanalysis,* p. 237.

20. Martin Freud, *Sigmund Freud: Man and Father* (New York: Vanguard Press, 1958), p. 44.

21. S. Freud, *The Origins of Psychoanalysis,* pp. 172-173.

CHAPTER 5

1. Eliane Amado-Levi-Valensi, *Les Voies et les pièges de la psychanalyse* (Paris: Editions Universitaires, 1971), p. 210.

2. Ernest Jones, *The Life and Work of Sigmund Freud,* 3 vols. (New York: Basic Books, 1953-57), 1:221.

3. Ibid., p. 224.

4. *S.E.* 2:34-35.

5. Jones, *The Life and Work of Sigmund Freud,* 1:224.

6. Sigmund Freud, *L'Homme aux rats: Journal d'une analyse* (Paris: Presses Universitaires de France, 1974), p. 21.

7. Jacques Lacan, "L'Ethique de la psychanalyse: Séminaire de l'année 1959-1960" (unpublished).

8. Jones, *The Life and Work of Sigmund Freud,* 1:224-25.

9. Ibid., 1:224-225.

10. Ibid., 1:226.

11. For Freud's change in direction, see ibid., 1:235; for Freud on the genesis of the symptom, see *An Autobiographical Study, S.E.* 20:19-28; for Jones on the above, see *The Life and Work of Sigmund Freud,* 1:242-43.

12. References to this case are from *S.E.* 2:125-34.

13. Ibid., pp. 100-101, n. 1.

14. Jones, *The Life and Work of Sigmund Freud,* 1:254.

15. *The Aetiology of Hysteria, S.E.* 3:191. Subsequent references to this case are from *S.E.* 3:191-221.

16. Habakkuk 2:9-11.

17. Ibid., 2:19-20.

18. Luke 19:40.

19. Jacques Lacan advises the young psychoanalyst to do crossword puzzles in *Ecrits* (Paris: Editions du Seuil, 1966), p. 266.

20. See Didier Anzieu, *L'Auto-analyse de Freud,* 2 vols. (Paris: Presses Universitaires de France, 1975), 1:253.

21. In *Letter 78* (December 3, 1897), Freud writes of the "anxiety about travel which I have had to overcome," (*The Origins of Psychoanalysis: Letters to Wilhelm Fliess,* ed. Marie Bonapart, Anna Freud, and Ernst Kris; trans. Eric Mosbacher and James Strachey [New York: Basic Books, 1977], p. 237).

22. The German proverb that means "like father, like son" is *der Apfel fallt nicht weit von Stamm* 'the apple falls no further than the trunk'.

23. Although we open the aetiology of neurosis to every kind of fault, we still continue to think that sexual faults have a special place, since sexuality is at the origin of every human being. We hope that this question will be posed differently following our research.

CHAPTER 6

1. Sigmund Freud, *The Origins of Psychoanalysis: Letters to Wilhelm Fliess,* ed. Marie Bonaparte, Anna Freud, and Ernst Kris; trans. Eric Mosbacher and James Strachey (New York: Basic Books, 1977), *Letter 16* (February 7, 1894), p. 80.

2. Ibid., *Letter 17* (April 19, 1894), p. 82.

3. Ibid., *Letter 18* (May 21, 1894), p. 83.

4. Ibid., *Draft E* (June 1894?), pp. 88-94.

5. Ibid., *Draft G: Melancholia* (January 1895?), p. 106.

6. Ibid., *Draft H: Paranoia* (January 1895?), p. 109.

7. Ibid., *Letter 29* (October 8, 1895), p. 126.

8. Ibid., *Letter 30* (October 15, 1895), p. 127.

9. Ibid., *Letter 34* (November 2, 1895), p. 132.

10. Ibid., *Letter 38* (December 8, 1895), p. 136.

11. Ibid., *Letter 39* (January 1, 1896), p. 141.

12. Ibid., *Letter 41* (February 13, 1896), p. 157.

13. Ibid., *Letter 46* (May 30, 1896), pp. 165-66.

14. Jacques Lacan, *Ecrits* (Paris: Editions du Seuil, 1966), pp. 254-55.

15. Freud, *The Origins of Psychoanalysis, Letter 50* (November 2, 1896), p. 170.

16. Ibid., *Letter 52* (December 6, 1896), pp. 179-80.

17. Ibid., *Letter 54* (January 3, 1897), p. 183.

18. Ibid., p. 184.

19. Ibid., *Letter 55* (January 11, 1897), p. 185.

20. Ibid., p. 186. The editors of the French edition of the Freud-Fliess correspondence regard Freud's "theory of seduction" as an uninteresting detour. They think that "in spite of this detour, he made, as a secondary by-product, a certain number of fruitful discoveries" (*Naissance de la psychanalyse* [Paris: Presses Universitaires de France, 1969], p. 163 n.). On the contrary, we find this "detour" singularly solid, well argued, and supported by clinical examples that are properly verified by the testimony of two people.

21. Freud, *The Origins of Psychoanalysis, Letter 55* (January 11, 1897), p. 187.

22. Ibid., *Letter 56* (January 17, 1897), p. 187.

23. Ibid., p. 188.

24. Ibid., *Letter 57* (January 24, 1897), p. 189.

25. Didier Anzieu, *L'Auto-analyse de Freud,* 2 vols. (Paris: Presses Universitaires de France, 1975), 1:296.

26. Freud, *The Origins of Psychoanalysis, Letter 60* (April 28, 1897), pp. 193-94, and *The Interpretation of Dreams, S.E.* 1:317-18.

27. Freud, *The Origins of Psychoanalysis, Letter 60* (April 28, 1897), pp. 195-96.

28. Ibid., *Letter 134* (May 7, 1900), p. 318.

29. Ibid., *Letter 61* (May 2, 1897), p. 196.

30. Ibid., *Draft L* (May 2, 1897), pp. 197-98.

31. Ibid., p. 198.

32. Ibid.

33. Ibid., p. 199.

34. Ibid., *Letter 62* (May 16, 1897), p. 200.

35. Ibid., *Draft M* (May 25, 1897), p. 203.

36. Ibid., p. 204.

37. Ibid., p. 205.

38. Ibid., p. 206.

39. Ibid.

40. Ibid., pp. 206-7.

41. *S.E.* 4:239-40; 247-48.

42. Ibid., p. 248, n. 1.

43. Ibid., p. 247.

44. Also see the dream from spring 1897 about the uncle with the yellow beard, a dream that can without difficulty be interpreted according to our hypothesis. There Freud is heir to a man who let himself get involved with evil. See the analysis by Anzieu, who sees the figure of the father behind that of the criminal uncle (*L'Auto-analyse de Freud,* 1:288-95).

45. Freud, *The Origins of Psychoanalysis,* p. 207.

46. Ibid., p. 208.

47. Ibid., p. 209.

48. Ibid., pp. 209-10.

49. Ibid., p. 210.

50. Ibid., p. 211.

51. Ibid., *Letter 66* (July 7, 1897), p. 212.

52. Ibid., *Letter 67* (August 14, 1897), p. 213.

53. Ibid., *Letter 68* (August 18, 1897), p. 214.

54. See Anzieu, *L'Auto-analyse de Freud,* ch. III. 4.

CHAPTER 7

1. Ernest Jones, *The Life and Work of Sigmund Freud,* 3 vols. (New York: Basic Books, 1953-57), 1:5-6.

2. *The Interpretation of Dreams, S.E.* 4:247-48.

3. Ibid., 4:248 n.

4. Sigmund Freud, *The Origins of Psychoanalysis: Letters to Wilhelm Fliess*, ed. Marie Bonaparte, Anna Freud, and Ernst King; trans. Eric Mosbacher and James Strachey (New York: Basic Books, 1977), *Letter 70* (October 3, 1897), p. 219.

5. Ibid., pp. 220-21.

6. Ibid., p. 221.

7. Ibid., *Letter 71* (October 15, 1897), p. 221. Translation modified. (N.L.)

8. Ibid., p. 221-22. Translation modified. (N.L.)

9. Ibid., p. 222.

10. Didier Anzieu, *L'Auto-analyse de Freud*, 2 vols. (Paris: Presses Universitaires de France, 1975), 1:38.

11. Joseph Sajner, "Sigmund Freuds Beziehungen zu Seinem Geburtsort Freiberg (Pribor) und zu Mähren," *Clio Medica* 3 (1968): 172-76. (Translator's note).

12. Ibid.

13. In German, to make the sign of the cross is said *ein Kreuz schlagen* — again, the verb *schlagen*, which we saw in *Schlagfertigkeit.*

14. Journal entry of Lou Andreas-Salomé on her visit to the Freuds in November-December 1921, in *The Sigmund Freud and Lou Andreas-Salomé Letters*, ed. Ernst Pfeiffer, trans. William Robson-Scott and Elaine Robson-Scott (New York: Harcourt Brace Jovanovich, 1972), p. 231, n. 142.

15. See Anzieu, *L'Auto-analyse de Freud.*

16. *The Interpretation of Dreams, S.E.* 4:166. Translation modified. (N.L.).

17. Jones, *The Life and Work of Sigmund Freud*, 1:13.

18. Sigmund Freud, cited by Jones, ibid., 2:350.

19. Ibid., p. 352.

20. Cf. René Girard, *Des Choses cachées depuis la fondation du monde* (Paris: Grasset, 1978).

21. Freud, *The Origins of Psychoanalysis*, p. 215.

22. These words, which we have here italicized, are included in neither the English nor the French translation of Freud's German. Interestingly, they appeared in neither the 1950 nor the 1962 German edition of the Freud-Fliess correspondence; they first came to light in the 1975 edition, which makes what appeared as a reprint a new edition. (Translator's note).

23. *Joke's and Their Relation to the Unconscious, S.E.* 8:62.

24. Jones concludes Freud's allusion by saying, "for fear that the daughters of the Philistines will rejoice about it."

25. Freud, *The Origins of Psychoanalysis*, pp. 216-17.

26. *Further Remarks on the Neuro-Psychoses of Defence, S.E.* 3:168, n. 1.

27. In German: *"Rebekka, zieh das Kleid aus, Du bist keine Kalle mehr."* A note in the German text explains that *Kalle* is *judischer Ausdruck für Braut* 'a Jewish expression for a bride'. A *Brautkleid* is therefore a wedding gown.

I have again altered the translation by Mosbacher and Strachey, which omits Freud's misquotation from Shakespeare (*The Origins of Psychoanalysis*, p. 218). (N.L.)

28. Ibid., p. 219.

29. Sajner, "Sigmund Freuds Beziehungen," p. 175.

30. Freud, *The Origins of Psychoanalysis*, p. 222.

31. Anzieu's account is at the end of the second volume of his *L'Auto-analyse de Freud.*

32. *The Interpretation of Dreams, S.E.* 4:197.

33. Jones, *The Life and Work of Sigmund Freud*, 1:22.

34. Freud, *The Origins of Psychoanalysis*, pp. 223-24.

CONCLUSION

1. One month after Tausk's suicide, Freud wrote to Lou Andreas-Salomé: "After all he spent his days wrestling with the father ghost. I confess that I do not really miss him; I had long realized that he could be of no further service, indeed that he constituted a threat to the future" (letter of August 1, 1919, in *Sigmund Freud and Lou Andreas-Salomé Letters*, ed. Ernst Pfeiffer, trans. William Robson-Scott and Elaine Robson-Scott [New York: Harcourt Brace Jovanovich, 1972], p. 98). This letter, which first appeared in Paul Roazen's *Brother Animal: The Story of Freud and Tausk* (New York: Knopf, 1969), p. 140, had been suppressed in the French edition of Lou Andreas-Salomé, *Correspondance avec Sigmund Freud* (Paris: Gallimard, 1970).

2. Unlike English- or German-speaking readers, French-speaking readers are without an authoritative and uniform edition of Freud's work. We are pleased that a new French translation is presently in progress, which will allow an authentic access to the German text.

3. Sigmund Freud, *L'Homme aux rats: Journal d'une analyse* (Paris: Presses Universitaires de France, 1974), p. 52. These notes have not yet appeared in English.

4. Morton Schatzman, *Soul Murder: Persecution in the Family* (New York: Random House, 1973), p. 11.

5. Ernest Jones, *The Life and Work of Sigmund Freud*, 3 vols. (New York: Basic Books, 1953-57), 2:341.

6. Ibid., p. 342.

7. Nancy Elisabeth Deaufils brought this to our attention. The bas-relief appears on the frontispiece of this book.

8. Edmund Engelman, *Berggasse 19: Sigmund Freud's Home and Offices, Vienna, 1938* (New York: Basic Books, 1976).

9. In French, *conscience* means both "consciousness" and "conscience." (Translator's note).

10. Lacan's phrase is *savoir avec l'Autre*. Who is this "Other" with whom one knows? In other words, who can be the witness? In which symbolic position is the witness located in relation to the subject? How can he guarantee, or answer for his discourse, for his verbal knowledge? The word *guarantee* leads us (by way of the Latin *auctor* 'he who guarantees') to the larger question of the relation to authority, or, more precisely, to the process of authorization. Another question arises here: Why do all these relations proceed from an interdiction against the possession of the other, of which the interdiction against incest is the most well known formulation? This is the point of departure for another study, which we can only suggest here.

11. Alfred Ernout and Antoine Meillet, *Dictionnaire etymologique de la langue latine* (Paris: Klincksieck, 1967).

12. In German, the word *bewusst* 'conscious of' apparently does not relate to the presence of another. Why has the word *mitwissen* (literally: "to know with") not undergone the same development as the words that derive from the Latin *cum-scire* 'to know with'? If Luther had to choose between these two words for his translation of the Bible, then that choice could well confirm rather than weaken our hypothesis on conscience/consciousness.

13. Daniel Lagache has forcefully emphasized the centrality of this question: "The relations of power doubtless constitute the most effective line of inquiry into the study of the individual's development and structuration" ("Pouvoir et personne," *L'évolution psychiatrique* 1 (1962):111-19).

14. At numerous points our work seems to cross and recross René Girard's thesis in *Des Choses cachées depuis la fondation du monde* (Paris: Grasset, 1978), of which we learned only late in the preparation of our research.

15. In French, the patient is called the *analysant*, which is also the present participle of the verb *analyser*; the activity suggested by the present participle (analyzing) is in opposition to the passivity of the past participle *analysé* 'analyzed'. English-speaking analysts use the term *analysand*. (Translator's note).

16. On this subject see Denis Vasse, *Un parmi d'autres* (Paris: Editions du Seuil, 1978), again a work that we came across only when we were concluding our project.

17. We read in Maurice Clavel's *Ce que je crois* (Paris: Grasset, 1975) that Kierkegaard "introduced repression to thought in 1844, fifty years before Freud. He even wrote: 'God has been repressed.' God was actually the first thing repressed in the Western World, well before human sexuality" (p. 106).

18. Sigmund Freud, *The Origins of Psychoanalysis: Letters to Wilhelm Fliess,* ed. Marie Bonaparte, Anna Freud, and Ernst Kris; trans. Eric Mosbacher and James Strachey (New York: Basic Books, 1977), *Letter 77,* December 3, 1897, p. 236.

19. See Marthe Robert, *D'Oedipe à Moïse* (Paris: Calmann-Lévy, 1974), p. 124, n. 2.

20. *The Interpretation of Dreams, S.E.* 5:606-7, n. 2. Translation modified. (N.L.)

21. Marie Cardinal, *Les Mots pour le dire* (Paris: Grasset, 1975).

22. *The Interpretation of Dreams, S.E.* 5:436.

23. Ibid., p. 435.

24. Ibid., 4:256. In the German and French translations the commandment in question is the fourth, while in the English it is the fifth. (Translator's note).

25. *The Psychopathology of Everyday Life, S.E.* 6:218.

26. Ibid., 6:219.

27. Ibid., 6:220.

28. Wladimir Granoff, *Filiations: L'avenir du complexe Oedipe* (Paris: Editions de Minuit, 1975), p. 318.

29. Jacques Lacan, *Télévision* (Paris: Editions du Seuil, 1973), p. 35. Lacan refers to the account in Genesis where the drunken and naked Noah is covered with a cloak by his sons. (Translator's note).

30. Granoff, *Filiations,* p. 323.

31. *Civilization and its Discontents, S.E.* 21:102.

32. *The Future of an Illusion, S.E.* 21:48.

33. Ibid., p. 54.

34. The primary meaning of the words *to exist* (or as Lacan writes it, to ex- ist) is to come from, to draw one's origin from, to arise from.

35. Michel Le Bris in *Le Nouvel Observateur,* no. 732 (November 1978).

36. Laurent Dispot, *La Machine à terreur* (Paris: Grasset, 1978), p. 159, cited by Philippe Sollers in *Le Monde,* November 28, 1978.